DE SADE

Ronald Hayman

DE SADE

A Critical Biography

Thomas Y. Crowell, Publishers
Established 1834
New York

Grateful acknowledgment is made for permission to reprint a selection from "The Voyage" from *Imitations* by Robert Lowell, copyright © 1958, 1959, 1960, 1961 by Robert Lowell. Reprinted with the permission of Farrar, Straus & Giroux, Inc.

FIRST U.S. EDITION

ISBN: 0-690-01416-3

LIBRARY OF CONGRESS CATALOG CARD NUMBER: 78-3170

78 79 80 81 82 10 9 8 7 6 5 4 3 2 1

For
Charles, Brenda, Justine and Juliette

I do not know if I am hangman or victim
for I imagine the most horrible tortures
and as I describe them I suffer them myself
There is nothing I could not do and everything
fills me with horror

Sade in Peter Weiss's *Marat/Sade*

The less natural and urgent needs are, the stronger the passions and what is worse, the greater the power to satisfy them; so that after long prosperity, after having swallowed up many treasures and ruined many men, my hero will end up by killing everything until he is sole master of the universe. Such is in brief the moral picture, if not of human life, at least of the secret aspirations in the heart of every civilized man.

Rousseau—*Discours sur l'inégalité*

Towards what is called evil, love made me pursue an adventure that led to prison. If they are not always beautiful, men bound to evil possess the manly virtues. By their own choice or a choice made for them by accident, they steep themselves knowingly, uncomplainingly into a reproachful shameful element like the one entered by victims of profound love. Erotic games uncover an ineffable world. The nocturnal language of lovers reveal it but such a language is not written down.

Jean Genet—*Journal du voleur*

Contents

Acknowledgements

I am most grateful to the French Government for making me its guest on a research visit to France. I would like to thank Comte Xavier-Marie-Henri de Sade, great-great-grandson of Sade's second son, Donatien-Claude-Armand, for showing me his private collection at Condé-en-Brie and allowing me to quote from unpublished letters written by Sade and his father. I was also glad to have access to unpublished material in the Archive National, the Bibliothèque National and the Archive de la Bastille.

I am greatly indebted to the friends who have read part or all of my typescript in draft and made comments—especially to Catharine Carver and Geoffrey Strickland.

The translations are my own except where another translator has been credited. The translation of Baudelaire on page 233 is reprinted by permission of Faber and Faber Ltd from *Imitations* by Robert Lowell.

Chronological Table

Page	Year	Biographical	Political	Cultural
2	1733	13 November: Marriage of parents	War of the Polish Succession. Alliance with Spain against Austria and Britain	
	1734			Marivaux's *Le Paysan parvenu* (1734–5) Saint-Simon's *Mémoires* (1734–1753)
	1735		Cardinal Fleury starts secret peace negotiations	
3	1737	Birth of daughter	Fall of Chauvelin, Foreign Secretary and leader of pro-war faction	Marivaux's *Les fausses confidences*; Crébillon fils's *Les Égarements du coeur et de l'esprit* (1736–8)
	1739	Daughter dies. Count becomes Lieutenant-General of Bresse, Bugey, Valromey and Gex	Secret treaties with Austria and Prussia	
	1740	Count sent as ambassador to Cologne. 2 June: Donatien-Alphonse-François born	Death of Emperor Charles VI. Succeeded by Maria-Theresa	

Page	Year	Biographical	Political	Cultural
12	1754	Begins at cavalry school		Rousseau's *Discours sur l'inégalité* Crébillon *fils*'s *Les Heureux Orphelins*
	1755	14 December: Commissioned as sub-lieutenant		Voltaire's *La Pucelle d' Orléans* Death of Montesquieu
13	1756		Treaty of Versailles with Austria. Outbreak of Seven Years War. July: French defeat Hanoverians at Sondershausen	Voltaire's '*Poème sur le désastre de Lisbon*'
12	1757	January: Promoted to rank of cornet	July: French defeat English at Hastenbeck	Diderot's *Le Fils naturel*
	1758		Duc de Choiseul appointed Secretary for Foreign Affairs	Rousseau's *Lettre à d' Alembert sur les spectacles*
14	1759	April: Promoted to rank of captain		Voltaire's *Candide*
23	1760	Count resigns Lieutenant-Generalcy in favour of his son		Diderot's *La Réligieuse*
	1761		Alliance with Spain	Rousseau's *La Nouvelle Héloïse*
17	1762		Calas executed; France withdraws from right bank of Rhine	Rousseau's *Emile* and *Le Contrat sociale* Diderot's *Le Neveu de Rameau*

Page	Year	Biographical	Political	Cultural
19	1763	Affair with Laure de Lauris	February: Peace of Paris ends Five Years War	Deaths of Marivaux and Prévost; Voltaire's Traité sur la tolérance
23		17 May: Marriage with Renée-Pélagie de Montreuil		
27		18 October: Sadistic night with Jeanne Testard		
33		October–November: Imprisoned at Vincennes		
35	1764	July: Affair with Colet begins. Succeeds to Lieutenant-Generalcy	April: Death of Pompadour; November: Expulsion of Jesuits	Rousseau begins writing Les Confessions
38	1765	Affair with Beauvoisin		
41	1766	Affair with Dorville	Lorraine becomes part of France	Mme de Staël born
43	1767	24 January: Death of Count; 16 April: Rejoins regiment		
44		27 August: Louis-Marie, eldest son born		
46	1768	3 April: Sadistic adventure with Rose Keller		
50		8 April: Arrested and taken to Saumur		
52		May: Transferred to Pierre-Encise		
54		November: Released. Stays at Lacoste		

Page	Year	Biographical	Political	Cultural
55	1769	May: Returns to Paris 27 June: Birth of Donatien-Claude-Armand, second son September–October: Journey to Holland		Diderot writes *Le Rêve d' Alembert*
56	1770	August: Rejoins regiment at Poitou	Dauphin marries Marie-Antoinette Fall of Choiseul Ministry of Maupeou and Terray begins	Holbach's *Système de la nature*
57	1771	17 April: Birth of Madeleine-Laure, daughter August: Imprisoned for debts September: Affair with sister-in-law, Anne-Prospère	Parlements exiled	
58	1772	January: Production of a comedy by Sade at Lacoste June: Journey to Marseilles. Sadistic adventure with prostitutes		Helvétius's *De l'homme* published
63		September: Death sentence passed by Aix Parlement. Escape to Italy		

Page	Year	Biographical	Political	Cultural
65		with Anne-Prospère November: Anne-Prospère returns to France		
66		5 December: Arrested at Chambéry and imprisoned at Miolans		
75	1773	30 April: Escapes		Diderot writes *Jacques le fataliste* Holbach's *Système sociale*
77	1774	6 January: Police raid on Lacoste. Sade hides	May: Death of Louis XV. Accession of Louis XVI. Maupeou and Terray replaced by Maurepas. Parlements recalled. Turgot in charge of finances	
80	1775	Scandal with young girls		Restif de la Bretonne's *Le Paysan perverti*
86		July: Escapes to Italy		Beaumarchais's *Le Barbier de Séville*
88	1776	June: Returns to France	Fall of Turgot	
91		November: Shots fired on him by a girl's irate father		
92	1777	January: Death of Countess	Necker put in charge of finances	
93		February: Arrested in Hotel		*Journal de Paris* (first French daily) starts

Page	Year	Biographical	Political	Cultural
132	1783	February: Trouble with eyes	War of American Independence ends	
142	1784	January: Death of Milli Rousset 29 February: Transferred to Bastille		Beaumarchais's *Le Mariage de Figaro*
149	1785	October: Transcribes *120 journées* on to roll of paper	Scandal of diamond necklace discredits Marie-Antoinette	
154	1786	Begins *Aline et Valcour*		
161	1787	July: Completes *Les Infortunes de la vertu*	August: Parlement of Paris exiled and (September) recalled	
	1788	October: Compiles a catalogue of his writings	May: Parlement suspended again and (September) recalled August: Convocation of Estates-General	
169	1789	2 July: Harangues crowd in street through improvised loudspeaker	Bread and grain riots in spring and early summer May: Estates-General meets June: Tennis Court oath July: Siege of Bastille August: Feudal privileges abolished	

Page	Year	Biographical	Political	Cultural
174	1790	2 April: Released		
177		9 June: Legal separation from Renée-Pélagie		
183		1 July: Given card as 'active citizen'		
		25 August: Beginning of relationship with Marie-Constance Renelle		
183	1791	June: *Justine* published	21 June: Louis XVI escapes to Varennes	
184		Writes 'L'*Adresse d'un citoyen de Paris au roi des Français*'	September: Dissolution of Constituent Assembly	
		October: Performance of *Le Comte Oxtiern*		
185	1792	March: Abortive production of *Le Suborneur*	August: Attack on the Tuileries	Mirabeau's *Lettres à Sophie*
186		September: Secretary of Section des Piques	September: Convention meets. Monarchy abolished	
		Lacoste vandalized		
		December: Sade's name appears on list of *émigrés*	December: Trial of Louis XVI	
192	1793	August: As President of his section he spares the Montreuils	January: Execution	Condorcet's *Esquisse d'un tableau historique*
		September: Makes speech in praise of Marat	March: Revolutionary tribunal set up	
			April: Committee of Public	

Page	Year	Biographical	Political	Cultural
193		November: Arrested and imprisoned	Safety established September: Law against suspects	
194 197	1794	March: Transferred to Picpus October: Released	July: Fall of Robespierre. Terror ends	
	1795	Publication of *La Philosophie dans le boudoir* and *Aline et Valcour*	October: Convention dissolved November: Directory begins	
203	1797	Publication of *La Nouvelle Justine* and *Juliette*	May: Napoleon occupies Venice	Chateaubriand's *Essai sur les révolutions*
212	1799	Employed at theatre in Versailles	July: Napoleon defeats Turks at Aboukir and (October) returns to France November: Directory overthrown December: Consulate established	Death of Beaumarchais
	1800	*Crimes de l'amour* published	February: Napoleon appointed First Consul June: Napoleon defeats Austrians at Marengo and conquers Italy	Mme de Staël's *De la littérature* Fouché establishes theatrical censorship
213	1801	March: Arrested and imprisoned April: Transferred to Sainte-Pélagie		Chateaubriand's *Atala*

Page	Year	Biographical	Political	Cultural
	1802		Napoleon appointed Consul	Mme de Staël's *Delphine*
216	1803	April: Transferred to Bicêtre and then to Charenton		Mme de Staël exiled. Death of Laclos
	1804		Napoleon crowned as Emperor	
	1805		Battle of Austerlitz	Chateaubriand's *René*
	1806		Battle of Iéna	
219	1807	Writes *Les Journées de Florbelle*		Benjamin Constant writes *Adolphe* (published 1815)
220	1808	Organizes theatrical performances in asylum / September: Donatien-Claude marries		
223	1809	June: Louis-Marie killed on army service in Italy		Benjamin Constant's *Cécile*
	1810	7 July: Renée-Pélagie dies		
	1812	Writes *Adelaide de Brunswick*		
	1813	Writes *L'Histoire secrète d'Isabelle de Bavière*. *La Marquise de la Gange* published		
224	1814	2 December: Dies, aged 74	Abdication of Napoleon. Louis XVIII crowned	Mme de Staël's *De l'Allemagne*

Introduction

'To explain evil,' said Baudelaire in his *Journaux intimes*, 'we must always go back to Sade—that is to natural man.' Eluard was making almost the same point when he said that Sade 'wanted to restore to civilized man the force of his primitive instincts. He wanted to liberate the erotic imagination for its own objectives.' But it was not until the 1960s that his complete works could be put on sale in France. The publisher who brought out a limited edition of *Juliette* in 1957 was found guilty of 'outrage to public morals'.

Camus and Simone de Beauvoir had been the most influential of Sade's champions during the '50s; recently Structuralism has tended to produce a more favourable valuation of the novels. Criteria have become less realistic, while fiction is no longer expected to adhere to the principle of temporal progression. Roland Barthes is not making an adverse judgement when he demonstrates that the journeys in Sade's fiction lead nowhere, or when he concedes that the novels are boring if we concentrate more on the actions narrated than on the narrative. Structuralism has encouraged literary critics to regard narrative as a system of internal relationships, in the same way that linguistic analysts ignore the historical evolution of a language in their efforts to unearth the system of rules that makes it operate in the way it does. Sade's fiction could be said to fulfil the demands made later by Gertrude Stein when she said that in the best writing 'there is at present not a sense of anything successively happening, moving is in every direction beginning and ending is not really exciting, anything is anything, anything is happening!'

Barthes regards Sade's novels as great classics; Philippe Sollers ranks them among 'the most varied and most exciting texts in our literature'. I do not rate Sade's novels as highly as this, but my view of his importance is extremely high. I think he is a key figure in the history of modernism, and, above all, in the history of alienation. He was a nihilist before the word 'nihilism' existed, anticipating Dostoevsky and Nietzsche. In 1878–9, Dostoevsky wrote in *The Brothers Karamazov*: if God is dead, anything is permissible. And in 1881, two years before *Also Sprach Zarathustra*, Nietzsche wrote his story about a madman who lit a lantern in bright daylight and ran into the market-place, looking for God: ' "Where is God?" he cried. "Well, I will tell you. We have murdered him—you and I." ' 'I foresee something terrible,' wrote Nietzsche. 'Chaos everywhere. Nothing left which is of any value. Nothing which commands: "Thou shalt".' The same idea is common to Kafka and Camus: that if humanity is cut off from its metaphysical roots, all action is absurd.

Sade exerted a dominant influence on the French *poètes maudits* from Baudelaire to Genet, and he was a precursor of Freud, not because he tried to make a catalogue of perversions, as he did in *Les 120 journées de Sodome*, but because the idea of the pleasure principle is implicit in his searching analysis of his own case-history in his fiction and in his letters. He was as much a masochist as a sadist, and more important as a theorist than as a practitioner of either perversion.

The word *sadism* is liable to be very confusing. Freud used it in three distinct senses, meaning:

1) the aggressive impulse which is a component of all normal sexuality.
2) the phase in the development of the normal personality during which 'anal-sadistic' aggression begins; reluctant to acknowledge the impossibility of loving fusion with the whole of the external world, the growing consciousness experiences its first frustration. Infantile narcissism asserts its independence through rebellious action.
3) the perversion that develops when the aggressive impulse, becoming exaggerated and independent of the other elements in sexuality, usurps the leading position.

All three uses of the term occur as early as 1905 in *Three Essays on the Theory of Sexuality*. Later, Freud changed his mind about whether the 'impulse of cruelty' could be independent of sexuality. In 1915 he said that it arose from the 'instinct for mastery', and in his later writings, he treated it as something secondary, arising out of the self-destructive death instinct. In any case, it is a mistake to regard sadism in either of the first two senses as abnormal. In the first sense it is not even peculiar to humanity; many male animals and birds inflict pain on the female before mating. Pain, as Havelock Ellis points out, is a nervous stimulant which can act powerfully on the sexual centres.[1] Another mistake is to imagine that Sade was the originator of sadism in the third sense. Abundant examples of sadistic cruelty are to be found in early mythology and in the Bible. Unlike the sadism of the late Roman emperors and the medieval Church's treatment of witches, Sade's sadism was not murderous. It was only in his fantasies and his fiction that bloodshed was involved.

He was, in any case, not a pervert in the cradle. Once the suffix *-ism* has been tacked on to a man's name, we tend to forget that his life was a process in which habits and attitudes developed in response to pressures both internal and external. How did Marx become a Marxist or Sade a sadist? The answer must be biographical. Another reason to study his life is that the best way to gauge the influence of each area of activity on the others is to analyse his development from phase to phase, putting mental events and physical facts into the same perspective.

Very little is known about his childhood, and several biographers have succumbed to the temptation of assuming that the autobiographical narratives of his heroes correspond exactly to his own experiences. In some parts of this book I have resorted to guesswork, but I have tried always to make it clear where fact ends and surmise begins.

Another difficulty is that the documentation is very uneven. Because police espionage was so efficient and dossiers so detailed, we know a great deal about his relationships with actresses and prostitutes. Thanks to legal records it is possible to write in great detail about 3 April 1768, when he celebrated Easter Sunday by flagellating a woman he found begging, and about the evening of 26 June 1772 when he and his valet had an orgy with four Marseilles prostitutes. But for the periods of his life where we are almost entirely dependent on letters, we have to make do with a very much less detailed narrative, and the early chapters tend (like Sade's novels) to be bare of descriptive details.

Of previous biographies, the best is the most scholarly. Gilbert Lely's *Vie du marquis de Sade* was first published in two volumes

[1] *Psychology of Sex*, Heinemann, 1933.

(1952, 1957) and then in a revised single-volume edition in 1965. Only the earlier edition has been translated into English. Admirably researched though it was, the book is too much like a massive catalogue of incidents with lengthy quotations from letters and legal documents. As a study of a man's development it is almost useless. Most of the book is written like a vicarious diary, with each day's events treated separately. So the reader is given an ant's-eye close-up of each blade of grass, but never allowed to fly up for a glimpse of the garden.

Nor is Lely sufficiently acute either in his psychological interpretations or his critical judgements. He is too much of a sentimentalist to arrive at a proper understanding of his subject. On his way to Sade's old château he wrote: 'I saw the heart of the Marquis de Sade. And I understood that in this heart there was something nobody knew about, and for the mysterious existence of which there was no proof. Six years went by and thanks to the power of love, my hands became the holders of those forgotten documents in which I recognized all the words which had been cried to me under the heaven of the miraculous stones of Lacoste.'

The sentimentality and the failures of understanding would have mattered less if Lely had told the story in such a way that the reader could make up his own mind about the pattern and the transitions in Sade's development. No one could have predicted that this titled child, born in the Condé palace, would become as alienated as any writer has ever been, or that the tempestuously active young profligate would grow into a habitual masturbator, or that after more than twenty years of promiscuity followed by thirteen of imprisonment, he would be capable of a monogamous relationship that would last twenty years. The story is worth telling in considerable detail, but there is nothing to stop us from flying between the grass and vantage points on the trees.

DE SADE

Chapter 1

Boyhood

The Sade family was of Italian origin. Different forms of the sur-
name—Sado, Sadone, Sazo, Sauza—can be found in documents
of the twelfth and thirteenth centuries, and it was in the twelfth
century that the family settled in Provence. The Marquis de Sade's
father, Jean-Baptiste-François-Joseph de Sade, was born at
Avignon in 1702. He had four younger brothers and five sisters.
He inherited the title of Count and the seigneuries of Saumane and
Lacoste, which is east of Avignon. The estate consisted of about
200 acres, as compared with the thousand acres owned by local
peasants. The château was on a hilltop outside the village. He also
became co-seigneur of Mazan and the owner of a lucrative estate
at Arles in the Camargue. After serving in the Prince de Condé's
regiment as a captain of dragoons, he was appointed at the age of
twenty-eight as ambassador to the Russian court. Though reserved
and apparently rather cold, he was attractive to both sexes. There
is an autograph letter to prove that the Tsar was enamoured of
him, and his mistresses included two princesses de Condé.

He did not marry until he was thirty-one, which means that he
must have selected his own wife, unlike most young noblemen
who married the girl their father chose. But we should not infer
that the Count's choice was based on either affection or sexual
attraction. Marie-Eléonore, the twenty-one-year-old daughter of
the Marquis de Carman and the Comtesse de Maillé, was a distant
relation of the royal family, and her fifth cousin, Cardinal Richelieu's niece, had married the Prince de Condé. Many of the old
families were trying to establish their *noblesse de race* more meaning-
fully by linking themselves to the blood royal. According to the
official genealogist, Chérin, there were less than a thousand families in France whose lineage could be traced back to the fourteenth
century, but there may by now have been as many as 200,000
noblemen—about 1 per cent of the total population. This was the
result of Louis XIV's policy of selling titles on a very large scale
by letters patent. Sixteenth-century kings had resorted to this

expedient only occasionally; in one month (March 1696) Louis raised 3,000,000 livres by ennobling 500 people at 6,000 livres apiece. He also left France with an unwieldy bureaucracy; having sold all the jobs there were to sell, he invented sinecures. One of his chancellors, Louis Pontchartrin, said: 'Every time your Majesty creates an office, God creates a fool to buy it.' The sale of jobs and titles continued after his death. Often the two were sold together; during the decade before the revolution 4,000 official posts carried titles. The most expensive of the sinecures, the fictitious position of secretary to the King, brought with it a *lettre d'honneur* which established nobility as hereditary in the purchaser's family. One consequence of Louis's fund-raising methods was the disappearance of all clear demarcation between nobility and bourgeoisie. In 1753, on the birth certificate of Louis-Marie Larevellière-Lepeaux (later a member of the revolutionary Directory) it was recorded that his father was the 'nobleman Jean-Baptiste de la Revellière, bourgeois of the town of Angers'. Among the old nobility, therefore, marriage was often used as a means to climb above the rising tide of upstart ennoblement.

The Comte de Sade and Marie-Eléonore de Maillé de Carman were married on 13 November 1733 in the chapel of the Hôtel de Condé, a group of palatial buildings with huge gardens facing the Palais de Luxembourg in the rue de Vaugirard. The Comtesse de Maillé had been lady-in-waiting to the Princesse de Condé: the Prince and Princess attended the wedding after which the new Comtesse de Sade was appointed as lady-in-waiting. Socially, then, the marriage was highly satisfactory; sexually, there is no reason to think it was expected to be. If the Prince de Ligne is to be believed,[1] aristocrats were conditioned by their upbringing to look outside marriage for sexual gratification:

> They teach a girl not to look a man in the face, not to reply to him, never to ask how she happened to be born. Then they bring along two men in black, accompanying a man in embroidered satin. After which they say to her: 'Go and spend the night with this gentleman.' This gentleman, all afire, brutally assumes his rights, asks nothing, but exacts a great deal; she rises in tears, at the very least, and he, at least, wet. If they have

[1] See D. H. Lawrence, 'The Duc de Lauzun' in *Phoenix* (London, 1936).

said a word, it was to quarrel. Both of them look sulky, and each is disposed to try elsewhere ... All delicate modesty is gone: and would modesty prevent this pretty woman from yielding, to a man she loves, that which has been forced from her by a man she doesn't love? But behold the most sacred union of hearts, profaned by parents and a lawyer.

As Pierre Manuel put it: 'At one time a good Christian could not sleep with his wife for the first three nights of the marriage. Today these are the only ones he devotes to her.'

The Comte de Sade was to have a mainly negative influence on his son, who scarcely came to know him until he had lost all sense of purpose. In his youth the Count succeeded brilliantly as a diplomat and a soldier, but his career kept him away from home, and the habit of success stiffened the aristocratic pride which precluded flexibility in dealing with his financial problems. From middle-age onwards he would decline with great dignity into bankrupt despondency.

The War of the Polish Succession broke out in 1733, so during the first two years of his marriage, campaigning as aide-de-camp to the Maréchal de Villars, the Count was mostly separated from his young wife. No child was born of the marriage until 1737, when the Countess gave birth to a daughter who survived only until 1739, the year in which the Count became Lieutenant-General of Bresse, Bugey, Valromey and Gex. These four provinces had been offered to him as a reward for his services, but he had to pay 135,000 livres to the heirs of the previous Lieutenant-General, the Marquis de Lassay.

In 1740 the Prince de Condé died, and the Count was sent as ambassador to the Court of Cologne. This is where he was on 2 June when his son was born in the Countess's apartment at the Hôtel de Condé. So many babies died within the first days of their life that it was usual to safeguard newborn souls by baptizing them as quickly as possible, and on the next day the infant Marquis was taken by two servants to the parish church of St Sulpice, where he was christened Donatien-Alphonse-François. His mother had wanted him to be called Louis-Aldonse-Donatien, but the bungling servants substituted François (which was one of the Count's names) for Louis, while Aldonse, an old Provençal name unfamiliar in Paris, was transformed into Alphonse.

The insouciance of entrusting the matter to servants was characteristic of the period. It is easy to be misled by fine clothes and happy expressions on children's faces in eighteenth-century family portraits. Until they were capable of rational behaviour, children were liable to be treated more like amusing animals than human beings. Christian moralists[1] condemned parents who coddled their children without paying attention to the state of their souls, but the recommended alternative was to impose a repressive discipline which took no account of physical and emotional needs. Even the richest of parents submitted children to appalling discomforts, both psychological and physical. The experiences recorded in the memoirs of the Duc de Lauzun, who was born seven years later than Sade, cannot have been untypical. D. H. Lawrence comments:

> No man on earth could have come through such an upbringing as this boy had without losing the best half of himself on the way, and emerging incalculably impoverished. Abandoned as a baby to the indifference of French servants in a palace, he was, as he says himself, 'like all the other children of my age and condition; the finest clothes for going out, at home half naked and dying of hunger'. And that this was so, we know from other cases. Even a Dauphin was begrudged clean sheets for his bed, and slept in a tattered night-shirt while he was a boy. It was no joke to be a child in that smart period.

Girls were generally treated even worse than boys; in aristocratic and upper middle-class families the birth of a daughter was an unwelcome event. But whatever the infant's sex, no one was much concerned about what it might be feeling. Mothers sometimes retired for several months after childbirth to recuperate in a convent, and even those who didn't were unlikely to spend time with the baby. It might be farmed out to a wet-nurse in the country, probably a peasant woman with children of her own who might enjoy priority over the nurseling, not only in feeding but in emotional nourishment. Lower down in society, parents were more liable to abandon their children totally. In Paris the annual intake of foundlings at the General Hospital was nearly 6,000, though it was known that 90 per cent of the infants there

[1] E.g. Fleury, *Traité de choix de la Méthode des Etudes*, 1686.

died within the first three months. Gibbon said that the hospitalization of foundlings was a form of infanticide acceptable to the Roman Catholic conscience.

Sade was brought up in the Hôtel de Condé, where the grandeur of the surroundings can hardly have compensated for the gloom and disorientation which must have ensued when the Prince died. The Princess died eighteen months after her husband and a fortnight after Sade's first birthday.

The Comte de Sade spent little time at the Hôtel de Condé. The last Habsburg Emperor, Charles VI, had died at the end of October 1740 without male issue. His daughter, Maria Theresa, Queen of Bohemia and Hungary, was only twenty-three and her army was weak. This presented France with a chance of seizing the Netherlands and putting Charles VI's brother, Charles Albert, the Elector of Bavaria, on to the imperial throne. Sent back to the Elector of Cologne as minister plenipotentiary to win him over to Charles Albert's cause, the Comte de Sade was prominently active in the negotiations that led to the alliance between Bavaria, France and Spain. The treaty was signed at Nymphenburg in May 1741, eight months before Charles Albert was proclaimed as the new Emperor, Charles VII. The Count seems at first to have succeeded brilliantly, winning the Elector's goodwill, but, according to the memoirs of his Minister for Foreign Affairs,[1] de Sade took advantage of his position. 'The Elector complained that the envoy had let himself be bought and entered into shady transactions. M. de Sade asked permission to make a journey to France. This was granted.'

The Countess was twenty-nine when the Princess's death ended her career as lady-in-waiting. She stayed on at the Hôtel de Condé, helping to bring up the orphaned prince. Her own son, four years his junior, must have felt overshadowed. There is a passage in Sade's 1788 novel *Aline et Valcour* which draws on memories of early childhood:

> Through my mother I was connected with everything that was most grand in the Kingdom, through my father to everything that was most distinguished in the province of Languedoc. I was born in Paris in the bosom of luxury and plenty. As soon as I could think, I believed that nature and fortune had joined hands

[1] R.-L. de Voyer d'Argenson.

to fill my lap with their gifts. I believed it because people were stupid enough to tell me so, and this ridiculous preconception made me haughty, despotic and quick-tempered. It seemed that everything ought to give in to me, that the whole universe should humour my whims, that it belonged only to me, that it was there for me to use in any way I pleased. I will give you only one fact about my childhood, but it will show you how dangerous were the principles that they stupidly allowed to take root inside me.

I was born and bred in the palace of the illustrious prince my mother had the honour to serve. He was about the same age as I was, and she took care that we should spend a great deal of time together, so that, having known him since childhood, I should be able to count on his patronage throughout my life. But in my vanity, and in my ignorance of this scheme, I lost my temper with him one day when we were playing a game. He was arguing about something, and it made me angry that he thought—and with some justification, no doubt—that his rank entitled him to have everything his own way. My response was to hit him and go on hitting. Nothing would stop me until I was dragged, with some violence, away from him.

It was at about this time that my father was engaged in negotiations and my mother went to join him. I was sent to the house of a grandmother in Languedoc and her uncritical fondness for me exacerbated all the faults I have just confessed.

The correspondences to Sade's own childhood are unmistakable. The Countess did travel with the Count on some of his diplomatic missions in 1745, and in 1744 the young Marquis was sent away to his grandmother's house in Avignon. But Sade was four years younger than the prince, and biographers have no right to assume—as they all have—that the narrative tallies with what happened. That the prince married at sixteen does not mean he cannot have been weak or under-developed at the age of eight, but he would not have been under-nourished, and a four-year-old could hardly have been a formidable opponent. Sade's account of the fight probably reflects not what he did but what he would have liked to do. He must have been constantly irked by the fact of being smaller, physically weaker and inferior in rank. He probably felt that everyone in the household, including his mother, loved the prince more than they loved him—an impression which can only have grown stronger when he was sent away. His banishment must have seemed like a punishment; guilt and resentment must have festered painfully as he puzzled about what he had done to deserve it.

The decision had possibly been taken simply because his parents wanted to be together again. Their third baby, another daughter, was born on 13 August 1746, but she was entrusted to a wetnurse and survived for only five days. No other children were born, but the death of the infant daughter did nothing to strengthen the emotional tie of either parent with their son. They were content to have him brought up by other members of the family until he was old enough to be sent to a Jesuit boarding-school.

His paternal grandmother, who had borne ten children, appears to have treated him kindly, but she was an old woman, and even if he had not felt rejected by his mother, his new life in the fifteenth-century mansion at Avignon would have seemed a poor substitute for life in the palatial Hôtel de Condé. The daughter of Jean, Marquis de Murs, Baron de Romanil, his grandmother had been married in 1699 to Gaspard François de Sade, a colonel in the light cavalry and the first member of the family to bear the title Marquis. He died six months before the birth of his grandson. Of their five daughters only one was married; two were abbesses and two were nuns.

The arrangement cannot have worked out satisfactorily; the boy stayed at Avignon for only about eight months. He was then entrusted to the care of his uncle, the Abbé de Sade d'Ebreuil, a sensual man of forty who divided his life between the Cistercian monastery at Ebreuil, near Limoges, and the château at Saumane, which belonged to the Count. It was quite usual for younger brothers to carve out lucrative careers in the Church without believing they had a vocation. He had been tempted into Holy Orders twelve years previously by the prospect of becoming Vicar-General of Toulouse. Voltaire's reaction had been: 'I hear you are going to be a priest and vicar-general. What a lot of holiness all at once in one family! So that's why you tell me you are going to give up making love.'[1] He was right to be sceptical; while at Saumane the Abbé was seldom without a concubine, and

[1] Letter of 25 November 1733.

when he was fifty-seven he was briefly imprisoned on charges of debauchery after a police-raid on the house of a procuress.

When he took charge of his young nephew's upbringing, the Abbé had plenty of money. A royal decree of 1741 had given him a pension of 2,000 livres from the Archbishop of Arles, and as abbott of Ebreuil he had a lucrative benefice. Meanwhile the Count's financial position was rapidly deteriorating. He had an annual income of 10,000 livres from his office as Lieutenant-General, and the Provençal estates could have yielded an annual 18,000 if properly managed, but letters exchanged between the brothers in the early '50s show that the Count was finding it hard to pay for his son's education. He had been borrowing money from one of his abbess sisters, and was several times on the verge of selling the château and estate at Saumane. Eventually, in 1760, he leased them to his brother who never paid any rent.

To the courtiers constellated around Louis XV at Versailles, vanity was an asset at least in so far as it gave them an appetite for the gratifications that could be won in the elaborate game of conforming to etiquette and vying for prestige and precedence. But like most provincial noblemen he could enjoy neither the pleasures of the court nor the profits of the entrepreneur. Fixated on an antique set of values, de Sade was averse to activities he associated with an inferior class. He had no interest in farming or in managing his estates. It was beneath his dignity to involve himself in trade or commerce, though it was not beneath the dignity of the Prince de Carignan and Monsieur de Gesvres to draw 120,000 livres a year from roulette tables in their Paris gaming house. Financially the Count was not so badly off as the noblemen whom the English traveller Arthur Young found near Auch, ploughing their own fields, or as the Breton gentry who 'went to market with a sword on one side and a basket on the other'.[1] But there were not many options open to him, although he went on feeling superior to the newly ennobled magistrates and to the bourgeois who were busying themselves to buy properties and privileges of the sort that he had inherited. To them his dignity seemed enviable, but they had what he lacked—incentive.

Life would have been pleasanter for him if only he had shared his younger brother's enthusiasms. The Abbé was living at

[1] J. McManners, 'France' in *The European Nobility in the Eighteenth Century*, ed. A. Goodwin. (see Bibliography)

Saumane less like a churchman than a cultured country gentleman with keen interests in history, classical antiquity and literature. He was later to write a stylish biography of Petrarch, his interest being largely based on the assumption that Laura was a member of the Sade family. Though he was no more hypocritical and no more debauched than many other contemporary churchmen, the dissociation between principle and practice made an impact on his nephew, who later populated much of his fiction with priests who have no virtues, no scruples and no likeable qualities. Later on he would find a combination of libertine thinking and libertine behaviour infinitely preferable to self-indulgence behind a façade of piety. Meanwhile, five years of observing his uncle's double life created mental habits which would condition Sade's reactions to the discipline imposed at the Jesuit Collège Louis-le-Grand.

Underlying the Jesuit system of education was the assumption that children's souls still possessed their baptismal innocence. To protect it, the Fathers kept their charges relentlessly under surveillance. In Jacqueline Pascal's 1721 appendix to the constitution at Port Royal it was suggested that: 'This constant supervision should be exercised gently and with a certain trustfulness calculated to make them think that one loves them, and that it is only to enjoy their company that one is with them.'[1] At the same time, teachers were required to hold themselves strictly at a distance from their pupils, never addressing them familiarly in the second person singular. The size of the classes—there were about 200 boys in each—also militated against personal contact between pupil and teacher. The success of the Jesuit colleges depended on an austere, almost monastic regimen. Swearing and fighting were forbidden while punishments were severe, though there were equally severe restrictions on the exposure of skin for birching. Breeches must not be removed, even from the younger boys, and no more of the body must be bared than was necessary to inflict the punishment.

On the other hand, there was nothing to restrain sadistic teachers who relished the humiliation they could inflict on a boy by beating him in the presence of his class-mates, and it is possible that Sade enjoyed watching punishment, especially if he thought of the victim as a rival he could identify with the Prince. Krafft-

[1] *Regelments pour les enfants*, cited by Philippe Ariès, *Centuries of Childhood*.

Ebing has recorded the case of a student who experienced sexual enjoyment from watching his father spanking his sisters or his teacher punishing fellow-pupils. Subsequently he would day-dream about punishment while masturbating, and at the age of twelve he persuaded a school-friend to let himself be beaten.

The Jesuits had adopted a more tolerant attitude towards games and dancing. Though condemned by seventeenth-century moralists, both were taught in the colleges during the eighteenth century. After learning Latin dialogues on sacred subjects, the boys proceeded to study and act in French tragedies with ballets in the intervals or pastorals with music and dancing. Between 1750 and 1753 there were productions at Louis-le-Grand of several comedies, including Molière's *Le Misanthrope*, as well as the inevitable tragedies on Biblical subjects and dramatizations of stories about saints.

The college was in the rue Saint-Jacques, tantalizingly close to the Hôtel de Condé. The Countess, who was accompanying the Count on his travels, still had a suite of rooms there, and it is not impossible that their son stayed there for some of the time during the four years he spent at the college, but even if he began his school career as a day-boy, his routine was no longer one of princely luxury. The boarders would be woken up at 5.30 in the morning to assemble for prayers at 6. They had to study scripture for an hour and a half before breakfast. The morning's work started at 8.15. It was interrupted at 10.30 for Mass. Afterwards they had to study privately until the midday break for dinner and recreation. The afternoon's work started at 1.15 and went on until the break for refreshment at 4.30. School work resumed at 5.0 to continue until 7.15. The final prayers of the day were at 8.45, and the boys went to bed at 9.

One of their main subjects was rhetoric. Though Sade was only fourteen when he left the college, he would by then have made at least a start on the critical study of classical and modern texts, and on practical exercises in writing and speaking. Diderot, who had also been at Louis-le-Grand, has described how he was taught to prefer the directness of Homer to 'the pompous declamation of Racine'. Like Flaubert, who (long after the Jesuits had been expelled from France in 1764) was launched into short-story writing by the 'imitations' he had to produce at the Lycée, Sade learnt the rudiments of constructing a fable and a speech.

Of the 3,000 boys then at Louis-le-Grand only 500 were boarders. Most of them slept in dormitories, about twenty to a room.
The most privileged had private rooms and valets to look after
them. Sade may have been a boarder or he may have lodged for at
least some of the time with the private tutor who had been engaged
for him, the Abbé Jacques-François Amblet, a thirty-four-year-
old tonsured priest from the diocese of Geneva. If Valcour's
experiences in Sade's novel correspond to the author's, the tutor
was 'strict but intelligent. He was certainly the right sort of man
to exert a good influence on me during this formative period, but
unfortunately I didn't keep him long enough.' Probably the Count
could not afford to go on paying the Abbé's salary for the whole
of his son's four years at the school. Nearly twenty years later,
when the Abbé had to testify about his ex-pupil at one of his many
trials, he described him as having 'a passionate temperament
which made him eager in the pursuit of pleasure'. But he had
always known, he said, that Sade had 'a good heart'. At the college
he had been 'extremely well liked by his fellow-pupils'.

When Sade caught the smallpox which was to leave his face
scarred, all his hair was shaved off for fear that he would lose it
permanently. Later, when the same precaution was taken with his
son, he wrote to his wife: 'I was much uglier than he was after my
smallpox. Ask Amblet. I would have scared the devil. But, without boasting, I think I became quite a pretty bastard.'

Apart from Amblet's testimony that Sade was well liked, we
have no evidence of how he got on with boys of his own age.
Aimed at preventing sinful intimacy, the Jesuit surveillance can
hardly have been conducive either to friendship or to friendliness,
and Sade does not seem to have begun any relationships which
survived into adult life or which can have served as models for
accounts of boyhood friendships in his fiction. Neither the example of his father nor anything else in his upbringing inculcated a
capacity for rapport with other people. Amblet seems to have
befriended him in a way that none of his other teachers could, and
to have offered something of a benevolent warmth that Sade had
not experienced from his family, but there was too little continuity in his relationship with Amblet to give him much chance
of reciprocating the interest that the Abbé was taking in him.
Sade never got into the habit of concerning himself with what
other people were thinking and feeling. As with Genet, the soil

in which perversion grew was habitual solitude and constant frustration of the need to feel loved.

In eighteenth-century society it was not axiomatic that children had a right to be educated. Sade became a soldier when he was fifteen; the Duc de Lauzun was forced into a Guards regiment when he was twelve, and this was not exceptional. For the nobility, the army was an important source for both money and honour; as in marriages to cement an alliance between two families, boys were used ruthlessly, quite without regard for their happiness or the effect the experience would have on the development of their character.

Commoners had not yet been barred, as they were in 1781, from rising to commissioned rank in the French army, but to help the impoverished nobility and keep out the *nouveaux riches*, cadet schools required entrants to prove four generations of nobility in the family. Before Sade could be admitted for training at the cavalry school attached to the Light Horse Regiment of the Royal Guards, he had to obtain a certificate from a genealogist. The school's fees were 3,000 livres a year.

The new routine of his life was less consistently austere but hardly less rigorous than the routine at the Jesuit school. Spurred on by rivalry with the military training school attached to the Musketeers, the instructors drilled their pupils on foot and in the saddle, preparing them for the battlefield by moving them about in formations, sometimes in one large group as if they were a batallion, sometimes in small, squadron-like units. While the regiment was garrisoned close to Versailles, the King paid frequent visits to the school.

After twenty months of training, Sade was commissioned as a sub-lieutenant on 14 December 1755, just over six months after his fifteenth birthday. He would receive no wages, but he now had the right to wear a blue tunic with twenty gold buttons, a white coat with pink trimmings and a blue lining, blue riding-breeches and a hat braided with gold. At the end of thirteen months as a sub-lieutenant, he was promoted to the rank of cornet (the officer who carries the flag) in the Brigade de S. André of the Comte de Provence's Carbine Regiment, which was commanded by the Marquis de Poyanne. He was not yet seventeen when he had his first experience of being under fire from the Prussian army.

Always alert for passages in the fiction that can be construed as factual, biographers have assumed that Sade acquitted himself as well as his hero Valcour:

> On the battlefield I can claim to have done well. The natural impetuosity of my temperament, the fieriness that nature had given me contributed only a greater degree of force and energy to that ferocious virtue which is called courage and which is regarded, no doubt wrongly, as the only one necessary to our condition.

Again, this may correspond more closely to the way Sade wished he had behaved than to the way he did, though the Marquis de Poyanne later recommended him for promotion.

In May 1756 France abandoned her old allies, Sweden, Poland and the German states, in favour of Austria and Russia. Maria-Theresa, hoping to recover the Silesian territory she had lost, had been angling diplomatically for French help. The peace treaty between France and Austria prompted Frederic II of Sweden to occupy Saxony before the hostile coalition could consolidate any more power. France retaliated by invading Hanover, and thanks to the military genius of François de Chevert, a lieutenant-general who was debarred by his birth from rising higher in the ranks, the French won a victory at Hastenbeck under the nominal command of the Duc d'Estrées. But military achievement was soon undermined by intrigue. D'Estrées had quarrelled with the powerful financier, Paris-Duverney, who was in control of supplies. He used his influence with Mme de Pompadour and the King to have d'Estrées replaced by the royal favourite, the Duc de Richelieu, who not only allowed undisciplined looting in Hanover but refused to join forces with the other French army which was under the command of Mme de Pompadour's old friend, the Prince de Soubise. The combination of court intrigue and dilettante generalship led to the rout of Soubise's troops by the Swedes in November 1757.

By then Sade had been transferred to the Brigade Malvoisin of the Carbine Regiment. Before being driven out of Hanover and Westphalia, the French defeated the Hanoverians at Sonders-

hausen and it was during the celebrations for this victory that
Sade had an accident with some fireworks. A rocket, which might
have caused a fire, fell on a house. No damage was done, but he
had to write a formal apology, promising to stage any future
firework displays further away from the town.

In April 1759 he was nominated for a cavalry captaincy which
was available because the Chevalier de Tocqueville had been taken
prisoner. The position was worth 10,000 livres. The Marquis de
Poyanne recommended Sade as being well-born and possessing
'beaucoup d'esprit'. Still in his nineteenth year, he was promoted.
By now he was giving full play to his amorous impulses. It
seemed to him that he had failed to win his mother's love; like
many men who are left with a compulsion to wipe out the memory
of failure, he used women ruthlessly. A letter to the Abbé Amblet
displays a remorse which cannot have been entirely genuine, but
may not have been entirely spurious:

> The many misdemeanours I committed during my stay in
> Paris, my dear Abbé, and the way I have treated the most loving
> father in the world are making him repent of ever bringing me
> into it. I am justly punished by remorse at having displeased
> him and by fear of losing his affection for good. Of the pleasures
> I believed to be real, nothing is now left except bitter grief at
> having annoyed the kindest of all fathers and the best of all
> friends. I rose from my bed each morning in quest of pleasure:
> this idea made me forget all others . . . In the evenings I was
> desperate. I knew it was wrong, but the knowledge came to me
> only in the evening, and the next morning I would again be
> prey to the appetite that would send me flying back to pleasure
> . . . At present, the more I think about my own behaviour, the
> stranger it seems. I can see that my father was quite right when
> he said that three-quarters of the things I did were for the sake
> of making an impression . . . Oh dear! Does one ever get real
> enjoyment from a pleasure which is bought, and can there ever
> be real affection in love without tenderness? My self-esteem is
> now suffering from the idea that I was loved only because I
> paid perhaps less ungenerously than other people.
>
> I have just received a letter from my father this minute. He
> tells me I must make a general confession to him. I am going
> to do it, but I assure you it will be sincere. I do not want to go

on deceiving a loving father, who still wants very much to forgive me if I confess my faults to him.

Adieu, my dear Abbé, please let me have your news, though I shall not receive your letter until I am back in the army. I cannot stop anywhere else on the way. So, my dear Abbé, do not be surprised if you do not hear any more news from me until I have arrived.

Writing from Saint-Dizier while the Abbé was staying with the Count, Sade knew both men well enough to anticipate that the priest would not remain silent about receiving a letter and that his imperious host would ask to read it. What Sade probably failed to anticipate was that his father would be angry with him for taking his old tutor into his confidence. The Count wanted his son's misdemeanours to remain a secret.

The letter was written in April 1759, when Sade was on his way back to rejoin his regiment in Germany after spending his leave in Paris. The Count had the letter copied, together with another letter, written to him from Saint-Dizier by a M. de Castéra who was travelling with Sade:

> The dear boy is marvellously well. He is a convivial, considerate and entertaining companion ... Travel is making him put on weight and restoring to his cheeks the colour that had been drained away from them by the pleasures of Paris. We are taking care ... Each time we make a stop, he leaves the place with regret. His little heart—or rather his body—is violently inflammable. Beware of the German girls! I shall do my best to prevent him from doing anything silly. He has given me his word not to gamble more than 20 livres a day in the army. But this is a secret I am not telling you. Your kindness and the flattering indications of your friendship etc ...

The Count then sent copies of both letters to his brother the Abbé: 'You see! The rogue has 20 livres a day to lose ... He'd promised me not to gamble a sou, but whatever he said or did not say, it makes no difference ... This M. de Castéra is only twenty, and he never does silly things. He is so astonished that he should be a libertine ...' This is the first recorded use of the word against the boy, who went on trying to win back the approval of his father, complying without protest when he was ordered to write 'with sincerity' about his life in camp. The letter he sent from Obertistein on 12 August 1760 appears to contain nothing but the truth, though it may not contain the whole truth:

I am accused of being fond of sleep and it is true that I am a little prone to this fault. I go to bed early and rise very late. I often ride out to study the position of the enemy, and ours. After three days in a battlefield I know every gully of it as well as the Marshal. Afterwards I make my comments and I am praised or criticized according to how much commonsense there is in them. Sometimes I pay visits, but only to M. de Poyanne or to my old friends in the Carbines and the Royal Guards. I'm not ceremonious with them. I cannot abide ceremony. But for M. de Poyanne I should never set foot in general headquarters throughout the campaign. I know that I am doing nothing to advance my career. To be a success one has to pay court. But I cannot bear to. It upsets me to hear someone trying to flatter someone else by saying a thousand things he does not believe. He must have more willpower than I have to be able to play such a stupid role. To be polite, honest, dignified without pride, considerate without obsequiousness; to have my own way fairly often when it does no harm either to us or to anyone; to live well, to have a good time without ruining myself or running wild . . . those are my virtues, those are the ones I aspire to.

If I could boast of having a friend, I believe I have one in the regiment. I am not entirely sure. He is called M—, the son of M. de — and he is even, I believe, related to me through the Simianes.[1] He is a most talented boy, very agreeable. He composes very pleasing verse and writes extremely well, applying himself in a highly professional way. I am truly his friend: I have reasons for believing him to be mine. As to the rest of them, how can one know? There are friends who are like women: put them to the test and one finds that money has bought only deception. That is the end of my confession. I am opening my heart to you, not as to a father who is often to be

[1] In 1627 Jean-Baptiste de Sade had married Diane de Simiane, which brought the seigneurie of Lacoste, an ancient fief of the Simianes, into the family.

feared and not loved, but as to the most sincere friend, the most affectionate that I believe I have in the world. Do not go on harbouring reasons for making out that you hate me. Give me your love, never again to withdraw it, and believe me—there is nothing I will neglect to do in the effort to keep it.

The compulsion to win back his father's approval must have grown even stronger when his mother withdrew at about this time into the Carmelite convent in the rue d'Enfer. She was not alone in using convent seclusion less as an advance towards godliness than as an escape from an unsuccessful marriage. Many noble girls went straight from convent schooling into an arranged marriage, and straight back to the convent when it became unendurable. The Count's relationship with her had been deteriorating steadily. From 1750 onwards, complaints of penury had been recurrent in his letters. His health was poor, and he had long spells of depression. He was living in the rue du Bac, and there were days when only his personal valet was allowed to go near him. The Countess, long deprived of the luxuries she loved, had not lost her interest in worldly possessions when she withdrew into the convent. As a boy Sade had not been allowed to play with her jewellery; when he married in 1763, she refused to sell her diamonds, although the Count was having difficulties in raising money to pay for the wedding.

The Seven Years War was now in its final stages. At the beginning of May 1762, Prussia made peace with Russia and, later on in the month, with Sweden. In July the French army suffered a major defeat, and at the beginning of November, after surrendering at Cassel, the French had to evacuate the right bank of the Rhine. Three weeks later a truce was made between Austria, Prussia and Saxony. A great many French officers were due to be discharged when the war ended, and cavalry captains would be paid only a notional 600 livres, which was in practice retained as a contribution towards the liabilities of the unit.

In a letter of February 1763, the Count was complaining about his twenty-two-year-old son: 'He never misses a ball or an entertainment. It is infuriating.' He had gone to a house-party in the country in preference to visiting his father, and a major in his regiment had been saying 'frightful things' about him to one M. de Saint-Germain. However seriously the boy had intended to

reform his life, he had been gambling and borrowing money during his final period of leave. He found actresses irresistible.
Quarrels could blow up very quickly when two men were trying
to outbid each other for a girl who could willingly sell herself to
both of them, and Sade had been involved in a duel with a M. de
Soyecourt and in an exchange of insults with 'M. de Ch'. After
receiving 'a terrible letter' from him, the Count came to the con-
clusion that marriage might have a stabilizing effect on his
headstrong son.

Some parents in positions comparable to the Count's—the
parents of the Marquis d'Argenson, for example—took a great
deal of trouble over arranging a strategic marriage for their son.
It was characteristic of the Count that without being immune to
financial inducements, he failed to exploit the value of the *noblesse
de race* he was putting on the market, and that instead of taking the
initiative on his son's behalf, he responded to an approach from
an official at the Invalides—the bride's uncle. Her father, Claude-
René de Montreuil, had been one of the Presidents—in some of
the sovereign courts there were as many as thirteen—of the *Cour
des Aides* in Paris from 1743 until 1754. Of the four courts con-
trolling indirect taxation on such commodities as salt and wine,
the one in Paris was the most important. In 1715 it had sixty-nine
officers—more than twice as many as any of the other three.
Monsieur de Montreuil kept the honorific title of President. He
had adopted the name de Montreuil in the year of his marriage,
when his father, Jacques-René de Launay, bought the baronial
estate of Echauffour and the subordinate domain of Montreuil-
Largille in Normandy from the Marquis de Saint-Pierre. When
newly ennobled members of the bureaucracy or non-noble members of the bourgeoisie bought seigneuries that had belonged to
the nobility, they simultaneously acquired seigneurial rights. Nor
were they stopped from styling themselves by aristocratic names
and affecting an aristocratic life-style. By 1781 22 per cent of the
lay seigneurs in the Election of Le Mans were not members of the
nobility. Even fiscal privileges could be acquired: in 1789, out of
1,715 names on the tax-roll in the town of Montargis, 852 were
marked as privileged or exempt. The de Launay family was
typical of the rising class: Jacques-René's three sisters all married
into the nobility, as did the two sisters of his wife, Marie-Madeleine
Masson de Plissay. His presidential robes and the precedence he

enjoyed at ceremonial occasions must have afforded some compensation both to him and to her for the lack of a title, and by securing a noble fiancé for their eldest daughter they were belatedly fulfilling an ambition they had renounced in marrying each other—the desire for a close link with the old *noblesse d'épée*. From the Comte de Sade's point of view, the incentive was mainly financial: he was ridding himself of all responsibility for the unreliable boy.

The father's decision could not have been taken at a worse moment for the son, who had just discovered, painfully, that it was possible to become emotionally involved in a sexual relationship. He had also contracted a venereal disease and failed to keep it a secret from his father. The twenty-two-year-old Laure-Victoire-Adeline de Lauris was the daughter of the Marquis de Lauris. Both fathers might have been willing for their children to marry, and Sade, after visiting her in Avignon, hurried back to obtain his father's consent, only to learn from the Count that she had gone down on her knees to beg her father not to allow the marriage. On 6 April 1763 Sade wrote to her:

> What has become of those promises to love me for the rest of your life? Who is forcing you to be inconstant, to break the bonds that were going to unite us for ever?

Already, apparently, she had found another lover she preferred, and Sade's letter swerves desperately between incredulity, anger and pleading.

> There will be a time, perhaps soon, when you will not be afraid to enter my family. When I am head of it, my choice will be in accordance with my own wishes. Perhaps you will show more determination then. I am in need of consolation, reassurance, proofs of your fidelity. Everything frightens me.

He was very willing to forgive her for infecting him with venereal disease:

> Take care of yourself. For the restoration of my own health I'm doing what I can. But whatever condition I find yours in, nothing shall prevent me from giving you the most tender proof of my love.

He also realized that the infection might give him power over her:

> The little business of the c— ought to make you tread carefully with me. I promise you I should not conceal it from my rival. Nor would it be the only secret I should confide in him. I swear to you, there are no lengths, however horrible, to which I would not go.

In previous sexual relationships, rank, money and persistence had given him all the power he needed. He would have been exceptional if he had not slept with many prostitutes and camp-followers when he was a teenage soldier. He may have had even earlier sexual adventures, as many boys did, with servants. According to Krafft-Ebing, an excessive sexual appetite must always be regarded as a basis for sadistic inclinations, and the likelihood is that Sade had a great deal of sexual experience during his youth. But Laure de Lauris seems to have been the first woman who could make him suffer so much. We can discount the conventional insistence in his letter that life without her would be unendurable, meaningless; what is genuinely revealing is the violent inconsistency in the tone. After reviling her, the letter rebounds into professions of adoration. Addressing her as 'my divine love, my heart's only support, my life's only delight', he implores her forgiveness for what he has just written. He is 'beside himself'. To lose her is to lose his life and die by the cruellest of deaths. Then suddenly he is making practical suggestions again. The last time they met, he says, she told him that she would be delighted if her parents put her into a convent.

> If you want us to be able to see each other, it is the only step you can take; for you know it will be impossible for me to visit you at home.

The letter was written, obviously, out of an urgent need to convince himself that he had not lost her. But he was contrite at having threatened that he would go to any horrible lengths: 'I blush at the thought of using means like these to keep you.' He is determined, he says, to resist the marriage his father is planning for him:

Be faithful to me if you don't want to see me die of grief. Goodbye, my beautiful child. I adore you and love you a thousand times more than my life. It is useless to tell me 'Go away'. I swear to you neither of us can exist without the other.

Meanwhile Mme de Montreuil had discovered that he was in Avignon. Eager though she was to ally the family with the royal blood, she cannot have been ignorant of the Marquis's reputation. The Count had done his diplomatic best to persuade the Montreuils that there was little foundation for the gossip, and that his son was in Avignon because he wanted to live there. He was making arrangements about a house. The Count even went to the lengths of manufacturing documentary evidence to account for the boy's delay in returning; he asked his brother, the Abbé, to write a letter reporting that he could not allow the Marquis to travel back until he had recovered from a fever.

A few days before the wedding, the Count wrote to one of his abbess sisters:

> I believe that since the last delivery of mail from Avignon, Mme de Montreuil has known everything. That and the other affair have made her furiously cold towards my son, but it is too late to go back on it now ... Whatever attitude he adopts, I am holding things together by being careful, polite and attentive. The whole family seems to be pleased with me. I dine and spend every day with one or other of them. They see no one else and their solicitousness is unbelievable. I cannot help pitying them for the acquisition they are about to make, and I feel guilty at deceiving them about his character. In his last letter the Abbé agrees that no one could be less placid. When I used to tell him that, he would not believe me, always assuring me that he knew how to handle the boy. Nothing is placid about him except his tone of voice. In big things and in small there is no bringing him to heel. I imagine I shall be in a hurry to leave Paris when he is living here.

The Count blamed his son's disposition on the Countess. 'She is a terrible woman,' he wrote to the Abbé on the day of the wedding, still furious at her refusal to part with her diamonds. 'Her son takes after her.' He was so eager to be rid of the boy that he had

not scrupled to do 'things one would never have done if one had
been more fond of him'.

Capable though he obviously was of believing in the possibility
of long-term sexual commitment, Sade submitted meekly to his
father's arrangements for a marriage of convenience. This is not as
strange as it seems. In eighteenth-century France it was not
assumed that people had the right to make their own decisions
about work, faith or sexual relationships. Children might find
themselves married at the age of twelve or thirteen for the sake of
bettering their parents' financial or social situation. In the family,
as in the state, government was autocratic. The authority of the
father continued into the adult life of his children, and it was up-
held by the law; it allowed him to force his sons and daughters
into the marriages he chose for them. A boy who disobeyed was
liable to be arrested by the police; a girl who became pregnant by
the wrong lover could be imprisoned in a convent. All the father
had to do was apply for a *lettre de cachet*. This was a letter which
would be signed by the King and countersigned by one of his
ministers. Once the royal seal had been affixed, the victim could
be imprisoned without a trial for as long as his father wished to
go on paying for his board and lodging in the gaol. The letter need
not even specify a reason for the arrest. Family honour was considered to be reason enough. The young Mirabeau was imprisoned
twenty-two times by *lettres de cachet* issued at the request of his
father, and this is how Mme de Montreuil was later to revenge
herself on Sade. During the ministry of Fleury (1726–43) 40,000
lettres de cachet were issued, mostly against Protestants and Jan-
senists.

If Mme de Montreuil's vengeance was sadistic, so was the
whole social and judicial system which encouraged the powerful
to abuse the human needs of the unprotected. The most public
manifestations of sadism were the spectacular tortures and savage
punishments inflicted on law-breakers and heretics, who were
degradingly tortured in front of large and appreciative audiences.
The degradation was integral to the punishment. The penalty for
sacrilege committed in church was death by burning, and in 1750
two peasants were burned to death for sodomy. Huguenots who
defied the ban on assemblies were liable to be whipped in the
street. A house-breaker could be sentenced to be broken on the
wheel, which meant that the executioner would bind him to a St

Andrew's cross and strike eleven blows to break his bones, finally crushing his chest in. The corpse was then exhibited on a wagon wheel. High prices were paid for space at the best vantage points.

In the spectacular ceremony of an aristocratic wedding, no cruelty was apparent. The pain would make its entrance later, privately and gradually, as the relationship developed. On 1 May, at Versailles, in the presence of the Comte de Sade, Monsieur le Président de Montreuil and Madame la Présidente, the King and Queen gave their consent to the marriage; on 15 May, at the Montreuils' town-house in the rue Neuve-du-Luxembourg, the contract was signed by the couple, and on the following day by their families. Whatever misgivings Mme de Montreuil was harbouring about the Marquis's escapade at Avignon, she wrote to the Abbé saying: 'No one could be more genial or more desirable as a son-in-law than your nephew. The pains that you took with him seem to have developed his appearance of being intelligent, quiet and well-educated.'

The woman who was to inflict so much damage on her son-in-law was extremely attractive, and she had given birth to her youngest daughter only three years before her eldest was married. Daintily built and still young-looking, she had an engaging laugh, a charming smile, a quick mind and a much more dominating personality than either her husband or her eldest daughter. It is probable that from the beginning she found Sade desirable: it would be galling for her to discover that two of her daughters would enjoy the man who was denied to her.

Her meanness was reflected in the marriage settlement, which was contrived to give the young couple a modest income with no opportunity of squandering capital. The Montreuils' caution was matched by the concern of the impoverished Count to protect what remained of the family resources. As was usual in marriages of convenience, the contract went into considerable detail. The Count made over the annual revenue of 10,000 livres from his post as Lieutenant-General, back-dated to March 1760 when he had relinquished it, and the Marquis received a certificate of credit from the King. The Count also made over his Provençal estates, with their annual revenue of about 20,000 livres, and all his other property, but reserved the right to dispose of land to the value of 30,000 livres. Of the 34,000 livres owed to the Comte de Sade by the Comte and Comtesse de Béthune, a credit of 10,000 livres was to be transferred to the Marquis, with interest payable from the date of the marriage. Meanwhile M. de Montreuil gave his daughter 10,000 livres in cash and 1,500 in rent, with the expectation of an additional 2,000 in rental income when his father died and an additional 80,000 in cash when he died. Mme de Montreuil did not give her daughter any cash, but left her 50,000 in her will. The bride received a rental income of 6,000 livres from her father's mother, with the prospect of large capital sums when both her father and her grandmother were dead. The Montreuils undertook to accommodate the young couple with two servants either in their town-house or in the Normandy château for the first five years of the marriage, or to pay an annual living allowance of 2,000 livres. At the end of this period they would provide 10,000 livres towards the couple's expenses in setting up house. The Count, in other words, was signing his son into what promised to be a fairly comfortable financial dependence on the family dominated by the formidable Mme de Montreuil.

On 17 May the marriage was solemnized in Paris at the church of Saint Roch. The Marquis's venereal disease must by now have been cured; there is no evidence that any infection passed on to the bride.

Chapter 2

Divertissements

In a sadistic relationship the victim is used like an instrument, as a means to an end, but the dehumanization is part of the point; it is impossible to be sadistic towards a thing. Though it would be inaccurate to describe a whole society as sadistic, the *ancien régime* tended to popularize the art of humiliation. One man's degradation was another man's honour. The bourgeoisie was no less rank-conscious than the aristocracy; the wife of a public prosecutor or notary would be addressed as Mademoiselle, the wife of a judge as Madame. Everyone had superiors and inferiors; there was no need to watch the eyes of inferiors for indications of what was going on in the mind.

Sons were superior to daughters, but all children were inferior to parents, and seeing his son with Mme de Montreuil, the Comte de Sade did not notice any sign of danger in the way she looked at him. After the newly united families had gone to see the parade of the royal household at Marly, the Count reported to his brother: 'She is mad about the Marquis, who has no idea in his head, except that he must have his pleasure and cannot find it anywhere.' In a week of living next door to his father, the boy had not troubled to pay him a single visit.

Within six weeks of marrying, the Marquis found his way towards a great deal of extra-marital pleasure. For 800 livres a year he rented a small house in Paris, near the rue Mouffetard and not far from the Collège Louis-le-Grand. It was easy for a nobleman to obtain credit from tradesmen and he furnished the house without paying. He had other uses for his cash. Without giving up hope of reviving his relationship with Laure de Lauris, he found the best sexual delights currently available were the ones he could buy.

Since the marriage Mme de Montreuil had taken less trouble to be charming to the Count, which made it all the more irritating for him to see her being so charming to his son. Blithely unaware that her daughter was being deceived, she supported Sade in the financial squabbles which started when his father wanted to deduct expenses before paying over the revenue from the Lieutenant-Generalcy.

At the beginning of August 1763 the Montreuils moved to Echauffour, their Normandy estate, where the young couple joined them a week later. Though the Marquise was not yet pregnant, Mme de Montreuil was exuberantly untroubled. The Abbé, who would hardly have been worrying about it, received a letter assuring him that: 'Neither of them comes from infertile stock.' A week later he heard from his brother, who was complaining that his son had 'turned the head' of Mme de Montreuil.

So the Count had to cope simultaneously with guilt at having behaved unscrupulously to rid himself of his troublesome son, with jealousy over the reactions of the attractive Mme de Montreuil, and with financial insecurity. It was too much for him: he started behaving like a sulky child. By October he was refusing to fulfil the commitments of the marriage contract. There was even trouble with a tailor. The account for the wedding garments had been sent to the Count who had ordered them, but he referred the man to the Marquis for what was owing to him.

In October Sade told the Montreuils that he was going to Fontainebleau where he would apply for a position at Court, and then to Dijon, where, as the new Lieutenant-General of Bresse, Bugey, Valromey and Gex, he would present himself to the Burgundian Parlement—one of the thirteen offshoots of the royal court, sovereign bodies dispensing civil and criminal justice in the King's name. Mme de Montreuil had no reason to suspect that his intention was to spend the whole time in Paris, and in a letter to the Abbé she fondly described her 'little son-in-law' as a 'funny child'.

> Sometimes I take the liberty of scolding him. We quarrel, but we soon make it up. It is never serious and never lasts long . . . He may be harum-scarum but marriage is giving him something to think about. Unless I am much mistaken, you will notice a big difference in him. As for your niece, much as she would like to please you and obey you, she will never scold him. She will love him as much as you like. It is very simple: he has always been very kind. He loves her very much. He could not treat her better than he does.

This letter was written on 20 October. The night of the 18th Sade spent with a twenty-year-old working-class girl, Jeanne Testard, a fan-maker, who afterwards testified in great detail about her experience with him. About three weeks previously she had met a procuress called du Rameau, who now offered Jeanne 48 livres to put herself into the hands of a man whose name would remain unknown. When she accepted, she met a man of about twenty-two, about five foot three inches tall, with light chestnut hair, a pale complexion and pock-marks. He was dressed in an overcoat made of blue cloth, with silver buttons, a red collar and red facings. He made her climb into a hired carriage. Waiting inside it was a servant, whom she was told to address as la Grange. She was taken to a small house near the rue Mouffetard. The carriage gateway was painted yellow and it had iron thistles above it. The man took her up to a room on the first floor. The servant, who had followed, was sent downstairs. The door was locked and bolted. The man asked her whether she was religious, whether she believed in God, in Jesus, in the Virgin Mary. She answered that she believed in the Christian religion. She had been brought up in it and followed it as much as she could. The man replied with insults and horrible blasphemies, saying that there was no God, that he had proved it, that he had masturbated into a chalice which had been at his disposal for two hours in a chapel. He blasphemed against Jesus and the Virgin Mary. He told her about having intercourse with a girl who had taken communion with him. He had kept the two hosts, put them inside the girl and enjoyed her carnally, saying: 'If you are God, revenge yourself.'

He then suggested to Jeanne Testard that they should go into an adjoining room, warning her that she would see something extraordinary. When she told him that she was pregnant and afraid of seeing anything which might give her a shock, he said there was nothing frightening about it. He took her into the next room, shutting himself in with her. She was astonished to see four birch-rods and five whips of different kinds hanging from the wall, three ivory crucifixes, two engravings of Christ, one of Calvary and one of the Virgin Mary. Also arranged around the walls were many drawings and engravings depicting nude bodies in indecent postures. After making her examine the different objects, he told her that when she had warmed him up, she would have to beat him, and that he would then beat her with any whip of her choice. She would not consent to any of these proposals, although he pressed her very hard. He then took down two of the crucifixes. He crushed one of them under his feet and polluted the other by masturbating on it, telling her to trample on it. When she hesitated, he pointed to two pistols on the table and held his hand on his sword, threatening to run her through with it. To save her life, she trampled on the crucifix and at the same time he forced her to say blasphemous words. He wanted to give her an enema to pollute the crucifix, but she refused.

She spent the whole night without eating or drinking or lying down. He read her several poems full of impieties and totally contrary to religion.[1] He said they had been given to him by friends who were as libertine as he was. He suggested making love to her in an unnatural way, and he made her promise to meet him the following Sunday at 7 o'clock in the morning, so that they could take communion together and keep the two hosts. His idea was to burn one and take her when the other was inside her. Before he left and before the procuress arrived to collect her, he forced her to take an oath not to divulge anything of what had happened. She also had to give him her signature on a blank piece of paper.

It is not easy to explain how Sade had acquired his taste for flagellation. Not that perversion of this type was rare. In August 1764, when a young count had himself beaten till blood was drawn, the police report contains the comment: 'Many people are being reduced to this extremity, and today there is no brothel without a number of birch-rods.' Antoine Adam[2] maintains that 'in these days of Anglomania', French gentlemen were inspired by the example of London's well-known Hell-Fire Club to behave viciously towards working-class girls. The chapter on flagellation in Dühren's history of sex-life in England[3] supports the view that 'le vice anglais' had its name because the practice had been more common in England than anywhere else. John Cleland's *Memoirs of a Woman of Pleasure* (better known as *Fanny Hill*) suggests that the perversion is more common among older men who are

---

[1] Lely suggests that one of the poems may have been the fifty-third erotic epigram in the Palatine Anthology, a hymn to pregnancy as the season in which the man should not lie on top of the girl. She should offer him the more impious sheath in her backside.

[2] Preface to Vol XXIX of Sade's *Oeuvres complètes*.

[3] *Das Geschlechtsleben in England*, Vol II, Berlin, 1903.

'obliged to have recourse to this experiment, for quickening the circulation of their sluggish spirits'.

But why should a man of twenty-three have recourse to such extremes? The explanation must be partly physiological, partly psychological. The letter Sade wrote from the Bastille twenty-one years later about the abnormal thickness of his seminal fluid and the extreme difficulty he had in ejaculating[1] cannot be wholly irrelevant to his situation in 1763. It would seem he could achieve an orgasm only when he was already in a state of extreme excitement. Renée-Pélagie, obviously, was incapable of exciting him as Laure de Lauris had, and though he had never before had the opportunity to establish himself in a house of his own, well equipped for simultaneous indulgence in flagellation and blasphemy, he may have discovered pleasure in inflicting pain during earlier relationships with actresses, prostitutes, camp followers and servants. But if all human behaviour is to some extent imitative, what was his model?

He may have been beaten before he was put into the hands of the Jesuits, or it may be that the Fathers gave him his first taste of corporal punishment. Many of them no doubt took profane pleasure in having so much power over young boys. (James Joyce wrote revealingly about twentieth-century Jesuits in *A Portrait of the Artist as a Young Man*, in which the preacher at the retreat, terrifying the boys by describing the torments of damnation with enormous relish, seems no less sadistic than the prefect of studies who canes Stephen on the hand for breaking his spectacles on the cinder path.) In eighteenth-century France, when boys were caned on the bottom, the rule about exposing a minimum of skin must have had the opposite of the intended effect: a chink of flesh is more erotically suggestive than bareness. After living for five years with his self-indulgent uncle, Sade may have seen a continuity between his behaviour and that of the Fathers. Like the Abbé, the teachers must have seemed very much like surrogate parents: if he sensed that they were enjoying themselves while beating him, he may at some level have enjoyed the combination of passivity with power to give pleasure. He had seldom been able to believe that he was giving pleasure to his real father.

Then suddenly, in the cavalry school, the fourteen-year-old boy was being trained to inflict pain on the horse between his legs. He

[1] See p. 146 below.

must win the approval of his masters by mastering the animal, applying the spurs, the bridle and the whip. Women could be mastered in much the same way, and after being born in a royal household where servants were treated as congenital inferiors, how could he have been expected to treat prostitutes or peasant girls as if they were his equals? In *Les 120 journées de Sodome* the Duke is described as being able to rape a girl without using more than one hand, and to kill a horse between his legs. Girls, like horses, were there to be used. Though the word *sadism* did not yet exist, Sade's first experiences of the activity must have given him a gratifying—and rather frightening—certainty that after the early pain of failing to make any apparent impact on his mother or on any of the other ladies who waited upon the prince, he was at least making himself felt. To some extent he may have been revenging himself for her inattention and indifference. No woman could be inattentive or indifferent to the whip. But surely Jean-Paul Sartre is wrong to suggest that the sadist wants to reach his victim 'in her particularity, in the depths of her consciousness'.[1] For Sade it was important that the victim was female, but he was unconcerned about her personality. Her consciousness must revolve, like a satellite, around him, but he is not concerned to penetrate it or even to know what it contains.

I had better say explicitly that I am not trying to justify Sade's behaviour, only to present the results of my efforts at understanding it. From his own point of view, everything he did must have seemed justifiable, and the biographer, like an actor playing an unsympathetic character, should identify at least enough to understand the strength of his subject's compulsions. It would be inadequate to write as if Sade merely did what he did because he wanted to. He may have experienced considerable ambivalence and almost as much fear as his victims. The sense of danger, probably, was integral to the excitement he needed if he was to achieve an orgasm.

If he thought all his actions were justifiable, this can only mean, paradoxically, that he thought it right to do wrong, good to do evil. At this stage of his development, the need to inflict pain and the need to blaspheme were interdependent. Alongside the whips and straps, crucifixes and holy pictures were on the wall, waiting to be defiled. If we compare the atheistic ideas he expounded to

[1] *Saint Genet, comédien et martyre*, Gallimard, 1952.

Jeanne Testard with his atheism of nineteen years later, as explained in his *Dialogue entre un prêtre et un moribond*, the differences are very striking. The *Dialogue* is the work of a man who has thought his way systematically through the problem, liberating himself from any compulsion towards obscenity, blasphemy or violence; the Sade of 1763 is a rebel and a hysteric, totally alienated from the world in which he found himself. He had not yet thought out his position philosophically, but he was reacting emotionally against the society that accepted all the anomalies and injustices, the parents who demanded love and gave none, the Jesuits who denied the body's natural right to pleasure but self-righteously took pleasure in the denial. In blaspheming against Jesus and the Virgin Mary, Sade was venting the hatred he felt not against them but against those who professed to love them. His mother had given them the love she owed to him.

Blasphemy is never logical. If an omnipotent God exists, the blasphemer can only be damaging himself by insulting him; if he does not exist, there is no one there to insult. With Sade, the need to behave outrageously was urgent enough for logic to become irrelevant, not only while defiling the crucifixes and unleashing his aggressions against the girl, but during the less heated moments of acquiring the paraphernalia and arranging the crucifixes and obscene pictures on the wall. The night had been as carefully prepared as a theatrical performance.

Unlike Dostoevsky, Sade would never have said that he wished he could believe. In a letter of 1854, calling himself 'a child of unbelief and scepticism', Dostoevsky wrote: 'How terribly it has tortured me (and tortures me even now) this longing for faith which is all the stronger for the proofs I have against it! And yet God gives me sometimes moments of perfect peace; in such moments I love and believe that I am loved.' Dostoevsky may have been thinking of Sade when he created Stavrogin in *The Devils*. In Chapter 1 of Part Two, Shatov asks Stavrogin: 'Is it true that the Marquis de Sade could have taken lessons from you?' When Stavrogin smashes a crucifix, the Bishop tells him: 'You honour the Holy Spirit without knowing it.' Dostoevsky makes Stavrogin confess: 'Every unusually disgraceful, utterly degrading, dastardly, and, above all, ridiculous situation in which I ever happened to be in my life, always roused in me, side by side with extreme anger, an incredible delight . . . It was not the vileness that I loved (here my mind was perfectly sound) but I enjoyed rapture from the tormenting consciousness of the baseness.' I. A. Richards has said the key to Stavrogin's religious dilemma is the combination of his pride with his lust for vileness;[1] the same could be said of Sade's.

Almost certainly Sade was perpetrating with Jeanne Testard the most evil actions that he could imagine, and, as with a child, one motive for the naughtiness was desire—overwhelming but unconscious—for punishment. He was putting himself at enormous risk. When the girl walked out of the house, there was nothing to stop her from going straight to the police, and nothing did.

Nine or ten days elapsed before Sade was arrested. The Lieutenant-General of Police had been consulted before a statement was taken from the girl, and he may have ordered his officers to interview other girls who had been procured for Sade. Louis XV took a close personal interest in the sexual activities of his subjects. It amused him to learn that the Bishop of Rennes was indebted to his mistress, Mme de Marsay, for many of his benefices, that the Baronne Blanche had slept with most of the diplomatic corps, that the Duchesse de la Vallière and the Duchesse de Luxembourg were having a Lesbian relationship, that the Princesse d'Enrichemont threatened her chambermaids that she would make them open their legs to her lackeys.[2]

M. de Sartine, the Lieutenant-General of Police, controlled a network of police espionage in which inspectors were required to pick up as much information as they could from stage-door keepers, procuresses and brothel-keepers. The King was an avid reader of the dossiers they compiled. He was kept informed about the specialities and tariffs in the various brothels. Nor was his interest merely academic; he benefited directly from the heavy taxes levied on them.

Sartine, a commoner, had been only thirty in 1759 when he was given his position—one which would never have been given to a commoner under Louis XIV. He had an almost fetishistic passion for wigs. De Fleury's memoirs describe him as having a large 'library' of wigs for different occasions. To cross-examine suspects he donned a wig which was called 'the inexorable'. It had curls like serpents, calculated to inspire guilt and fear.

[1] *Complementarities*, Carcanet Press, 1977.
[2] See Louis Marais, *Mémoires*, and Pierre Manuel, *La Police dévoilée*.

When Sade was arrested, he was escorted by Inspector Marais—who was to play the leading role in the police surveillance of his activities—to Fontainebleau, where he was cross-examined by M. de Saint-Florentin, Minister of the Royal Household. The dossier was passed to the King with the suggestion that such excesses merited the severest punishment. The royal warrant was then issued for Sade to be imprisoned in the fortress at Vincennes, just outside Paris. It was one of about twenty state prisons. In most of them the lavatory was a gutter on one side of the cell, while the straw the prisoners slept on was changed only once or twice a month.

After three days in his cell, Sade was asking to see a priest. On 2 November he wrote to M. de Sartine:

It serves me right that God should avenge himself on me, and that is what is happening. All I can do now is weep for my faults and despise the mistakes I have made. Alas, God could have annihilated me without allowing me time to see them for what they were. I must be thankful to him for permitting me the opportunity to find myself again. I beg you, Monsieur, give me the means by letting me see a priest. Only with good instruction and sincere repentance can I hope soon to approach the divine sacraments which I have been entirely neglecting. This was the prime cause of my downfall.

As in the letters to his father, his contrition should not be dismissed as insincere. On the contrary, to the extent that he had been courting punishment, he must have responded gratefully to the debasement that made self-castigation seem inevitable. In the fantasies behind his acts of sacrilege, fear of divine punishment must have been mixed with the hope that he would not escape it. He had been the sole author of the drama that Jeanne Testard had helped him to act out, but not of the epilogue in which the scene disconcertingly shifted from the rue Mouffetard to a dark, smelly, uncomfortable dungeon in a fortress. Was there a genuine possibility that God was revenging himself? If not, the drama had been meaningless.

But he still had to concern himself with the consequences that disgrace could have on his career. He had already written to M. de Sartine on 29 October asking for the affair to be hushed up. His career would be ruined, he said, if the details of his arrest became public knowledge. He also wrote to the governor of the prison for permission to send a letter to his mother-in-law so that his wife could visit him: 'Grant me the pleasure of making peace with the woman who is so dear to me and whom, in my feebleness, I have wounded so grievously . . . I implore you, Monsieur, not to refuse me the comfort of seeing the woman who means more to me than anyone else in the world. If she had the honour of knowing you, you would recognize that her conversation is more likely than anything else to put an unhappy man back on the right road, when nothing could be greater than his despair at having strayed from it.'

In his second letter to the Lieutenant-General of Police, Sade begged that his family should not be told of the reasons for his imprisonment. Besides, he had succumbed to temptation for scarcely a week. Though that, admittedly, was 'long enough to anger the Supreme Being'. In the same letter he asked whether he could be allowed to have his valet in prison. The young man, he said, had taken no part in the debauches.

Two days later, the Preacher of the Royal Household wrote to a confessor asking him to visit the prisoner, while M. de Saint-Florentin gave instructions that Sade should not receive 'distinguished treatment' in the dungeon. He could be allowed a servant, but not his own valet. It was not until the Count had paid a tearful visit to Fontainebleau, pleading for his son's release, that the King authorized it. The Marquis was required to stay at Echauffour, and Inspector Marais accompanied him there. Writing to the Abbé three days later, the Count briefed him to deny any rumours that might reach Provence. Above all, their sisters must know nothing of what had happened.

Soon after Sade's return, Renée-Pélagie was pregnant. Writing to the Abbé on 21 January 1764, Mme de Montreuil described her daughter as about three months gone and quite well, apart from some morning-sickness. The Marquis would have to make reparations for past events by behaving irreproachably. So far, the family was satisfied with him. But if the child was born alive, it can have survived only for a few hours. In an undated letter to his uncle Sade wrote: 'Heaven did not want me to go on enjoying the happiness of being a father.'

At the beginning of April the King granted the family's request that the Marquis should be allowed to spend three months in

Paris, but he did not go there till late June or early July. Meanwhile, he had his first practical experience of theatre, directing some amateur productions with members of the family at the Chateau d'Evry. In the comedy *L'Avocat Patelin* by Brueys et Palaprat, he played opposite his wife and sang to her some additional verses which he had composed himself. They included a promise of fidelity and the reflection: 'From evil to good is but a single step.'

He paid little attention to the admonitory letter his father wrote on 21 April 1764:

> The trouble you caused which led to your arrest is more serious than you believe and you should reflect on the grievous transgression you have committed. Everything that concerns God and the religion is beyond the forgiveness of men appointed to render justice. God is good and compassionate and he does not want to lose us when there is sincere repentance, but men do not forgive in this manner. When I ordered you to stay at Echauffour I had my reasons for wishing it and I do not know why M. and Mme de Montreuil went against my judgement after all my instructions which in one word were to have you compelled to stay there.

In June Sade finally paid the visit that had been planned for the previous year to the Burgundian Parlement at Dijon. Royal permission had been given for him to go there, but to stay only as long as necessary. He was formally installed as the King's Lieutenant-General for the provinces of Bresse, Bugey, Valromey and Gex. In his address to the Parlement he described the day as the happiest in his life.

One of the functions of theatre was to provide a shop-window in which actresses and dancers could sell themselves, and soon after his arrival in Paris Sade became eager to buy an outstandingly attractive eighteen-year-old. Mlle Colet had made her debut at the age of fifteen and a half, and soon had several noblemen outbidding each other for her. When she was seventeen, she was infected by a Duke with a venereal disease. The husband of his titular mistress took her to a surgeon and, after the six-week cure, himself started an affair with her, but lost her to a viscount, whom she abandoned for the Marquis de Lignerac. He was paying her 480 livres a month, but within six months had to share her with a count who paid 720 a month, besides taking responsibility for debts to the value of 6,000. She was described as svelte with signs of incipient plumpness. Her eyes were small but expressive, sometimes gentle, sometimes fiery. Inspector Marais, whose prose betrays the pleasure he took in his job, described her as having 'a small spider face and eyes like holes in a bit-brace'. About three weeks before Sade met her, an English nobleman, Elchin, paid 700 livres for one night with her.

Sade had probably been in the audience many times before he was introduced to her after a performance at the Comédie-Italienne in July 1764 and succeeded in accompanying her to her home. The following day he wrote two letters to her, each more passionate than any he is known to have written since his affair with Laure de Lauris ended fifteen months previously. In the first letter he told Mlle Colet that he was madly in love. There could be no happiness for him except to share his life and his fortune with her. To the message that she was outraged by his declaration, he responded with a longer letter, a whirlwind of abject apology and ecstatic promises. He would die a thousand times rather than give her offence. He should not have given rein in his earlier letter to the violence of his passion for her, but the only way to stop loving her would be to stop living. His feelings are more delicate than she believes. If only she would let him die at her feet, her tender and virtuous heart would be witness of the frightful state to which she had reduced him. His love has become the guiding principle of his life. Had she thought he was offering her his fortune merely to buy favours? No, for a heart like hers the price he is willing to pay includes his tears, sighs, fidelity, obedience, repentance and respect.

After this, the eighteen-year-old actress did not refuse to meet him, but the rendezvous she proposed was not soon enough: 'How cruel you are so to postpone the moment of my happiness. I can no longer live, no longer exist. For pity's sake, can it not be at four o'clock today?'

In a report dated 7 December, Inspector Marais recorded that she was accepting 500 livres a month from Sade though she was still living with de Lignerac, who turned a blind eye to her double-dealing. Sade, much less tolerant of his rival, was venting his spleen on the procuress, La Brissault, nicknamed La Présidente, who kept a brothel on the Barrière-Blanche while her husband managed another on the rue Tire-Boudin. Sade was by now on the alert for police espionage. On one of his visits to the Présidente's brothel he asked her whether she knew Inspector Marais. She said no, and told Marais about the enquiry. Without explaining why it was dangerous, he warned her not let Sade take any girls to private apartments.

Two weeks later the Inspector was reporting that de Lignerac, who was under pressure from his family, had abandoned Colet to Sade, but he found the situation embarrassing. Like many of the more successful actresses, she was expecting her salary to be subsidized very substantially by lovers, while he was nervous that the liaison might cause a scandal. He confided in la Présidente, who advised him that the girl was beyond his means. It was not in the procuress's interest to lose him as a casual customer. He had been coming regularly and paying generously.

According to a report the Inspector filed a week later, on 28 December Colet was still meeting de Lignerac, though his family had now cut off his allowance. The jealous Sade was worried about the present she had received on Christmas Day, a pair of ear-rings worth 3,000 livres. She was showing them off as a curiosity to all her visitors. No longer ignorant of Sade's extra-marital affairs, Mme de Montreuil was characteristically both practical and shrewd about prising her son-in-law away from his mistress. Before the end of the year she had convinced him that Colet was deceiving him, though according to Marais he slept with her three times between 21 and 28 December. It is unlikely that he made love to her sadistically, but she probably found nothing 'unnatural' in being taken from behind, while his growing preference for anal sex derived partly from feeling it to be more impious. His involvement with Colet was quite passionate. But the ear-rings had been sent by a Duke with very much more money than Sade, who was soon asking for his letters to be returned. She was still going to bed with de Lignerac, and in 1765 she had another affair with Elchin. But she had only a year to live; in 1766 her theatrical and sexual career was abruptly cut short when she died—not yet twenty-one.

In helping to free Sade from one infatuation, Madame de Montreuil had only been clearing the way for the next two, which both occurred early in 1765. The first was with a girl of noble birth whom he met at a ball in February. What 'delicious days' he could have spent with her if it had not been for 'an unhappy marriage of convenience'.

The royal order confining him to Echauffour had been repealed in September 1764, and in March 1765 he was preparing to leave for Provence. He did not go until May, and it was in April that his name first figured in police reports on the actress Beauvoisin, who was about twenty-two. According to the well-informed Marais, 'there are few women with such a well-stocked wardrobe, or who look so alluring in lace. At home she is always dressed with seductive propriety in elegant *déshabillés*, and no one is more expert at exploiting her figure. She is now considered to be one of our prettiest women and thought to be fairly faithful to her lovers, though I am assured that she denies herself nothing, and her temperament is very lively despite her air of reserve. Last Wednesday the Marquis of Louvois left to join his regiment, and the same night she slept with the Chevalier de la Tour, who is reckoned by all these beauties to be quite a stallion.'

Sade left Echauffour on 9 May, ostensibly on his way to Avignon, but eleven days later there had been no news of him or from him, and when he arrived at the Château de Lacoste he was with Beauvoisin. He must have been passing her off either as his wife, who was not yet known in Provence, or as a relation of hers. He spent a great deal of money on redecorating the castle's private theatre and inviting the nobility of the district to dramatic entertainments, balls and banquets. The Provençal nobility was known to set a high value on private theatricals, and Sade, paying his first protracted visit to Lacoste since his marriage, was anxious to make a good impression. His neighbours included the dissolute Dane, Count Rantzau, who was living in exile at the village of Menerbes; while the debts of the Comte de Mirabeau, who was not far away, were not preventing him from living recklessly. The noblemen of Provence could allow themselves considerable licence. One night in about 1750, when some gentlefolk on their way back to Aix met a peasant on the Tholomet road, they amused themselves by conducting a trial, condemning the man to death by hanging, and carrying out the sentence on the spot.[1]

[1] Guibal, *Mirabeau et la Provence*.

Meanwhile, at Versailles, the *noblesse dorée* was setting an example of elegant sensuality. 'The court today', wrote the Marquis d'Argenson in 1756, 'is nothing but a *bordello*. A quantity of women inundate the apartments of our princesses, not paying court gallantly but licentiously. One sees only great ladies running out of their apartments dressed for battle and their maidservants carrying letters of assignation; that attracts the young people; there have never been so many courtiers.' To some extent, therefore, Sade was following fashion. At the same time he was reacting, perhaps unconsciously, against a sense of having been betrayed by both his mother, who had opted out of social life, and his father, who had opted out of financial responsibility for him by marrying him into a middle-class family. It is not hard to see how Sade could have explained his behaviour—at least to himself.

The Abbé accepted his nephew's hospitality for a week, doing the honours with the other guests—which outraged Mme de Montreuil, who did not understand how such a man could condone the presence of a courtesan. The ageing libertine probably felt more envy than disapproval, but his participation in the revelry did cause gossip. After returning to Saumane, he sometimes pretended that he had never been to Lacoste, and sometimes complained that he had been outrageously deceived. 'I see nothing of my nephew, and would be very angry to see anyone who behaved so badly.'

Sade also received a reproachful letter from one of his abbess aunts, who had heard from her brother about the goings-on at the château. But he was not intimidated:

To tell you the truth, I was not expecting to hear such strong language from the mouth of a religious saint. I am not allowing the person who is with me to be taken for my wife. Everyone has been told the contrary. 'Never introduce her as such,' M. l'Abbé told me, 'but don't prevent people from saying she is if they want to. Even if what you are telling them is absolutely the opposite.' It is his advice I am following. When one of your sisters, married like me, lived here openly with her lover, were you already thinking Lacoste was an accursed place? I am doing no more harm than she, and that is very little. In spite of being a priest, the man who gave you the information about me always has a couple of whores living with him. Forgive me for using the same language that you do. Is his château a seraglio? No it's better. It's a b . . .

Forgive me my failings. I have inherited the family temperament, and if I have anything to reproach myself for, it's the bad luck of being born into it.

As with some of his unrestrained letters to his mistresses, Sade afterwards felt compunction at having given vent to his passion, and in October 1765 he was blaming Beauvoisin: how could he have written such a letter to an aunt he respected if it had not been dictated by the siren who was turning his head? But it was too late. The abbess had passed the letter on to the Abbé, who never quite forgave his nephew.

Mme de Montreuil was still keeping her daughter in ignorance of the affair, and worrying about the debt of 5,000 livres that Sade was expecting the Marquise to settle. In August, writing another of her friendly letters to the Abbé, the mother-in-law was working like a Machiavellian politician for the separation of the lovers. Shrewdly gauging his involvement with Beauvoisin to be livelier and less frenetic than his previous affair, she asked the Abbé to invent a pretext for going back to Lacoste. He could speak firmly to his nephew about the need to live less extravagantly, and to take his mistress to a secret retreat, where he should receive no visitors. Then the girl would be more likely to leave him.

If, as I suspect from his last letter, which I sent you, he is beginning to tire of her, you will profit from the moods and quarrels that he is too weak to profit from himself. If she leaves him, do not let him follow her. Keep him in your company. Occupy him. Do not leave him alone. And then we shall see. So long as this madness continues, I would rather have him in Provence than here.

Less than two weeks after this was written, Sade's valet appeared at rue Neuve-du-Luxembourg with the luggage of his master, who would soon be arriving, he said. When the news reached Mme de Montreuil at Echauffour, she surmised—correctly—that her son-in-law was already in Paris, staying with his mistress. Beauvoisin had agreed to help him out of his immediate financial difficulties.

They employed the royal notary to make out a contract by which he was to pay her an annual 500 livres in perpetuity. In return she would provide him with 10,000 livres in cash, which she could raise by selling jewellery.

He did not make contact with the Montreuils until about ten days later, and even then it was only to inform them that two pieces of business were keeping him in Paris. As soon as these were settled, he would come to Echauffour. He arrived late in the evening of 15 September. Renée-Pélagie, who had not seen him since May, was still ignorant of his infidelity, but he was attentive and seemed eager to be on good terms with her. He stayed in Normandy for less than two months. Hearing, early in November, that Beauvoisin was in an advanced state of pregnancy, he hurried to Paris, where he stayed at her house. The baby was born in December, which means that unless the birth was premature, the infant had been conceived before his affair with her began. When he left Echauffour he could neither have known that Beauvoisin's pregnancy was so advanced nor that the woman he was leaving behind had started a pregnancy for which he indubitably *was* responsible. Renée-Pélagie had just conceived the first of the children who were to survive. Beauvoisin was soon acting again at the Comédie-Italienne and winning new adorers. In the opinion of Inspector Marais, 'Childbirth has made her more beautiful.' A cluster of noblemen was competing for her favours. 'But the most dangerous of all is the Chevalier de Choiseul. Yesterday I noticed him eyeing her. When I congratulated him, he answered, "I caught an expression on her face that assures me she will be mine within a few days."'

He was not wrong. He did not even have to give her money. By the beginning of the new year she had broken with Sade. She was living at the expense of another marquis and giving herself to the forty-six-year-old Duc de Choiseul, the Minister for Foreign Affairs, a man greatly admired by Mme de Pompadour.

Sade consoled himself with Mlle Dorville, a tall prostitute who had been working until recently in the brothel of Mme Hecquet. He paid her only 240 livres a month but again his taste coincided with that of the munificent Elchin, who was sleeping with her at least once a week and paying 100 livres each time. Sade was also sleeping with a blonde dancer at the Opera whose ambition was to become an actress at the Comédie-Française. She was being paid by the Comte de Bintheim to whip him till the blood came. She had a good figure, a voracious sexual appetite and a playful disposition. But in spite of all the pleasure and all the pain he was enjoying with her and with Dorville, Sade did not lose interest in Beauvoisin. Nor had she grown indifferent to him, or she would not have gone on attacking him in anonymous letters. 'I shall take no revenge,' he wrote to her. 'You are not worth the trouble. The most utter contempt for you is the only feeling left in my heart. Take your latest conquest and break away from him by the same foul tricks you used with me. When you have finally squeezed him dry, when the illusion of pleasure and ambition has passed, there will be nothing to save your heart from the torments of remorse it deserves.'

The mutual animosity was so feverish that by the end of January they were making love again, and in April he joined her in Lyons to accompany her on a tour. Afterwards, he went on to Avignon for his first meeting with his uncle since describing his castle as a brothel. In a letter to Mme de Montreuil written on 1 June, the Abbé said that she and he were the only two people with some influence over the boy, but that they must not repeat the Count's mistake of brushing him up the wrong way. Nothing could be done until he had let off more steam.

> As you can imagine, I have spoken to him a great deal about his wife. He esteems her highly and sings her praises. He feels friendship and great respect for her. He would hate to upset her, but finds her too frigid and too pious for him. That is what makes him look elsewhere for amusement. When he is older, he will appreciate the value of the woman you have given him. ... He says she knows nothing of his escapades, and he would be in despair if she did. That is something.

An affair with another dancer came to an end in September, when she left him for the chief tax-farmer.[1] According to her police

---

[1] Since 1726 the government had been accepting a lump sum from a syndicate of 60 financiers for the right to collect (and keep) all the indirect taxes—on salt, wine, tobacco and so on. There was a great deal of irregularity and bribery, which increased the unpopularity of the tax-farmers. But the trade was vastly profitable in spite of rivalry with the Parlements for what could be extorted from the peasantry. By the time of the Revolution, the farmers-general had 30,000 employees.

dossier, she was a charming girl but at the mercy of an avaricious aunt who appropriated all her earnings. Later on in the month Sade rented an apartment at Versailles, and in November a furnished house at Arcueil, four miles outside Paris. During a performance at the Royal Academy of Music he felt desire for one of the dancers, and used a guards officer as go-between. Two days later he wrote to tell her that he knew another man was paying dearly for the happiness of possessing her. Though not so rich as his rival, he is younger, with more love to offer. Will she accord him 'the second place', which is all he aspires to ? He will be at her disposal always. He will be her slave. In January 1767 Inspector Marais learned from Beauvoisin's official lover, the Chevalier de Jeancourt, that she was deceiving him with several men, including Sade. She 'gives him her hand in public'.

The day after this report was written, the Comte de Sade died suddenly. He was sixty-five. The Marquis, who had been with him five days previously and thought his health had improved, appeared to be so upset by the death that his mother-in-law became conciliatory. This, at least, is the reason she gave for her willingness to forgive, though the real reason may have been that her daughter was pregnant. In April, when Sade was promoted to a captaincy in the du Mestre cavalry regiment and ordered to rejoin his company without delay, Mme de Montreuil was quite pleased. At least he would be kept away from temptation. But, presumably after obtaining a reprieve from his colonel, he went back to Lyons to be with Beauvoisin. In June he was at Lacoste. The local community had to recognize him formally as its lord, and to pay him the usual homage by kneeling to him.

The château and the estate had originally been received in fief from the King, to whom the feudal lord owed the homage that his vassals owed to him. It was for him to administer justice from a seigneurial court, and he had the right to impose tolls, together with the rights of hunting, fishing and pasturing cattle on the mountain. The villagers had to pay him feudal dues and tithes— a proportion of the grain, vegetables, olives, grapes, hemp and acorns they grew on his land. The feudal lord also had the exclusive right to press wine and oil and to bake, which meant that his vassals could be required to pay for using his wine-press, his oil-press and his bakehouse. Until the revolution, feudal monopolies like this survived all over France and on many estates they were harshly enforced, but not at Lacoste, where the villagers were even allowed to shoot in the seigneur's parkland.

Like his father, Sade never became interested in the practical problems of managing the estate; he bought books on a variety of subjects but among the 440 in his library at Lacoste there was only one about agriculture—the Abbé de Champvalon's *Manuel des Champs*. Nor did he wish to be involved in the collection of his seigneurial dues. A notary at Apt, Elzéar Fage, who had managed the estates for the Count, supervised the various leases. At Lacoste a farmer, working more like a small-scale tax-farmer than a bailiff, paid Sade a lump sum for the right to collect the dues. At Mazan a farmer and at Arles a merchant acted in the same capacity. From Saumane no income was to be expected until the Abbé died. Sade's proceeds varied, but around 1770 he was receiving about 17,500 livres a year which was quite a high income compared, for instance, with the average income of the Toulouse nobility at this time—5,748 livres. Generally he had little desire for conversation or contact of any kind with the villagers, who were mostly illiterate.[1] His aloofness is reflected in his fiction: there is no characterization of farmers or farm-labourers, no observation of country life. He was never popular with the villagers, who were aware of his lack of interest.

The old Count died just too soon to become a grandfather; a son was born to the new Count (who scarcely ever used the title) on 27 August 1767. The boy was called Louis-Marie. Neither the death nor the birth caused Sade to change the pattern in his pursuit of pleasure, but he had some difficulty in negotiating with his next dancer. Attractive, lively and loose-living, Mlle Rivière turned down his offer of 500 livres a month for her company on the evenings she was not performing at the Opera. Sade went on pursuing her until she succumbed in November. The affair lasted for about two months. Meanwhile he had been badgering la Brissault to send girls to have supper with him at Arcueil. According to Marais's report: 'This woman has consistently refused, knowing more or less what he is capable of doing, but he will have approached others, who are less scrupulous, or less aware of his habits. We shall be hearing more of him before long.' The policeman was not wrong. It is safe to assume that there was much less

[1] Michel Vovelle, 'Sade, Seigneur de village', in *Le Marquis de Sade*, Centre Aixois d'Etudes et de recherches sur le 18e siècle.

sadism in the long-term relationships than with the girls hired for a single night. The house at Arcueil was isolated enough for any but the loudest screams to go unheard, so the girls would be entirely in his power.

The villagers did not fail to notice the frequency of arrivals and departures. According to police records, there were fifteen months of scandal in the village as Sade brought men and women, day and night, to his small rented house. One evening at the beginning of February he had four girls there. He whipped them, and then ate dinner with them, giving his valet 20 livres to reward them. The man kept three for himself as compensation for the trouble he had had finding them in the Faubourg Saint-Antoine.

Chapter 3

Flagellation and Aphrodisiacs

On Easter Sunday, 3 April 1768, at 9 o'clock in the morning, Sade saw a woman begging in the place des Victoires. If he had reported her to the police the punishment might have been more severe than any that a libertine would have meted out. Treated as potential rioters, beggars and tramps were interned in *dépôts de mendicité*. She spoke French haltingly, with a German accent. He signalled her to come close. When he promised her 3 livres if she would go with him, she protested that she was an honest woman. The widow of a pastry-cook, she had been working as a cotton-spinner until she lost her job a month ago. Sade reassured her: all he wanted her to do was clean his room. (At least, this is what he said according to the testimony she gave at the trial. His version was that he told her he wanted her for a debauch.)

After making her wait for an hour in a house near the new market, he reappeared with a carriage to take her to his country house. Seating himself next to her, he closed the wooden shutters. Her name was Rose Keller and she was about sixteen years older than Jeanne Testard. He spoke very little. As they were approaching the barrière d'Enfer, he promised her that no harm would come to her. She would be well fed and treated kindly. After that he slept, or pretended to. They drove past fields. It was about 12.30 when they arrived in the village. Making her wait outside the house, he went through the front entrance to open a small green door from inside.

He led her up to the first floor and into a rather dark room. The apertures in the shutters were blocked. There were two beds with canopies. He told her not to worry and to wait there while he went to look for bread and something to drink. He locked her in. After an hour he came back with a lighted candle and said: 'Come down, my pet.' He led her to a downstairs room that was no less dark. As soon as the door was shut he ordered her to take off her clothes. She asked why. To have fun, he said. That was not what she had come for, she told him. He threatened to kill her and bury her in the garden. He then went out of the room. She took off most of her clothes, but not her shift.

When he came back and ordered her to remove it, she said she would prefer to die. Tearing it off, he pushed her into the neighbouring room and threw her, face downwards, on to a divan. He tied her arms and legs with ropes, covering her neck with a bolster and a muff. (According to his evidence, he did not push her and did not tie her down.) Taking off his jacket and shirt to don a sleeveless waistcoat and tie a handkerchief around his head, he snatched up a birch and whipped her savagely. She screamed. Showing her a knife, he swore he would kill her unless she kept quiet, and again he threatened to bury her with his own hands. She tried to hold back her cries. According to her, he whipped her seven or eight times; according to him it was only three or four. According to him, he used only a cat-o'-nine tails; according to her, he alternated between it and the birch. Two or three times he stopped to rub ointment into the abrasions, but resumed the whipping vigorously. According to her, he cut her flesh with a small knife, rubbing red and white wax into the wounds, but the evidence of the surgeon supports his insistence that this never happened. She begged for pity, imploring him to spare her life: she did not want to die without making her Easter confession. This was of little importance, he told her, he would confess her himself. As she went on trying to make him relent, the blows became faster and more agitated. Suddenly he was emitting cries himself, 'very loud and very frightening'.

Having finally achieved satisfaction, he untied her and took her back into the other room for her to put her clothes on. He left her alone, soon returning with a towel, a bowl and a jug of water. She washed and dried herself, leaving bloodstains on the towel, which he ordered her to wash. Afterwards he brought a small bottle of brandy, telling her to rub it on the wounds. Within an hour, he said, the marks would have disappeared. Despite the smarting, she did as she was told.

When she was dressed, he gave her a piece of bread, a plateful of boiled beef and a flask of wine. He took her back to the room on the first floor, and before locking her in for the second time he advised her not to go near the window or to make any noise. In the evening, he promised, she would be at liberty again. She begged him to let her go early. She did not know where she was, and she had no money. She did not want to sleep in the street. She need not worry on that account, he said.

Left alone, she bolted the door on the inside, pulled the blankets off the beds and knotted them together. With a knife, she unblocked a vent in one of the shutters, opened it without difficulty, tied her improvised rope around the cross-bar of the window-frame, and slid down it into the back garden. Thanks to a trellis she was able to climb the wall and jump down on to some waste ground, grazing her left arm and her hand. Just as she had found her way to the street, the Marquis's valet came running after her, shouting to her to come back because his master wanted to talk with her. She refused. The man pulled out a purse to pay her. She pushed him out of the way.

Her hand was hurting. Her shift was torn and dangling between her legs. Meeting a village woman, she tearfully described her adventure. Two other women came up. After taking her into a courtyard, where they lifted up her skirt to inspect the wounds, they took her to a taxation official, who sent them to the château of a court official. His wife was so upset at Rose Keller's story that she had to leave the room. In the absence of the local magistrate, a Brigadier of the Mounted Constabulary came to the château. When he had taken a statement, he had the woman examined by a surgeon. She was then bedded down for the night in a neighbour's cow-stall. On Easter Monday, 4 April, she made a statement to the magistrate, and on the Tuesday she was allowed to move into the château. On Wednesday the magistrate heard evidence from the villagers.

Sade would not have been alone in refusing to differentiate between a beggar-woman and a prostitute, or in considering any prostitute fair game for flagellation. Nor was this attitude peculiar to the eighteenth century. Writing in the 1930s André Javalier said: 'Such episodes are daily occurrences in modern brothels, and the idea of complaining scarcely enters the victims' heads.'

But clearly Sade's choice of day was not accidental. When the libertines in *Juliette* arrange a sacrilegious debauch for Easter Day, Lady Clairwil talks about 'the pleasure of desecrating the holiest mystery of the Christian religion on the day of the year it regards as one of its greatest festivals'. There was still a strong element of anti-religious ritual in his sadism which, like the Black Mass, bore an inverse relationship to Catholic ceremonial. Over four years had passed since he tried to make Jeanne Testard pollute crucifixes with him and suggested they should go to communion together before committing sacrilege with the host. The offer he made to Rose Keller just before he reached his orgasm—that he would hear her Easter confession—was not merely a joke. Nor could he seriously have expected her to agree: it was enough if he could picture himself parodying the priestly role in a situation already designed partly to parody the crucifixion and the resurrection. If God existed, why did he not intervene? If he did not exist, Sade could behave as outrageously as he liked. So it was important to test how far he could go, and this could be done only by trying to shock the part of himself that acted as audience for his own actions.

Again we should not take it for granted that Sade was enjoying himself. Was he even doing what he felt he wanted to do? As Gide said: 'One can never know to what extent one feels and to what extent one plays at feeling. This ambivalence constitutes the feeling.' The choice of day indicates that the episode may have been planned in advance. Nor can he have been unaware that in spite of the ointment and the brandy he would be leaving dangerously incriminating evidence on Rose Keller's body. After being denounced by Jeanne Testard, why should he take such a risk? He may, of course, have taken it many times. The Rose Keller case is the first to be recorded since he had acquired the house at Arcueil, but other girls may have been treated equally badly and kept silent. Obviously, though, he was not deriving enough satisfaction from the long succession of affairs with actresses and dancers, none of whom could have either needed or afforded to put their bodies at such risk.

In a normal sex relationship the mental pleasure, which consists partly in the awareness of giving physical pleasure, is inseparable from the physical pleasure received. Homosexuals can hardly ever achieve simultaneous orgasm but the lovers can exchange roles. With flagellation, Sade seems always to have been interested in exchanging roles—Jeanne Testard was one of many women ordered to beat him before or after being beaten by him—but with most partners he was uninterested in the simultaneous exchange of sensation. As one of his fictional libertines will say, a girl who is concentrating on her own pleasure is not concentrating on the man's, and one of Sade's prime needs was to be confident of having the total attention of the woman. If he preferred anal love-making, it was partly because he could be sure that the pleasure he was giving was negligible in relation to the pleasure he was receiving. With flagellation he was either totally at his partner's mercy or had her totally at his. If he could ever tolerate the idea of sharing sexual pleasure, it was only with the few women who most excited him.

On Thursday morning, the Abbé Amblet and a lawyer were summoned to the rue Neuve-du-Luxembourg, where Mme de Montreuil told them that a girl at Arcueil was laying charges against Sade. Would they go there to find out whether there was any way of settling the case without a law-suit?

They found Rose Keller in bed. Since her ordeal, she said, she could neither stand nor sit, so she was in no state to work. Would she be willing to consider withdrawing her charges? Not for less than 3,000 livres. This was an exorbitant amount, said the lawyer, and even if she won her case, she would not make so much out of it. After withdrawing to consult with the Abbé, he offered her 1,800. She said she would accept 2,400. When they went back to discuss the proposition with Mme de Montreuil, she agreed to pay any price to get the business settled. Returning to Arcueil, they found the victim sitting up in bed, chatting. Nevertheless, the undertaking to withdraw the charge was drawn up in the presence of the court official. When she signed it, she was given 2,400 livres plus 140 for dressings and medications.

However unpleasant the events I have been describing in this chapter, there was nothing extraordinary about any of them. Scores of men were taking their pleasure in very much the same way; scores of girls, no doubt, were exploiting the situation for what it was worth. Money was an effective pain-killer. The only extraordinary fact about the Rose Keller case was that it was tried in front of the highest court in the country, the Paris Parlement, the court where 185 officials belonged to the *noblesse de robe* and all the fifty-odd *Ducs et pairs* of France had the right to attend as 'councillors-born'.

On 8 April, the Friday after Easter Sunday, the Minister of the Royal Household instructed the commandant of the Château de Saumur, which is on the Loire nearly 200 miles from Paris, that the Marquis de Sade was to be imprisoned there immediately. He was to be locked up and never allowed outside the castle walls. M.

de Sartine was ordered to have Sade arrested and taken to Saumur. Renée-Pélagie sent the Abbé Amblet to the house at Arcueil, ostensibly to pay some debts and bring away the articles of value. Probably he was briefed to search for letters and incriminating evidence. Sade was given permission to travel without a police escort to Saumur. Amblet accompanied him, and they were not quite half-way there when he wrote a propitiatory letter to his uncle, asking him to co-operate in quashing any rumours that might penetrate to Provence. 'Say I am with my regiment.' On 15 April he was denounced at a session of the Parlement's criminal council, the Chambre de la Tournelle, which agreed that the Royal Prosecutor should investigate the affair. It was unfortunate for Sade that the chairman of the council, M. Pinon, had a house at Arcueil.

Why was the case being tried on such a high judicial level? Maurice Heine's[1] explanation is that: 'An enfeebled central authority was having to reckon more and more with public opinion, which had long been outraged at the impunity accorded to misdemeanours and even to crimes of libertinage provided that they were committed by the bearer of a distinguished name. A scapegoat was needed to compensate, as it were, for the indulgence or ineffectuality shown towards certain guilty parties, especially a prince of the royal blood, the Comte de Charolais, who was notorious for his sanguinary fantasies.'[2]

Several copies of the charge against Sade and the witnesses' statements were circulated in Paris. On 18 April Mme de Saint-Germain, an old friend of the family who had always been fond of the Marquis, was writing to his uncle: 'The inexpressible way in which public opinion has been whipped up against him! Judge for yourself: they want him to have done this stupid flagellation in mockery of the Passion . . . He is being penalized for the affair of M. de Fronsac and so many others. There is no doubt that in the last ten years courtiers have done an inconceivable quantity of

[1] Maurice Heine, *Le Marquis de Sade*, Gallimard, 1950.

[2] The Comte de Charolais, the King's brother, emerged with impunity from a series of sadistic escapades. In one of them he invited a woman, Mme de Saint-Sulpice, to supper, made her drunk and undressed her. Inserting a firework into her vagina, he said, 'The little lapdog has to eat too.' When he set it off, she was badly burned. She was wrapped in a sheet and sent home in a cab. (Jean A. Chérasse and G. Guicheney, *Sade j'écris ton nom Liberté*, Pygmalion, 1976.)

horrible things.' The Duc de Fronsac had enthusiastically followed the example of his libertine father, the Duc de Richelieu, but Mme de Saint-Germain seems to have been unaware of the rumours that Sade had been involved in some of de Fronsac's escapades.

M. de Montreuil asked the Abbé to come to Paris and use his influence on his nephew's behalf. Meanwhile Sade's one married aunt received a letter from the Duc de Montpezat, warning her that her nephew was in considerable danger because of the Parlement's interest in the case. On 19 April the evidence was considered in detail by its criminal council, which ended up by ordering that the investigation should continue, that statements should be taken from Sade and others named by the Prosecutor-General, that Sade should be made a prisoner of the law-court, that all his goods should be confiscated and inventoried, that his victim should be examined by the court's doctors. The Parlement's bailiff accordingly presented himself at the rue Neuve-du-Luxembourg. Though Sade had already been a prisoner for nearly two weeks, the gate-keeper was given a copy of the order for his arrest and a summons for him to put in an appearance within a fortnight. Anomalies and overlaps resulted very frequently from the division of judicial authority between the King and the law-courts. The bailiff was unable to remove the furniture from Sade's rooms because it belonged to his father-in-law. On the same day two members of the Parlement's council visited the house at Arcueil to collect evidence, or as much of it as remained after Amblet's visit. At 7 o'clock the following morning, one of these councillors, Jacques de Chavanne, heard evidence from Rose Keller and from witnesses including the women she had met in the street, the Abbé Amblet, the gardener who worked for Sade at Arcueil, and the servant who looked after him at the rue Neuve-du-Luxembourg. Amblet emphasized Sade's good qualities. He was 'a long way from being capable of the horrors imputed to him'. An example of his generosity was the help he had given to a carpenter called Moulin during the long illness which had ended in his death, and one of his children was being brought up at Sade's expense.

Sade had been at Saumur for less than two weeks when it was decided that he should be transferred to the fortress of Pierre-Encise, near Lyons. Inspector Marais, who was to escort him on his journey, arrived at Saumur to find him enjoying complete freedom within the castle walls, and taking his meals with the commandant, who asked Marais not to say that he had found Sade at his table. Sade was very frightened by the news of the move. On the journey he told the policeman that his only intention had been to give the girl a whipping, not to leave any scars. He seemed to be sorry, Marais reported, but at heart 'he is still the same'. He was expecting that when he was released from Pierre-Encise he would be sent into exile, or be confined to his estate or his father-in-law's.

The commandant at Pierre-Encise had received instructions from the Minister of the Royal Household that the King did not wish the Marquis to be allowed outside his room or to have any contact with the other prisoners. When he needed fresh air, he should be under escort. However, since he was suffering from a fistula which needed treatment, he could be attended by a surgeon from Lyons and by his valet, who was used to bathing the sore morning and evening.

There was a new tone of alarm in Mme de Montreuil's letters to the Abbé, flattered though she was that the Duc de Montpezat was taking such an interest in her son-in-law. The Abbé thought the Parlement had acted too hastily and too severely, but at least his nephew would have been taught 'a lesson for the future'. To the Dowager Countess, who made one of her rare interventions on her son's behalf, the Minister said it would be wiser not to inform the King of her complaints about the treatment he had received in prison. 'His Majesty might decide to put him back into the hands of the Parlement, which would not be to his advantage.'

Sade was naturally unable to present himself to the Parlement within a fortnight of the bailiff's visit to the rue Neuve-du-Luxembourg, and one of the most absurd sequences of the cruel comedy was played out on 11 May outside the Montreuils' house, at the pillory in Les Halles and in 'all the usual places'. Two royal trumpeters sounded a fanfare which was followed by a stentorian announcement from the Usher of the Rod and Public Crier. The Sieur de Sade, who was 'absent and fugitive', must present himself within a week to the criminal court of the Parlement and must surrender himself as a prisoner to be examined. If he failed to appear, the trial would be conducted in his absence and in contempt of court.

When he did fail to appear, his default was recorded, and it was not until two days later that the two lines of legal retribution converged. The Lieutenant-General of Police received the royal

command that Sade was to be taken to the conciergerie so that the
Parlement could ratify the royal Letters of Annulment which had
been issued. Letters of Annulment were very rare. The King
could issue them to private citizens charged with capital offences:
the theory was that royal omnipotence was being used to abolish
the crime itself. No further investigation, therefore, was possible
once the letters had been ratified. So Jacques de Chavanne cross-
examined the Marquis before the ratification. Without denying
most of the accusations, Sade insisted that Rose Keller had known
she was letting herself in for a sexual adventure.

If the crime no longer existed, the prisoner ought logically to be
released, but the *ancien régime* was not logical and Sade was sent
back to Pierre-Encise to remain there under the same conditions
as before until the King decided to release him. In July the Minister granted the Marquise's request that her husband should be
allowed out in the fresh air for reasons of health. In August, after
selling some diamonds to cover her travelling expenses and leaving her eleven-months-old son in the care of her mother, she went
to Lyons. The Minister gave permission for her to see the prisoner
twice during her visit. He advised her not to stay long in the town
and to use the two meetings to make arrangements for her husband's affairs. 'I cannot hide from you the fact that it is not the
King's intention to restore his liberty in the near future.' But the
commandant of the fortress must have been generous in giving
them privacy. In September she became pregnant again, and she
was still in Lyons at the beginning of November. The Minister
now gave permission for her to see Sade as often as she wanted to.
Royal orders for his release arrived in the middle of the month, but
he was required to stay at Lacoste and not even to spend any time
at Lyons en route. The Dowager Countess was warned that the
amount of liberty accorded to her son would depend on his
behaviour.

Writing to the Abbé on 19 November 1768, Mme de Montreuil
said he would soon meet her daughter, who was about to stay at
Lacoste with her husband. Instead, after spending a few days with
him in Lyons, Renée-Pélagie left for Paris, while he went alone to
the château. He was not alone for long. During the five months he
stayed there, he was less concerned to redeem his reputation than

to make up for the opportunities of self-indulgence missed during seven months of enforced solitude.

He was as lavish as before in the balls and theatrical entertainments he staged for his neighbours. His mother-in-law, understandably anxious about the actresses he was employing, said she would not have had a moment's peace if her daughter had been shut up in an isolated château with that madman. When she learned that the Abbé was a frequent visitor there, her letters to him became very much less courteous. In his shoes, she would have set the place on fire. His nephew was on the verge of destroying himself totally, she wrote on 2 March 1769. If he went on refusing to sign a promissory note for 20,000 livres, his creditors would win the right to impound furniture and valuables, and his name would 'once again be dragged through the mud'. Ever since the wedding he had been living well above his income, and merely for the sake of his own pleasures. He was very mean over household expenses, and even now, with his wife pregnant, he was sending her barely enough to live on. Meanwhile Renée-Pélagie was petitioning for an end to her husband's confinement at the château. His health, she said, demanded careful treatment. Royal permission was granted for him to move close to Paris on condition that he lived quietly in a country house, devoting himself to his convalescence. He returned in time for the birth of his second son on 27 June. It was a difficult childbirth, but the boy was big and healthy. He was baptized Donatien-Claude-Armand. The godparents were his maternal grandfather and his paternal grandmother, who was at last willing to sell her diamonds. She offered them to the King, who refused to buy them.

Sade soon had complete liberty again. He was behaving considerately to his wife and seemed to enjoy the company of Louis-Marie, who was not quite two. His ambitious mother-in-law was soon thinking about his abortive journey to Fontainebleau six years earlier. Was it too soon for him to think of reappearing at court? The Minister said it was. More time should be allowed for the unfavourable impression to disappear from His Majesty's mind.

After this rebuff, which came towards the end of March, Sade stayed on with the family for more than four months, but as always he had less money at his disposal than he wanted, and domestic life was boring him. Renée-Pélagie was in the first month of a new pregnancy when he announced his decision to rejoin his regiment at Poitou, and in her second month when he left in August. Arriving at Poitou, he found that the Lieutenant-Colonel, the Comte de Saignes, was at Compiègne and the officer commanding in his absence would not allow Sade to take up his duties as captain. He protested strenuously, but the only result was that he was put under arrest. An indignant letter to the Count produced better results. By March 1771 he was able to apply to the Minister of War for an unsalaried commission as Colonel of Cavalry. The Prince de Condé supported the application, and Sade was promoted.

On 17 April the Marquise gave birth to a daughter, Madeleine-Laure. Writing on the 27th to the Abbé, who still hadn't met Renée-Pélagie, Mme de Montreuil reported that she was as well as could be expected. If he were able to meet her soon he would be favourably impressed with her intelligence and her gentleness. 'Beauty and grace are gifts that cannot be won by effort.'

At the beginning of June Sade made a profit of 10,000 livres by selling his unsalaried position as colonel to the Comte d'Osmont, but by the end of the month he was in the debtors' prison at Fort l'Evèque. He secured his release by paying 3,000 livres and making out a promissory note which would fall due on 15 October. He then took his wife and children to Lacoste. An entry in the local archives shows that the impending arrival of the Marquise was the subject of 'communal deliberations': she must be welcomed with a present, but what should they buy?

After the abortive affair with Laure de Lauris, none of Sade's involvements with women seems to have made him feel anything that could be called 'love', but he did come to experience a deep and intense emotional commitment to his sister-in-law, Anne-Prospère de Launay, who now came to stay at Lacoste. The second of Mme de Montreuil's five children, she was a couple of years younger than Renée-Pélagie and a canoness—a privileged nun who was not yet sworn to a life of chastity. No doubt this made her all the more alluring to Sade: to woo a bride away from Christ would be more gratifying than to win her from any human rival. Instructing one of the notaries he used in Apt to have some locks sent to Lacoste, Sade jokingly demanded a particularly good one for her bedroom: 'It is not, I believe, necessary to emphasize the need to lock this little treasure up.'

Anne-Prospère was attractive, intelligent and impetuous. Her arrival at Lacoste made an impact on the Abbé, who at sixty-six was still very susceptible to the charm of young girls. In November he was sufficiently hopeful to make her a present of a small Corsican horse, and she was sufficiently flirtatious to write: 'Oh, my dear uncle, how fond of you I am! You have not been out of my mind ever since I met you.' In a later, undated letter written from a convent in or near Clermont, she begged him not to go on writing such compromising letters: her reputation, her honour and perhaps even her life were in danger. So the old man's interest in her was still keen, but he had been eclipsed by Sade.

Renée-Pélagie was aware of the mutual attraction between her husband and her sister and she was oddly complaisant, though she was later to claim that her sister had come 'under the pretext of keeping her company and enjoying the peaceful atmosphere of the château', and that the 'attentiveness' of her husband prevented her from suspecting that a 'fatal passion' for his sister-in-law would soon precipitate 'a series of misfortunes'. Initially, the opportunity of making her elder sister jealous may have had an aphrodisiac effect on Anne-Prospère, but by the spring she had become more possessive about Sade than Renée-Pélagie was.

Once again he was lavish in the entertainments he staged for his neighbours. He wrote a comedy which was performed in January 1772. The actor Bourdais and his actress wife, who had worked at the private theatre during Sade's previous stay at Lacoste, were invited back in February. By the end of May Mme de Montreuil was extremely worried. She had received no news of her grandchildren, and she was apprehensive that her two daughters might both be harmed by the plays and frivolities that Sade still found irresistible, regardless of the debts he had accumulated both in Provence and in Paris.

Rivals though they were, the Abbé and Sade were effectively combining to seduce Anne-Prospère away from ascetic devotion. Sade obviously played the larger role, and later, in his fiction, he could draw on the experience whenever he wanted to make one of his heroines fall under the influence of experienced men and women of the world. He also wrote factually about Anne-Prospère's openness to argument against the prejudices imposed by monkish mentors, who had conditioned her 'to regard the sweetest emotions and natural impulses as crimes'. Even her beauty was enhanced by her new enlightenment. 'What a chill has descended on her former pleasures! And how warm her new ideas are!'

Her attitude to life—and to him—had changed totally by the time he left Lacoste in June 1772 on his way to Marseilles, where some money was owing to him. He was accompanied by a valet known as Latour, though his name was d'Armand. He may have been the illegitimate son of a nobleman. Sade stayed at the Hôtel des Treize-Cantons, and he paid several visits to a nineteen-year-old prostitute called Jeanne Nicou. He also asked her to come to his hotel, but she refused. On Thursday 25 June, two days before he was due to leave the town, he told Latour to round up some 'really young' girls. Accosting an eighteen-year-old called Mari-anne Laverne in the street, Latour told her that his master was in Marseilles to have fun with girls. This evening he was due to sup with some actors, but he would come to visit her at 11 o'clock the next evening. She gave him her address, a lodging house in the rue d'Aubagne, but when the two men arrived they were told she was out. She had gone somewhere on a boat. She was back when Latour called at 8 o'clock in the morning and she was quite willing to meet his master, but he said it had better be somewhere else. There was not enough privacy here. Could she come at 10 o'clock to the flat of Mariette Borelly on the third floor of a house at the corner of the rue des Capucins? The previous evening Latour had made the same arrangement with two other tenants of the lodging-house, Marianette Laugier and Rose Coste. The rue d'Aubagne is only a few blocks away from the old port, so they were well placed for taking sailors home. Jeanne Nicou had also been invited to the rendezvous but had refused to come. Her earlier encounters with the Marquis had presumably been too painful.

The subsequent legal investigation revealed that Latour made his first appearance alone. He went out again to reappear with a good-looking, full-faced, fair-haired man of medium height, who was wearing a grey coat, a feather in his hat, and waistcoat and breeches of marigold-coloured silk. There was a sword at his side, and he carried a cane with a gold knob. The valet, who was taller than his master, had a pock-marked face and long hair. He wore a sailor's outfit with blue and yellow stripes.

At twenty-three, Mariette Borelly was the oldest of the four girls, and the eighteen-year-old Marianne was the youngest. Rose and Marianette were both twenty. The Marquis took a handful of gold crowns[1] from his pocket. Who can guess how many? The girl who gives the right answer will be taken first. Marianne won. (He may have cheated in order to start with the youngest, whose flesh was likely to be the softest.) Everyone else except Latour was sent out of the room, and the door was locked. Both Latour and Marianne were made to lie down on the bed. Using one hand to beat the girl, he used the other to masturbate his valet, whom he addressed as 'Monsieur le Marquis'. The valet was then dismissed. The girl was offered a glass bowl containing aniseed sweets. The sugar-coating may have been soaked in Spanish Fly. She was told to eat a lot of them. They would put wind in her stomach. She ate seven or eight. He offered her 20 livres to let herself be buggered either by Latour or by him. Whether she refused is uncertain. According to her testimony she did, but since active and passive sodomy were both punishable by death she would hardly have admitted to it, and since most of her clients, presumably, were sailors, she would hardly have been averse to it.

From his pocket he then produced a cat-o'-nine-tails made of parchment with bent nails. He asked her to beat him with it. She hit him three times but could not go on. Not yet satisfied, he told her to send out for a broom. The door was unlocked and the maid dispatched to buy one. It cost one sou. He was right in thinking that she would feel less qualms about hitting him with a broom, and she beat his bottom, but when he kept shouting encouragement to hit harder, her stomach again began to feel queasy. She went into the kitchen. Moans were heard. The maid gave her a glass of water.

Latour came back with Mariette. Sade made her strip and bend over the foot of the bed. He beat her with the broom and then ordered her to beat him. He counted the strokes given and received, using a knife to carve the totals into the mantelpiece: 215, 179, 225, 240. Then, turning the girl over, he began to enjoy her. At the same time, after starting to masturbate Latour, he let the man bugger him. This is the first evidence of practical experience in the simultaneous sexual penetrations that were to figure so prominently in his fiction.

When they had finished with Mariette, Rose was brought in. She was asked to strip and lie down next to Latour. He stroked

[1] A crown was worth 3 livres.

her body and fucked her. Then Sade whipped her with his right hand, using his left to masturbate Latour. He then gave her 20 livres to let the energetic young Latour bugger her. In the game of role-reversal, the man addressed his master as Lafleur.

The last girl was Marianette. After caressing her, Sade was about to give her a beating. He still had twenty-five strokes to go, he said. Seeing the whip on the bed, all bloody, the frightened girl tried to run out of the room, but Sade held on to her and called back Marianne, who was feeling ill after eating the sweets. She had been in the kitchen, where the maid had given her coffee. Sade offered sweets to both girls, but Marianne had had more than enough already. Marianette took some but threw them on to the floor without even tasting them. Marianne was lowered on to the bed and her skirt deftly lifted. The Marquis's nose approached her bottom as he sniffed for evidence of the aniseed.

When he started whipping her, he told Marianette to watch from the bed-head. Then he took his clothes off to bugger Marianne while Latour buggered him. Marianette, who could neither leave the room nor bear to watch, looked out of the window. When Marianne was released, Marianette was told to let Latour bugger her, but she refused. She wanted to go. Marianne was also in tears. Sade threatened them, but finally released them, giving them each 6 livres and promising them more if they would join a boating-party in the evening.

Towards the end of the afternoon, Latour came for them but they refused to go with him. If Sade had not been so unwilling to waste his last evening in Marseilles, he might have escaped with impunity, but Latour was sent out to find another prostitute. He picked up a twenty-five-year-old girl called Marguerite Coste, leaving a handkerchief with her as a pledge. Sade greatly enjoyed the company of actors, and when Des Rosières called on him he was invited to stay for supper. But after Latour had whispered in his master's ear, the meal was finished hastily and, making excuses to the actor, the Marquis left with his valet, who took him to Marguerite's flat. This time Latour did not stay. The Marquis sat on the bed, the girl on a chair. Offered sweets, she sucked some. She was pressed to more. He gave them to all the girls, he told her. After coaxing her into eating quite a lot, he asked whether she felt anything in her stomach. He then wanted to take her from the rear 'and in several other ways, all more horrible'. She would afterwards claim that she steadfastly refused, giving him permission 'to approach her only in the way that God intended'. When he went, he left 6 livres on the table, which may mean that she was telling the truth: he had been more munificent in the morning. At cock-crow on Sunday he set out on his homeward journey.

It is thanks to legal records that we know so much about the events of 27 June 1772, and not one of the five girls mentioned any blasphemy. He had outgrown the need for it but he was still compulsive about taking outrageous risks.

On Tuesday Marguerite made her first statement to the Royal Prosecutor at the local law-court. After being given sweets by a stranger she had not only suffered for several days from gastric pains but had vomited blood and black bile. She was examined by a doctor, while a chemist analysed samples of her vomit, finding no trace of arsenic. On Wednesday the Lieutenant-General for Criminal Affairs cross-examined the four prostitutes from the rue d'Aubagne and seven other witnesses. After studying the medical reports on Marguerite and Marianne, the Lieutenant-General submitted the statements he had collected to the Royal Prosecutor, who gave orders for Sade and Latour to be arrested. After being unfairly accused of fleeing from justice when he was imprisoned in Pierre-Encise, that is what Sade now did as soon as he heard rumours of the proceedings against him. He left Lacoste with Latour and Anne-Prospère a week before the bailiff arrived on 11 July. Renée-Pélagie helped them to plan their flight.

Chapter 4

Madame de Montreuil's Revenge

People as adept as Mme de Montreuil at flattery tend to be adept at rationalization, and her true feelings towards her son-in-law may have been as effectively concealed from herself as from the rest of the world. Between a man and his mother-in-law, as between a woman and her father-in-law, unacknowledged sexual desire can easily open a wound which will go on festering with jealousy, resentment and hatred, but no woman has ever waged war against her son-in-law more relentlessly than she did. After nine years of remarkable tolerance towards his insatiable sexual appetite and his infidelities, she persecuted him ruthlessly for twenty years. What seems to have turned her irreconcilably against him was his affair with Anne-Prospère, her favourite daughter—her Dulcinea, as Renée-Pélagie once put it in a letter, oddly equating her mother with Don Quixote. What remains unclear is whether Mme de Montreuil was more jealous of Sade or of Anne-Prospère.

For the first nine years she may have felt that through the daughter she could so easily dominate, she was having a vicarious relationship with Sade. Besides, the marriage had been planned; she was fully in control of the situation. Anne-Prospère was less tractable and more passionate, while the flight to Italy took her and Sade beyond the reach of Mme de Montreuil. Whatever the emotional undercurrents of her anger, it was easy to justify it when the news-sheets made the affair into a scandal. The reputation of the family had been sullied, the name borne by Renée-Pélagie and her children disgraced. But Mme de Montreuil was nothing if not practical, and the urgent practical considerations were that an eligible suitor, M. de Beaumont, wanted to win Anne-Prospère away from the religious life, and that his family's consent to the marriage was conditional on Sade's being permanently incarcerated. So this time instead of intervening to help the miscreant Marquis, Mme de Montreuil had him put in prison.

Her inoffensive husband did nothing deliberate to harm his son-in-law, but as a President of the *Cour des Aides*, he had attracted the enmity of the ambitious and influential lawyer, René-Nicolas de Maupeou, a small, fractious man known as the Seville orange. He had played a leading role in the Parlement's persecution of Sade during the Rose Keller case. Even in Marseilles his presence could make itself felt: the magistrates were anxious to please him. He went on rising irresistibly to power, finally becoming Chancellor in 1770. His hostility to the royal courts culminated in his suppressions of the Parlements (1771).

When the bailiff arrived at Lacoste a week too late to catch Sade and his valet, warrants were immediately issued for their arrest and for the distraint of all Sade's possessions and feudal revenues. Both men were charged to present themselves within a fortnight. When Renée-Pélagie went to plead with the Marseilles magistrates on her husband's behalf, she found their minds were closed. On 3 August 1772 the family name was disgraced: the town crier called it out in front of the château and in all the squares and cross-roads of the village. Both men must present themselves within a week. Even when Marguerite and Marianne appeared in front of a local notary to withdraw their charges, it made no difference. On 26 August the Royal Prosecutor ordered 'special proceedings' against the two absentees. On 3 September he presented his case to the Council Chamber, which pronounced its sentence. Both men were found guilty *in absentia* of poisoning and sodomy. They were required to 'make honourable amends' in front of the cathedral porch. 'There, on their knees, with head and feet bare, in shirts, a rope round their necks, each of them holding in his hand a candle of yellow wax weighing one pound, they must ask for pardon before God and King.' They would then be taken into the Place Saint-Louis 'for the aforesaid Sieur de Sade to have his head cut off on a scaffold, and the aforesaid Latour to be hanged by the neck and strangled on a gallows, and then the bodies of the afore-said Sieur de Sade and the aforesaid Latour shall be burned and their ashes thrown to the wind.' Eight days later the verdict was laid at the bar of the Parlement of Provence at Aix, and the sentence was confirmed. The next day, 12 September 1772, in the Place des Prêcheurs at Aix, Sade and Latour were burned in effigy.

Sade was lucky to have escaped a sentence which was remarkably harsh, and pronounced with remarkable speed. The judicial proceedings took barely two months, despite the August holidays.[1] Though sodomy was a capital offence, it hardly ever led to the death sentence and there was no conclusive proof that Sade was guilty of it, while it was obvious that the poisoning was accidental. Aphrodisiac sweets were used quite often: the ones impregnated with Spanish Fly were usually known as *pilles galantes* and sometimes as *pastilles de Richelieu*, because the Duc de Richelieu was so notorious for using them. The ones Sade offered the prostitutes had obviously been prepared with too strong a solution of *cantharides*, the drug taken from the cantharis beetle, but he had no conceivable motive for wanting to murder them.

The speed and severity of the Aix magistrates creates a mystery which is not adequately explained by enmity between Sade's father-in-law and Maupeou or by the constant anxiety of the Marseilles authorities about the use of imported aphrodisiacs. A likelier hypothesis has recently been suggested by André Bourde.[2] Living in the vicinity was another branch of the Sade family. Joseph-David de Sade, Seigneur d'Eyguières, had two sons, Jean-Baptiste-Joseph-David, who was now twenty-three, and Joseph-Henry Véran, who was just nineteen. They could hardly have been indifferent to a local scandal which did so much harm to the family name, but they may have had an even stronger reason for putting pressure on the venal magistrates. Ten years later Véran de Sade was imprisoned under a *lettre de cachet* issued at the request of the family. Is it possible, speculated Bourde, that he came under the influence of the cousin who was thirteen years his senior, that he was involved in some of Sade's escapades? If he was converted to sadistic habits, the family's acrimony would be understandable, and so would the letter written by the Intendant of Provence after Véran's arrest: 'The motives of the family are that no confidence can be placed in the young man and that it is essential he should be allowed no correspondence with his former associates, who would have caused his complete ruin if he had not been rescued by imprisonment.'

[1] This point was made by the Marseilles barrister Marcel Parrat at the 1966 colloquium on Sade in Aix: '*Le Marquis de Sade*, Centre Aixois d'Etudes et de recherches sur le 18e siècle'.

[2] Ibid.

At the end of August 1772, Mme de Montreuil came to stay in Provence with her daughter, and at the beginning of October, after three months of travelling all over Italy with her brother-in-law, Anne-Prospère returned to the château accompanied by Latour; but they probably left again after two weeks to rejoin Sade at Nice, which was then on the far side of the French border. The Duchy of Savoy was not annexed by France until 1792, and the territory around the papal city of Avignon did not come under French sovereignty. Corsica was French, but Sardinia was not. The Kingdom of Piedmont-Sardinia had been united under the House of Savoy by the Treaty of Aix-la-Chapelle in 1748, and the King had his court at Turin.

The Marquis was no longer using the name de Sade, but calling himself the Comte de Mazan. Anne-Prospère was sometimes introduced as the Comtesse de Mazan, sometimes as his sister-in-law. Latour was still with them, and they had another valet, who was known as La Jeunesse. Leaving their baggage in Nice, Sade and Anne-Prospère travelled northwards, keeping east of the frontier and arriving on 27 October at Chambéry. Had it not been for Mme de Montreuil, there would have been no question of extraditing them from the Duchy of Savoy, but she used her influence with the powerful Duc d'Aiguillon, the Minister for Foreign Affairs, who persuaded the Sardinian Ambassador to arrange for an order to be issued in the name of Charles Emmanuel III, the Sardinian King: the French nobleman known as the Comte de Mazan was to be arrested and imprisoned in a Savoyard fortress.

At Chambéry, Sade, Anne-Prospère and the two valets stayed at an inn called Le Pomme d'Or. After a few days there, Sade took a six-month lease on a country house just outside the gates of the city. Instead of venturing out into society, Sade was trying to live as quietly as he could, meeting very few people, though at the inn he did win the friendship of one Frenchman, M. de Vaulx, who later tried to help him.

Sade's relationship with Anne-Prospère had become very unstable. At the beginning of November she again left him, and Latour again accompanied her on her travels. She had said she was going to Italy, but her real intention was to go back either to Lacoste or withdraw into a convent. Left alone with La Jeunesse, Sade became ill. After being treated by a local surgeon, he sent a message for Latour to come back and look after him. He also sent

La Jeunesse to deliver some letters in Paris, where the Marquise was now living with the children. By the end of the month Count Lascaris, the Sardinian Minister of State for Foreign Affairs, was able to tell his ambassador that the King was pleased to oblige the Duc d'Aiguillon in the affair of the Marquis de Sade, and at the beginning of December the Governor of the Duchy of Savoy was ordered to have him incarcerated.

At 9 o'clock in the evening of 8 December 1772, Sade's house was surrounded and the Comte de la Chavanne entered it to find Sade alone with Latour. Relieving the astonished fugitive of his sword and two pistols, the Count searched his clothes. Finding no papers of any consequence, he left two adjutants to guard the prisoner. At 7 o'clock in the morning four cavalry soldiers arrived to escort him in a post-chaise to Miolans twelve miles from Chambéry, where the twelfth-century fortress (which is still there) had been used as a prison since the sixteenth century. Though Latour was also a fugitive from French justice, he was not arrested, but he voluntarily joined his master in prison.

The commandant of the fortress, M. de Launay, a former captain in the Savoyard grenadiers, had been instructed that Sade was to be kept under close arrest and allowed out of his dungeon only for his daily exercise under surveillance in the inner courtyard. No unidentified visitors were to have access to him and he must neither write nor receive letters. Latour would be allowed to sleep in the cell with his master, but not to go outside the inner ring of the building, which had three walls, with double moats. The keep and the Saint-Pierre tower were separate from the lower ramparts. The keep was square and five-storeyed. The dungeon situated on the lowest level was called 'Hell'. It was in a bad state of repair and level with the water in the moat under the drawbridge. There was so little air to counteract the poisonous fumes that few prisoners in it survived for long. Above it was 'Purgatory', and on the next level was the 'Treasure', consisting of two rooms for prisoners, one of which had a south-facing window and a fireplace. The Governor's rooms were on the floor above that, and on the next level were two cells. The one which faced north was known as 'Little Hope'; 'Great Hope' which faced south, had a big window with two grilles. It commanded a superb view of the Alps and the Isère valley. Sade was accommodated here. The top floor, 107 steps further up, was called 'Paradise'.

Sade immediately wrote to the Governor of the Duchy, asking him to intercede for the restoration of his liberty. In the meantime he asked for the right to write and receive letters and to send his valet out on errands. To his signature he appended his rank: cavalry colonel. Within a week the request produced results. Letters would be permitted, subject to censorship by the commandant, and the valet would sometimes be allowed out on errands.

Under the *ancien régime*, hierarchical power could be wielded internationally. After having Sade thrown into a Savoyard prison by orders that issued from the King of Sardinia, Mme de Montreuil could even influence the way her victim was treated. She sent a memorandum to the Sardinian Ambassador, who sent it on to the Governor, who gave the appropriate orders to de Launay. Remembering the stipulations of the de Beaumont family, she was primarily concerned that Sade should not make up his mind to escape. She asked for him to be made as comfortable as a man of his standing could expect to be, requesting that

> the personal effects he had with him, either for his use or for the entertainment necessary to such a lively mind, should be returned to him, with the exception of his papers, manuscripts, letters, of whatever sort they might be. His family asks that these should be forwarded to Paris, together with a small wooden box or coffer, believed to be red, with copper clasps. This contains papers. If he has taken it into the cell with him, please try to obtain possession of it and to extract the papers from it before he realizes it is missing.

Towards the end of December La Jeunesse was on his way to Miolans from Nice, bringing the luggage Sade had left there. The Governor, Comte de la Tour, wrote to assure the Montreuils that the trunks would be carefully searched and any papers of importance would be taken out and kept at the family's disposal. For the moment the prisoner had nothing to wear except a shabby coat, but no doubt the luggage contained a quantity of garments, so there was no need for the Marquis's relations to supply new ones.

Though Sade suspected that Mme de Montreuil was denigrating him to his captors, there was little he could do either to convince the family that he had been behaving well or to convince de

Launay and de la Tour that the Montreuils were telling lies about him. He asked the Count to issue a certificate, stating, for the benefit of his family, that from his arrival at Chambéry on 27 October until his arrest on 8 December, his conduct had been impeccable. And on New Year's Eve he informed the Count that the Montreuils, who in spite of all the evidence had been denying responsibility for his arrest, had forced him to defend himself by writing some memoirs. They were intended for his friends but they would be submitted initially to the Count.

On New Year's Day 1773, de Launay wrote to tell him that Sade was 'very dangerous. He is irascible, unpredictable and unreliable.' Why not encourage the family to petition for him to be removed to France? He had already hinted that he might use bribery to effect an escape. De Launay did not want to go on taking responsibility for him so long as he was given freedom 'to walk about all day in the fortress, which is not one of the most secure'. Besides, his letters were 'so badly written' it was hard to decipher them, and, not knowing the reasons for his confinement, de Launay could not judge which letters ought to be intercepted.

In fact the prisoner was under constant surveillance whenever he was outside his cell. When he walked in the keep, the sentry watched him; and when he walked on the lower ramparts, the guard was briefed not to lose sight of him. On 2 January 1773 the Count told the Ambassador he could reassure the Montreuils that all possibility of escape had been removed.

Still unable, after four weeks of imprisonment, to see any prospect of freedom, and frustrated even in his desire for a certificate of good behaviour, Sade became ill. On 8 January de Launay wrote to tell the Count that severe pains in the head and chest had given his prisoner several sleepless nights. Could a doctor be sent in order to prevent any deterioration? When one of the best local doctors arrived at the fortress with instructions to stay as long as necessary, his purgative treatment produced rapid results.

Meanwhile Mme de Montreuil was worrying about the memoirs Sade was writing. They must be censored by the Count, she insisted, and if they contained anything detrimental to his wife's family, which had never done him anything but good, it would be wrong to let them be circulated, and still worse if they were printed in Geneva as he had threatened they might be. The only men who could be looking after Sade's manuscripts were M. de

Vaulx or possibly Latour, a very bad type who ought to be kept under close surveillance. It would be wise never to let him leave the fortress without searching him carefully. 'He will hide the papers wherever he can.' In another letter, Mme de Montreuil specified what should be confiscated when the trunks arrived from Nice: all documents, letters and immoral books; valuable crockery, which might be abused by a prisoner; and clothes which he would not use. It may have occurred to her that some of her younger daughter's wardrobe might have found its way into her lover's trunks.

The relationship between commandant and prisoner was deteriorating. Sade tried to propitiate de Launay by having a gift of wine, coffee and chocolate sent up from the kitchen, but it was sent straight back; and by the middle of January the two men were exchanging not only insults but blows. According to Sade's subsequent letter of complaint to the Count, de Launay provoked the attack by swearing at him; according to de Launay's report, the bad language came only from Sade: in front of Lieutenant Duclos and an upholsterer, he blamed de Launay for having the door of the keep locked and ruling that he could exercise only on the lower ramparts.

Renée-Pélagie had been brought up to believe that her mother was always right, but by the end of January she had begun to feel her husband was being unfairly victimized. She wrote to tell de Launay that he had been excessively harsh and insufficiently respectful to his prisoner. She would inform the Ambassador. De Launay replied that in spite of the Marquis's discourtesy, he had done as much as he could to ameliorate his situation and had always regarded him as 'a man of the greatest distinction, who should not have deserved to be incarcerated in such a grim place as this.' But the next day, 5 February 1773, writing to the Count, de Launay adopted a very different attitude. 'My secret investigations indicate that he is completely untrustworthy. I believe that all his manœuvring is directed towards a single objective: escape. Quite apart from the suggestions he made to me, he has had all his Piedmontese money changed into livres and has been enquiring whether there is a bridge over the Isère.'

Circumventing the Count, Sade used M. de Vaulx as an intermediary for a direct appeal to the Sardinian Court at Turin. The petition deployed all the literary skill he had acquired. As soon as

it was safely in M. de Vaulx's hands, the Count was informed that
he would be welcome to read it and to judge for himself whether
it contained anything damaging either to the Marquise or to the
French court. At the same time, he asked the Count to pass on to
de Vaulx a package containing letters for his wife and his mother-
in-law. A few days later a peasant arrived with another letter from
Sade to the Count, asking him for 300 livres to pay for a watch.
Sade had had only 24 livres on him at the time of his arrest—when
the Count questioned the peasant, he revealed that it was Lieutenant Duclos who had handed him Sade's letter. Could it be that
Sade wanted to buy the watch for the Lieutenant as a reward for
being helpful in some way? De Launay was ordered to keep
Duclos under the same close surveillance as the prisoner. Without
being stopped altogether from going to see Sade, he should
somehow be prevented from seeing quite so much of him.

With no access to women and little conversation with men,
Sade had nothing to do except walk, eat, drink, sleep, read and
write. He knew he was being punished not for the pain he had
inflicted on the Marseilles prostitutes but for sleeping with his
sister-in-law, not for his defiance of the French law but because
his mother-in-law wanted him to be locked up. If self-justification
became a major motif in his mature writing, one of the reasons is
that in this formative period he cultivated the art of apologia. He
wrote another petition to the King of Sardinia, denouncing Mme
de Montreuil for seeking his 'total ruin' and his 'eternal absence'.
Her slanders had 'augmented the authority' of the Marseilles
tribunal which had condemned him. He had been given no chance
to defend himself. Surely His Majesty would not want to go on
supporting the cause of avarice and self-interest. If his enemy were
not aware that his cause was just, why was she using such devious
methods to keep him incarcerated in a country where he could not
complain? Sade's literary bombardment on the court had an effect,
though not the one he desired. The Ambassador reminded the
Count that nothing written by the prisoner must be allowed to
leave the fortress, 'because he is inundating us with rhapsodies
and memoirs in which the facts are as false as their presentation
is artistic'.

Meanwhile de Launay, who was not on good terms with
Lieutenant Duclos, had failed to keep him away from Sade. They
were eating supper together every evening. Sade did not seem

unsettled: he strolled a great deal on both upper and lower ramparts. But he was still sending and receiving clandestine letters.

All this time the Sardinian government had been paying for Sade's board and lodging. On 1 March the Ambassador asked the Montreuils to appoint a representative in Chambéry who would make monthly payments. Otherwise it might be necessary to release the Marquis. The implied threat was certain to be effective.

On 20 February 1773 the King of Sardinia died. He was succeeded by his son, Victor-Amédée III. A few days later Renée-Pélagie left Paris in a post-chaise, saying that she was on her way to Lacoste, but the Ambassador warned the Count that she was likely to be on her way to Miolans. She must not be allowed to see her husband. It was an expensive way of travelling, and the journey took her about ten days. On 6 March she arrived in Chambéry, dressed as a man and accompanied by another man. They spent the night at the inn, giving their names as Dumont. They said they were brothers and on their way to Piedmont. They left at midday, but stopped again after nine miles, as if they had had a slight accident. They were in the village of Montmélian, where the only inn was very uncomfortable, but they stopped there for a week. The man, Albaret, went up to the fortress in the evening to hand the commandant a letter from the Marquise, headed as if she were writing from Barraux, which was on the other side of the frontier. She asked that the bearer of the letter should be allowed to spend fifteen minutes alone with Sade to bring him news. De Launay refused, and in the morning he reported the incident to the Count in an express letter which must have arrived shortly before Albaret appeared at his palace with another letter from the Marquise. It was dated as if it were three days old, and it said she had been detained in Barraux by a chill, but felt some comfort in knowing that her friend, M. Dumont, would no doubt be permitted a meeting with the Marquis to discuss his affairs. Very courteously, the Count refused permission. It was against the King's instructions. But if the Marquise would like to write to her husband, the letter would be conveyed to him and his reply conveyed to her. Frustrated again, she wrote to ask the Minister for Internal Affairs at Turin for the permission the Governor had refused, complaining that her husband was constantly being denied the consolation of visits from friends he had made in Chambéry.

On Renée-Pélagie's third day in Montmélian, Albaret again called on the Count, this time with an unsealed letter from her to her husband. The letter was accepted, while Albaret, after again being refused permission to see the prisoner, was given a message for the Marquise: she should not prolong her stay in such an unpleasant place. But on the same day, Lieutenant Duclos visited her there, though not without increasing de Launay's suspicions that something was afoot. He wrote to tell the Count that he would ask to be relieved of his duties unless a means were found of removing the Lieutenant, 'who has always been prickly with his superiors'.

Reluctantly convinced that nothing was to be gained by staying in the village, Renée-Pélagie drove off towards Lyons without stopping at Chambéry. She had no doubt been in secret correspondence with Sade before she left Paris, planning for his escape. Arriving back at Lacoste, she wrote to tell the King that her husband had done nothing to deserve such severe treatment. 'An excessively lively imagination has produced, Sire, a kind of misdemeanour which prejudice has made into a crime, and the Law has hurled down its thunderbolts. And why? For a youthful turbulence that damages neither human life, nor honour, nor reputation.'

Meanwhile another dangerous prisoner had arrived at the fortress. Fifteen months previously the Baron de l'Allée had engineered the escape of a friend who had been imprisoned for debt at Bonneville. Together with several companions the Baron had stayed eating and drinking in the prisoner's cell until, at 10.30 in the evening, they hustled him out of the prison, disguised in the clothes of one man and the wig of another. The Baron's police record described him as 'very dangerous when drunk; a disturber of the peace; homicidal. Everyone gives him a wide berth.' For fourteen months he had been avoiding arrest in Geneva, after almost killing a soldier who had come out of a guard-house at Chêne to investigate the uproar that was going on. Drawing a sword from under his frock-coat, the Baron had lunged at the man's chest, piercing his shoulder-strap and his coat. But for a brass button which deflected it, the thrust might have been fatal.

The Baron was brought to Miolans on 22 February 1772. Five days later Sade told the Count that he had been gambling with the Baron and lost 250 livres. This, he said, was why he had invented the story about the watch: de l'Allée had been demanding immediate payment and making threats. He was also having a bad influence on Latour, who came from a good family and might one day be a man of property. Within two days the Baron had won 2,400 livres from him, which could hardly have been done without cheating. De Launay should have stopped them from playing, and the Count ought to make the Baron return to Latour the promissory note which was payable in three years' time. Meanwhile the Count need have no fear that the Marquis was planning to escape. He was incapable of breaking the promise he had made in writing when he arrived at Miolans.

When the Count wrote to him about the gambling and the quarrel, de Launay's answer was that he had known nothing of either. Sade, as he had said before, was a dangerous character, and now he was trying to spread the rumour that his valet was the Duke of Bavaria's illegitimate son.

During the next few days precautionary measures were taken. M. de Vaulx was expelled from Chambéry, and Lieutenant Duclos was dismissed from the castle. Sade appears to have sunk into a depression. 'He never speaks to anyone, not even to his valet,' reported de Launay in his letter of 19 March.

I have always shown him every courtesy, although he has never set foot in my quarters, and if he wished to take me into his confidence, I would try to afford him every possible consolation, without infringing my orders, and I would suggest certain approaches he could make to his relations and to the Minister in France.

Sade now wrote to the Count, trying to convince him that the Montreuils had nothing to gain by prolonging his imprisonment. The affair with Anne-Prospère was over, never to be resumed. An undertaking to that effect, couched in the most explicit terms, was enclosed. Would His Excellency send it to Paris by Monday's post? Sade also promised not to conduct any correspondence that could not be read by everybody in the land. He offered not to come within a hundred leagues of Paris for as long as they wanted to bar him from it. Beyond that, what could he propose? How could he make them believe him?

His despondency was exacerbated by a quarrel with de l'Allée, who interrupted a card-game to advise Sade's opponent never to play with men who could not lose without complaining. A very unjustified remark, said the Marquis. He was himself in a position to prove it, said the Baron. Livid, Sade protested to de Launay, who asked the Baron to withdraw to his room. He did not want to be punished because of Sade's grievances, the Baron said. De Launay prevaricated. The real reason for his request, he said, was that the Governor did not want him to grant any more privileges to de l'Allée. This enraged the Baron, who found a knife and stabbed himself several times in the stomach. A surgeon was called, but none of the wounds was more than a quarter of an inch deep.

As the time passed, still with no prospect of reprieve, Sade began to express fears—probably genuine—that his health was deteriorating. According to de Launay's report, confinement was making him very nervous and very melancholic. By the middle of April, having lost all hope of persuading the Count to help him, he was again complaining directly to the King. But at least he had made peace with the Baron. They were taking strolls together, and Sade asked whether his friend could eat meals with him. He also succeeded finally in winning the goodwill of de Launay, who pointed out to the Count that the budget fixed for the board and lodging of the Marquis and his valet made no provision for clothes or for messengers (who were always tipped very generously). At Easter, de Launay reported, Sade performed 'his duties as a Christian', afterwards undergoing such a change of heart that he begged the commandant to forgive everything he had said or written against him, and asked 'to make honourable amends to certain officers and under-officers of the garrison who had been upset by his outbursts of temper'. It seemed to the Count that the change of attitude must be 'due to sacramental grace'.

Now that he was taking his meals with the Baron, Sade began to complain that the food was almost invariably cold by the time it reached his room. Could they not be allowed to eat in the canteen? A room formerly used by Lieutenant Duclos became their dining-room. It was in a recently built extension to the canteen containing two communicating rooms. The other, which was almost always kept locked, was used by the cook as a store-room, and in the corner there was a lavatory which had a window without iron bars.

At 7 o'clock in the evening of 30 April 1772, Sade and the Baron came down for their supper. Latour, who served them, was waiting for the moment when the cook and his staff would stop going in and out of the store-room. As soon as they had sat down to their own meal, he pocketed the store-room key and slipped upstairs to his master's cell, where he lit the candles. Sade and the Baron had both written letters for de Launay which Latour left on the table. At 8.30 the two noblemen and the valet climbed through the lavatory window. An eighteen-year-old peasant boy called Joseph Violon was waiting to help them down the wall. Until a few days ago, when he had been banned from the fortress, he had been employed by Sade as a messenger. After years of working on the land, he knew his way in the dark, and he led the three runaways towards the frontier.

Just before 9 o'clock the guard Jacquet came back on duty after finishing his supper. Seeing through the keyhole that there were lights on in the Marquis's room, he assumed that the two noblemen were playing cards. Not wanting to interrupt the game, he threw himself down, still fully clothed, on the bed of the adjoining room, intending to take the Baron back to his own cell later on. But with all the food and drink inside him, Jacquet could not keep his eyes open, and it was 3 o'clock in the morning before he was conscious again. Candles were still burning in Sade's room. In a panic, Jacquet rushed to de Launay, who got up and, finding Sade's door locked, forced it open. He read Sade's letter. 'My joy at breaking free from my chains is marred only by the fear that you will be held responsible for my escape. After all your decency and your courtesy, I cannot conceal the anxiety that this consideration causes me.'

Not expecting that over six hours would elapse before the escape was discovered, Sade had concocted a fiction that might deter, or at least delay, any pursuit: 'Fifteen men, well mounted and well armed, are waiting on the hillside . . . all determined to die sooner than let me be taken prisoner again.' The letter continued with a mixture of threats and thanks. 'I have a wife and children whose vengeance for my death would carry you to your last breath . . . I hope the day will come when I shall be able to give myself up entirely to the feelings of gratitude you have inspired in me.' Would the Commandant also be good enough to forward to Lacoste the things he had left in his cell, including the six maps on the walls, the blue frock-coat, which was fairly new, and the two little china dogs, to which he had become quite attached. One was black all over, the other was spotted with white.

The fugitives kept on the move all night, and by daybreak they had crossed the frontier. From the village of Chapareillant, Sade wrote to the Count. If he had seemed unappreciative of the Governor's kindness it was thanks to the horror of his situation. 'I cannot abide punishments of this kind. To the loss of liberty I prefer death.'

It was the Sardinian Ambassador who had to break the news to Mme de Montreuil. She took it badly, but wrote very politely to the Count. She was distressed that His Excellency's goodness to the Marquis's family had not been effective for as long as she would have wished, but she and the other members of the family were none the less grateful for the consideration he had accorded to their interests. Suspecting that her daughter had been a party to the escape, she asked for the return of all the letters she and the Marquise had written to the prisoner. But these had been impounded for the enquiry into the escape and they could not be recovered until nearly a year later.

Chapter 5

Prime of Libertine Life

When he arrived in Grenoble at the beginning of May 1773, Sade was intending to take refuge in Spain, and hoping that Mme de Montreuil would send funds to help him. He wrote to her from Bordeaux and, in July, from Cadiz, but he does not seem to have gone any further. In the autumn he rejoined Renée-Pélagie at Lacoste, knowing that he might have to leave very quickly to escape arrest.

Elzéar Fage, the notary who had been managing Sade's estates, allowed himself to be seduced by Mme de Montreuil into betraying his master and collaborating with her in a plot to have him imprisoned again. The preparations were elaborate. The royal order for Sade's arrest was issued on 16 December 1773 and 8,000 livres were spent on the police raid. Mme de Montreuil consulted the Abbé, who had turned against his nephew once again, and she had ten meetings with Inspector Goupil of the Paris police—some before the raid, some after. Two peasant costumes were bought as disguise, although the plan was to arrive at Lacoste in the middle of the night. In any case, they moved too slowly. By the time Goupil arrived at Lacoste on 6 January, with four archers and a troop of cavalry soldiers from Marseilles, Sade had been alerted of the danger. They had brought ladders to scale the walls; after climbing in with swords and pistols in their hands, they searched for him unsuccessfully all over the château. One of the archers carried an iron bar which he used for smashing doors and furniture. They turned out the contents of Sade's study, burning some papers and taking others away. Before going, Goupil said he had not yet finished with that bugger. Sade did not reappear at Lacoste for several weeks.

To replace the disloyal Fage as manager of the estates, Sade chose the man who was as close as anyone to having been his childhood friend, Gaspard François Xavier Gaufridy, another notary in the same town, Apt, which was seven miles from Lacoste. He was the same age as Sade, and the two boys had played together when Gaufridy's father had worked for the Count. Notaries were authorized to carry out legal business, and Sade often addressed Gaufridy as 'my dear lawyer', though he had no legal qualifications. Sade greatly enjoyed his company: they disagreed about religion and agreed about the need for political reform. Sade was to go on employing Gaufridy for twenty-two years, not only in legal matters but in dozens of more personal ways. The whole Sade family used him as a factotum: he brought game and vegetables to the abbess aunts, advised the Abbé on legal and business affairs and he was always on hand to run errands. The bailiffs at Saumane, Mazan and Arles were all kept under his supervision.

Two months after the raid, Renée-Pélagie briefed Gaufridy to file a complaint against her mother. He sent the documents to a lawyer at the Châtelet Court in Paris, but this did not help Sade. By the end of the month, a royal warrant had been issued for his arrest. He was alternating between hiding-places in Bordeaux and Grenoble, while Renée-Pélagie was finding it very difficult to cope with the estate which was burdened with debts bequeathed by her father-in-law. Nor was help to be had either from her parents or from the Abbé, who was saying that Sade ought to give himself up.

In June 1774 he came back to Lacoste. He was worried that nothing had been done to quash the judgement against him at Aix. Renée-Pélagie had appealed to the Parlement, but to no effect. In reality, the main danger lay in the *lettre de cachet*, which had nothing to do with the judgement at Aix and which could have been enforced at any minute. After four months there was still no news of whether the law-court at Châtelet had issued a summons against Madame de Montreuil. Habituated at Miolans to producing apologias for his behaviour, Sade had written an ineffectual memorandum expressing his outrage that Mme de Montreuil should be content to leave things as they were. 'It is protracting the disgrace,' he complained in a letter to Gaufridy, 'dishonouring her daughter and her grandchildren, plunging the estates into disorder and making my life dismal and unhappy.' Renée-Pélagie was going to be in Paris for four months: could Gaufridy advise her on how to arrange things so that Sade would not have to go on leading 'a vagabond life. I am ill-suited to play the role of an adventurer.'

When Anne-Prospère arrived at Lacoste, it was clear that the affair had ended, and she travelled with her sister to Paris, leaving Sade with the servants. The reigning favourite, Gothon, the attractive daughter of a Swiss Huguenot, was sleeping both with Sade and with his valet, La Jeunesse, who had left his wife and children starving in Langres. With free trade and a better system of internal distribution the famines of 1769–72 could have been largely obviated, but the administrators were incompetent. Though Louis XV was not trying to continue Louis XIV's policy of excluding the nobility from positions of administrative responsibility, they had become irresponsible. Without concerning themselves with what happened in the country, high-ranking churchmen and civic officials were living off the tithes, taxes and feudal dues paid by the predominantly rural population. Abandoning his family to share the life of a dissipated master, La Jeunesse was only paralleling the insouciance of his social superiors. Sade himself, in *Les 120 journées de Sodome*, was to blame the moral decrepitude on the wars of Louis XIV, which 'in exhausting the state's finances and the people's energy, found the secret of enriching an enormous number of those bloodsuckers who are always lying in wait for public calamities. They do not help to repair the damage but to cause it, putting themselves in a position to profit from it.'

Hippolyte Taine's *Origines de la France contemporaine* compares the rural population with a man walking through a pond, the water up to his chin. The slightest change of economic level would make him go under. 'You have not the least idea of what goes on in times of famine,' wrote Diderot, who witnessed the starvation at Langres, where he owned property. 'To represent country life by four rich farmers is to forget the misery of the multitude.'[1] Insurrections were frequent. 'In riots one would say that everybody is sovereign, arrogating the rights of life and death.'

Renée-Pélagie's journey to Paris took about twelve days. Her first task was to expedite the legal proceedings against her mother, but the obstacles were formidable and the situation extremely confusing. When she was told that Madame de Montreuil was madly in love with Sade, and less angry with him than with her, her reaction was 'So much the better'.[2] The Royal Attorney, who could have intervened in the legal proceedings, was saying that

[1] 'Apologie de l'abbé Galiani'.
[2] Letter to Gaufridy, 29 July 1774.

Renée-Pélagie was mad. There was even a possibility that police spies were keeping her under observation. She was staying at a hotel, but she warned Gaufridy to send all letters to the address of a tailor in the rue Saint-Nicaise. Later (perhaps to economize) she moved out of the hotel into the Dowager Countess's rooms at the Carmelite convent in the rue d'Enfer.

Two months earlier, the sixty-four-year-old Louis XV had died of smallpox. Until then the government had been dominated by an unpopular triumvirate—Maupeou, the Chancellor, Abbé Terray, and the Duc d'Aiguillon. But with the twenty-year-old Louis XVI on the throne, they did not survive for long once the seventy-three-year-old Jean-Frédéric Maurepas had emerged as the effective prime mover. But not Prime Minister. 'I understand,' he told the King at their first interview. 'Your Majesty wishes me to show him how to do without one.' The Parlements, which had been in dissolution since 1771 were to be reconvened, which seemed likely to help the Marquise's cause. Encouraged by the responsiveness of the Châtelet magistrates, she saw that the best chance of quashing the Aix judgement lay in making an outright denial of sodomy. Mme de Montreuil's contacts at court were no longer quite so good, and she seemed nervous about the outcome of the Châtelet proceedings. She was still in touch with the Abbé, who was convinced that Renée-Pélagie would be ineffectual in serving her husband's interests; in fact she did very well. By the beginning of September she had received a formal promise that when the Parlement assembled in October, it would be presented with an appeal for the sentence to be quashed. After that, the *lettre de cachet*, which had been signed by Louis XV, could be cancelled.

But Sade behaved exactly as if he could not tolerate the possibility that his troubles might be over. He launched immediately into a new bout of provocative debauchery. After meeting Renée-Pélagie at Lyons when she was on her way back from Paris, he employed a twenty-three-year-old girl called Anna Sablonnière and known as Nanon. Either there or at Vienne they also recruited five other girls (all about fifteen years old) and a young secretary, possibly without the knowledge of their parents. Nanon, who was described by Sade as a procuress, probably helped them to find the others. At the château she worked as a chambermaid, and Gothon was very impressed with her.

In starting legal proceedings against her mother, Renée-

Pélagie had, at the age of thirty-one, repudiated her lifelong habit of daughterly submissiveness. Though she had come to realize that her mother was a savagely vengeful woman, the feelings of guilt and disloyalty generated a compulsion to compensate by being totally loyal to her savagely perverted husband. Without understanding his tastes she may have been hoping to acquire them, believing that having done so well for him in Paris she had a chance of winning back his love. It is also possible that she wanted to emulate her younger sister, whose sexual appetite was larger and more complementary to Sade's. Whatever Renée-Pélagie's motives, and whatever her misgivings, she took part in the orgies. Later on, in the testimony of the young girls, she was described as 'the first victim of a fury which can be described only as madness'. This could also be said of the recklessness that was characteristic of Sade. After so much legal trouble and such prolonged spells of imprisonment, he was taking the risk that new legal proceedings would be started, as they soon were. Renée-Pélagie went to Lyons in the hope of appeasing the three parents who had complained, but one of the girls was taken secretly to Saumane where the Abbé, nervous of becoming compromised, made accusations on her behalf against his nephew, adding his own testimony to hers. Well versed by now in the art of apologia, Sade prepared a refutation of the charges.

Frightened by the legal repercussions and enervated by the orgies, Renée-Pélagie was in a state of hysteria. She contradicted herself, threatened to go into a convent, insisted that she must be paid for the girls' board and lodging before they were given back to their parents. All this made a very bad impression on the priests and the Royal Attorney. Even in her more lucid moments, she felt guilty about lapsing from the moral habits of a lifetime. Desperate, she tried to revert to being a dutiful daughter. Discarding the independence and the aplomb she had acquired in Paris from litigating against her mother, she wrote to her for advice.

It was characteristic of Mme de Montreuil that she neither refused help nor gave it wholeheartedly. She could not trust Renée-Pélagie to cope adequately with the situation. Already the Marquise had made strategic mistakes in answering questions put to her by the Royal Attorney and the local priests. No, it was to Gaufridy that Mme de Montreuil addressed her letters. Later she would manœuvre him into acting as her agent, but there was no indication in her letter of 11 February 1775 that she would ever ask him to act against the Sades' interests. The matter could be settled, she said, only by delivering the girls back to their parents, preferably in the presence of the Royal Attorney and the priests who had received complaints. In any case it would be necessary to obtain adequate clearance certificates. The accusations must be formally withdrawn and it must be established that there was no question of kidnapping the children. Mme de Montreuil had already written to tell the attorney at Lyons that far from wanting to keep them against their parents' wishes, the Marquise had taken them as an act of charity. All she wanted to do now was give them back against a proper discharge of liability. But it was essential to act quickly. The rumours spreading at Lyons must be quelled. Gaufridy must take charge of the situation, supervising personally while the girls were handed back.

He did not do this, but when one of the irate mothers arrived at Lacoste, he took her to his own house at Apt where he did his best to reassure her, bribing her with some old clothes. Meanwhile Mme de Montreuil had intervened quite effectively by making contact with the Royal Attorney at Lyons, but she was still worried about the girl at Saumane, who was the most talkative of the five. A convent would be the best place for her, said Mme de Montreuil. The girl appears to have been hurt during the orgies, and Renée-Pélagie asked the Abbé not to let her be examined by a doctor.

The letter she wrote to the Abbé in February 1775 seems (as Lely suggests) to have been dictated by Sade. It is full of recrimination, fiction and implied threats:

> Last year, when the whole of Provence was reverberating with the story of a girl you are concealing in your château at Saumane, a girl said to have been stolen from her parents, your secretary was obeying your orders, when, pistol in hand, he repelled those who came to search for her. Recently, when two Lyonnaise girls sought me out in Lyons to complain about the very bad treatment which, they alleged, they had received at your château, I did my utmost to appease them and silence their odious calumnies. I trust that you will do the same with this girl and her slanders. Above all she should be prevented from returning to Vienne. I have heard that it is your intention to take her there. This would be dangerous, because of the hor-

rible things she says everywhere she goes. It would be better to keep her in your château, where she will have her liberty. This she could not be allowed in mine, for political reasons which make my house into a kind of prison, though not for the reasons you seem to suppose and not for reasons which have anything to do with the nephew you choose to slander and to treat like a madman.

The letter refers obliquely to Renée-Pélagie's role in the orgies:

What horrible things may this creature say about me! And how can you possibly believe in what you tell me? Your letter treats me very prettily and, if you were to be believed, I would be the director of my husband's pleasures. No, monsieur, that is not and never has been the case. How could it be, when it is quite certain that he has not set foot in Lacoste for a year?

If the girl was attacked, it must have been by the servants. How could the Abbé believe that she or his nephew would be party to such violence?

The fictions in the letter are transparent, but the Abbé was sufficiently intimidated to scribble out certain words. The section he censored most heavily concerned a girl called Rose and a pregnancy that had occurred eight years previously. Among the words that are still legible are: 'that you owe the silence of this girl who was saying that you . . .' The blackmail was effective: the Abbé kept the Lyonnaise girl at Saumane. But he adamantly refused to plead for the revocation of the Aix sentence. Mme de Montreuil's policy towards the Sades had now changed radically enough for her to be quite angry at his refusal to co-operate. In a letter to Gaufridy he complained that she was a woman 'who regards us as automata made to move according to her whims'. He had kept the girl in his château 'out of excessive obligingness towards people who do not deserve it from me, and with whom I wish to have nothing to do. When I have the pleasure of seeing you, I will tell you things I cannot commit to paper.'

By the beginning of April 1775 one of the fathers had made a second accusation, but he could not prove his case simply by asserting that evidence was to be found on the children's bodies. In Mme de Montreuil's letter of 8 April to Gaufridy, she asked whether these were not fables, modelled on the old stories, created for the sake of raising money to buy silence. But she was in such a state of anxiety, she said, that each letter she opened made her shudder. If the stories were true, anything could happen from one moment to the next. How could Renée-Pélagie be so uncomplaining? 'She would let herself be chopped in pieces rather than agree to anything that could harm him.' She was in fact continuing imperturbably with her domestic duties, concerning herself with repairs to the building, cooking, and the servants' clothes.

Meanwhile Sade, like a gambler raising the stakes, had installed some more girls at the château. There was a Marseilles dancer called Du Plan, who was described as a governess (Louis-Marie was now seven, Madeleine-Laure four). At least three other adolescent girls, including Nanon's niece, were employed as servants, and there was a small floating population of kitchen-maids. If Sade's letters are to be believed, it was Du Plan who was responsible for the fact that human bones were found in the garden. There had been rumours during the Rose Keller scandal that Sade's garden was a graveyard for the victims of his experiments, but there is no proof that his sadism was ever lethal, and, according to him, Du Plan brought these bones from Marseilles. 'She is full of life and . . . as a practical joke—whether good or bad I leave you to judge—they were used to decorate a small room.'

In November or December, Renée-Pélagie had told her mother that she was pregnant again. In April, Gaufridy reported that she was not. Possibly the 'pregnancy' was no more than a fiction she had designed to ease the reconciliation with her mother, whose help she needed, both financially and in the affair of the little girls.

On 3 May a President of the Provençal Parlement, Bruny d'Entrecastaux, announced that he knew Sade to be at Lacoste, where he was 'giving himself up to all kinds of excesses with young people of both sexes'.[1]

[1] D'Entrecastaux himself was as much of a monster as any of the libertines in Sade's novels. After a childhood apprenticeship of snaring birds and sticking pins into them, he plotted with his mistress to murder his wife. During the last of her pregnancies, he scattered cherry-pips all over the staircase; while she was lying-in he gave her a glass of poisoned lemonade, but it tasted so bitter she left it undrunk. Finally he cut her throat with a razor.

Nanon was responsible for most of the household storms. When she gave birth to a girl on 11 May, Sade was rumoured to be the father. On the 18th, the Abbé appealed to the Minister of the Royal Household to have him arrested and interned, because his acts of madness were not only a menace to society but a source of continual alarm to his family. In the middle of June Gaufridy handed Renée-Pélagie a message from Mme de Montreuil: a *lettre de cachet* had been issued for Nanon's arrest. It was better to have the young procuress locked up, she said, than to run the risk of her going to Lyons and renewing the accusations. Gaufridy's instructions had been to deliver the message while out walking with the Marquise. Inside the château, wherever they were, it was quite possible that Sade would be eavesdropping from behind a screen.

A few days later, there was a violent row between Renée-Pélagie and Nanon, who finally ran away to the convent of Jumiège for asylum. The Marquise immediately laid accusations against her for stealing some silver, but this was only to put the girl out of action until the *lettre de cachet* arrived. After protecting her from three of Sade's servants, who arrived at Jumiège in pursuit, the Prior wrote to tell the Abbé that his nephew deserved to spend the rest of his days in prison. No one in the château had been to confession at Easter. And the Marquise could be no better than her husband: she allowed her young maids to have conversations with a married woman who was a Lutheran. The Prior was possibly unaware that more than half the villagers were Protestants.

At the beginning of July 1775, the Minister for the Royal Household was able to inform Mme de Montreuil that he had made arrangements for Nanon to be sent to the prison in Arles. This was the one Mme de Montreuil had recommended, knowing the gaolers would be nuns who could be induced to prevent the girl from communicating with her parents. By the end of the month her baby was dead. Left at Lacoste with a wet-nurse who was herself pregnant, the infant had died at the age of ten weeks when the woman's milk had dried up. Cut off from all contact with the outside world, Nanon had already been threatening to kill herself before she was told of her baby's death.

Meanwhile Sade had found another actress. He wrote to her in Marseilles to describe the torments he was undergoing at seeing she preferred a rival. Nothing in the world would persuade him to give her up. Confident of his ability to win her love, he offered to take responsibility for her young child. But he did not have time to pursue the relationship. Towards the end of June, the mother of the boy employed as 'secretary' arrived rather tardily in Lyons to cause trouble with the magistrates. Sade was convinced that she had been put up to it by the Royal Attorney. Later he discovered that M. de Castillon, the Advocate-General of the Provençal Parlement, who had seemed so well disposed, had told her what to say. Meanwhile Mme de Montreuil was finding herself unable to mother Sade's children as she would have liked to. 'His wretched sons,' she told Gaufridy, 'are breaking my heart. They are here under my eyes. But I cannot do the impossible. My plans are constantly being wrecked, just as they are coming to fruition, by the behaviour of their father and mother.'

Sade could not have escaped arrest for much longer if he had stayed in France. Once at Lacoste when a search-party arrived, he hid in a narrow space under the roof. In July 1775 he escaped across the Italian frontier. Again he called himself the Comte de Mazan, but this time he had no lively travelling companion—only a footman, Carteron. He felt very isolated. He wrote that there was 'not a soul who speaks French' in the whole country, and he was 'a very long way from speaking Italian', though he was working at it 'like a devil'. In Florence he did not go into any of the churches, feeling too much revulsion against anything connected with religion, but he did visit the galleries, enjoying some of the more erotic paintings and sculptures.

Renée-Pélagie had no notion of how long he would stay abroad or what his prospects were of escaping imprisonment when he returned. He sent her news of his movements, as when he was about to leave Florence for Rome, but his letters were liable to be full of detailed demands. Instructing her to have shirts made for him, he specified how the collars should be tailored.

The girl, who had been in the Abbé's château since the beginning of the year, had still not recovered by the end of September. He arranged for her to be taken into the hospital at L'Isle-sur-la-Sorgue, which was only two miles away from Saumane. Offering to pay the expenses, Renée-Pélagie asked for the girl to be kept incommunicado. After a month in hospital, she was well enough to be taken out and lodged with a farmer at Mazan, where few people would meet her. By then, questions were being asked about the death of Nanon's baby. The wet-nurse, who gave birth to a child, insisted that she had been unaware of her pregnancy when she accepted the foster-child. She had thought that the lack of milk was due to fatigue after working at silk-making in Lacoste.

The Abbé still maintained that there was no hope of quashing the sentence at Aix unless Sade gave himself up. Disregarding his advice, Renée-Pélagie made the journey to Aix, accompanied by La Jeunesse, who had returned from Italy in August. She even bought him new clothes for the journey—a peach-coloured jacket, black breeches and a grey ratteen frock-coat. Making a second trip to Aix with Gaufridy, she appointed two lawyers to represent her.

Gaufridy was the still point at the centre of the family quarrels, receiving stormy letters from the Abbé, Mme de Montreuil, Renée-Pélagie and Sade himself, who said he had been counting on the lawyer to make a firm stand against Mme de Montreuil.

But that unhappy creature, with a charm she has from the devil (to whom she has doubtless bequeathed her soul) carries away everything she touches. The moment her magical qualities have made their impact on anyone's eyes, I am abandoned ... I can hear you saying 'Monsieur, if your misfortunes have continued it is because of your latest misdemeanours.' But listen to my answer: Monsieur, it is my misfortunes, my dishonour, my situation which make me continue with my misdemeanours, and until I am rehabilitated, every time a cat is whipped in the province there will be someone who says 'This is the doing of the Marquis de Sade'.

It was true that few people could resist Mme de Montreuil's combination of physical attractiveness, charm, determination, practicality and apparent reliability. A typical letter of hers to Gaufridy said:

You can be quite assured, Monsieur, that none of your letters has passed or will pass into anyone else's hands ... So if any of them were intercepted, it could only have been before they arrived. In any case, when one is acting reasonably and honestly, as you and I both are, one can walk with one's head held high.

In Naples early in 1776, Sade had to divulge his identity in order to clear up a confusion: the French *chargé d'affaires* mistook him for a cashier who had embezzled 80,000 livres from a salt-warehouse at Lyons. Calling himself Colonel le Comte de Mazan, Sade met another French officer who insisted that there was no Colonel le Comte de Mazan in the army. After admitting that he was the Marquis de Sade, he had to write to Provence for documentary evidence. Waiting for it to arrive, he was unable to appease the suspicious *chargé d'affaires*, who arranged for him to be dogged by the King of Naples's police. Desperate to prove his identity, he agreed to be presented at court in the uniform of a colonel, though he was nervous that he might be snubbed because of his reputation.

Tired of Italy, he soon announced his intention of coming back to Lacoste via Marseilles. Renée-Pélagie immediately sent La Jeunesse to Naples with orders to dissuade his master from taking such a risk. But Sade was too headstrong. He left Naples in May, dispatching two huge chests of antiques and curiosities ahead of him by boat. On 1 June he was in Rome, and by the 18th he had reached Turin. When he arrived in Grenoble towards the end of the month, he sent La Jeunesse to Lacoste with the news that he was to be expected within two weeks.

Sade had begun working on the book he intended to call *Descriptions critiques et philosophiques de Rome, Florence, etc*. He had already collected a great deal of material and for a long time after his return to France, letters went on arriving from Florence, where the Grand Duke's physician, Dr Mesny, had become one of his most wholehearted collaborators. Another was Dr Giuseppe Iberti, who had been asked to report on any outstanding cases of libertinism, whether culled from the classics or from contemporary Roman life. It was unlucky that one of Sade's letters to Iberti fell into the hands of the Inquisition, and even unluckier that the papal soldiers who burst into the doctor's room caught him copying out some lubricious stories for his correspondent. He was dragged off to a papal cell and kept there for 120 days. Meanwhile rumours were circulating in Provence that Sade had undergone a religious conversion, and, far from wanting to deny them, Renée-Pélagie encouraged the belief that the Pope had given him an audience.

The scandal about the little girls was not over. After being lodged on a farm by the Abbé, one of them ran away to make a statement before the magistrates at Orange, while another, who had stayed at Lacoste, caught a malignant fever. Though the doctor from Bonnieux paid eleven visits to the château within a fortnight, she was dead by the end of August.

The practice of libertinism was not altogether divorced from theory, and while working on his book about Roman and Italian debauchery, Sade was reading philosophy. It was at about this time that he studied Holbach's *Système de la nature*, which impressed him deeply. Later, in 1783, he would describe it as 'the basis of my philosophy'. Baron d'Holbach, the German-born friend and patron of the French *philosophes*, had published it in 1770. It takes a strong stand against the argument that Nature needs to be explained in terms of cause and result. The universe has always been in a state of continual movement: the energy is produced by interaction between the parts. The soul is entirely physical and dies with the body. Human behaviour, therefore, must be oriented towards earthly rewards. 'It would be futile and perhaps unjust to require a man to be virtuous at the cost of making himself unhappy. If vice makes him happy, he ought to love vice.'[1]

Holbach himself did not love vice or libertinism. 'Debauchery, when it becomes habitual, extinguishes all feeling in the heart, all activity in the mind; the excesses of the libertine suffocate the remorse which his initial misdeeds might have provoked.' But he was uncompromisingly hostile to organized religion. Everyone should be taught that beyond Nature there is nothing; though a religion without mystery 'would be of little use to the priests' who are 'the most dangerous and the most useless members of society'. It was nonsensical to affirm God's existence and to make statements about his qualities. The idea of God was 'an idea without a prototype, and is this anything more than a chimera?' This was why Holbach was described as 'the personal enemy of the Almighty'. Sade follows him in repeatedly applying the words 'chimera' and 'phantom' to God. The phrase about suffocating remorse seems to have stuck in Sade's mind. Twenty years later, in *Juliette*, he made Lady Clairwil say that the libertine should carry his excesses far enough for there to be no possibility of remorse or reform, and in *La Nouvelle Justine* (1797) he wrote: 'It

[1] *Système de la nature*, Vol I.

is unfortunately only too common for lechery to extinguish pity in man's heart.'

So Sade preserved the letter and subverted the spirit of Holbach's argument. Meanwhile, if he felt any remorse at the death of the girl, his reaction was to plunge further into libertinism. In the middle of October 1776 he left the château to stay in Montpellier, where he met Rosette who had worked at Lacoste for two months during the summer of the previous year. She not only gave herself to her old master but found another girl for him, Adelaide. When Père Durand, a monk, was asked to provide a third girl willing to work at the château, he made contact with a pretty twenty-two-year-old, assuring her father, a blanket-weaver called Trillet, that the moral discipline at the château was as strict as at any convent. Catherine Trillet was tearful when she arrived, but Renée-Pélagie comforted her.

In his eagerness to employ new girls, Sade was recklessly extravagant. He had offered Catherine a rise of 30 livres above the 120 she was earning in Montpellier, while Renée-Pélagie was so short of housekeeping money that she could not afford to repair the broken windows in her draughty bedroom. There was neither enough fire-wood to burn nor enough food. Her clothes were shabby and inadequate. A bad cold was making her even more depressed, and despite the broken windows, she took to her bed. Sade's income from the Lieutenant-Generalcy was still under sequester but, incapable of economizing, he spent money on expensive book-bindings and picture-frames. The desperation of Renée-Pélagie's appeal to her mother produced 1,200 livres, but the money was sent to Gaufridy, who was instructed that it must be used for housekeeping and paid out only as needed. Both the Sades were angry at these restrictions and, put into the position of paymaster, Gaufridy found it hard to preserve his appearance of neutrality, especially when Sade forbade him to show his face at Lacoste.

In December the helpful Père Durand was again commissioned to procure servants. About the middle of the month he drove up to the château in a cart with a secretary called du Rolland, a Parisian wig-maker whose brother was a lackey for the Count du Périgord, a chambermaid called Cavanis and a foreign kitchen-maid. After giving them supper, Sade shut them into separate rooms, and during the night he tried to seduce all four, offering each of them money. At 4 o'clock in the morning, all except the kitchen-maid returned with the monk in the same cart. When they described the events of the night to the blanket-weaver, he was alarmed about his daughter, who had been in the château since All Saints' Day. He was furious with Père Durand, who said he had heard stories about the Marquis in the past but felt sure he was cured. Durand's advice was that the girl should be left at the château, but when the illiterate Trillet insisted, the monk wrote a letter to the Marquis. Suspicious, the weaver took the letter to the monastery, where the superior confirmed that it did not say what the monk said it said. He had to write another letter before being expelled from the monastery.

A month elapsed before Trillet attempted to rescue his daughter, but on Friday 17 January 1777 he arrived at Lacoste, determined she should not go on working there. During an argument, he fired a pistol at Sade, but missed and ran away. About four hours later, after his daughter had sent someone out to calm him down, he reappeared, not at all calm, accompanied by four villagers. Seeing a movement in the courtyard, he fired again, and the four men ran away. Trillet went off to drink in a tavern. He was not arrested, though the local Registrar soon arrived there. The following day the junior magistrate at Lacoste took statements from witnesses of the attempted murder, and it is an index of Sade's unpopularity that it was safe for Trillet to stay in the village for two days. When he left he was talking about his 'sincere feelings of friendship and attachment' to the Marquis.

Apprehensive, none the less, that the man might have gone off to make accusations, Sade instructed Gaufridy to ask the lawyer Mouret in Aix for advice on how to proceed. Gaufridy did nothing, while Trillet did in fact start proceedings, alleging that Sade had refused to give up his daughter. Sade said Trillet was lying and asked for him to be arrested. Catherine signed a confirmation that she had no complaints about the way she had been treated. Nevertheless, the Attorney-General ordered that the girl should be returned to her father.

If Mme de Montreuil's gift of 1,200 livres had represented a step towards reconciliation, she had since recoiled several paces towards enmity. She had been intending—or said she had—to submit a plea to the King on her son-in-law's behalf, but in January 1777, after receiving from Renée-Pélagie a very long threatening letter, which Sade must have dictated, she said she would never again intervene in their affairs. Let them find their own way out of trouble. But she did not find it easy to remain passive, especially when she had been threatened. As she told Gaufridy, 'I have my answer ready and I have nothing in the world to fear.'

At the end of December, Gaufridy had received an anonymous warning that a police officer and ten horsemen had been ordered to go to the Saint Clair fair in Apt on 2 January to arrest Sade. He succeeded, without much difficulty, in keeping out of sight on 2 January, but he did not take the step that ought to have followed logically. Anyone with an instinct for self-preservation would have made immediate arrangements to leave the country. Sade's instinct was not for self-destruction but for calling down punishment on his own head. Like Kafka, whose incurable fear of his father ramified into guilty stories about punishment savagely disproportionate to the offence, Sade could never believe that he deserved to be forgiven. In January 1777 he could hardly have courted Nemesis more provocatively than by going to Paris, but when he heard that his mother was dying this is what he decided to do. Even his servants tried to dissuade him.

She had done him little good during her life, and she did him great harm by dying when she did, though it was not her fault that she was used as bait to trap him. She was sixty-five when she died at the Carmelite convent on 14 January, and she was buried the following day; Mme de Montreuil made sure that the news did not reach Lacoste. A fortnight after the funeral, the Sades set out on the journey that would last over a week. Catherine Trillet, frightened of returning to her belligerent father, had volunteered to accompany them to Paris, and the other servant they took was La Jeunesse. The roads were in a bad state and their carriage kept having to be repaired. They arrived, exhausted, on the evening of 8 February, to learn that they were three weeks too late.

Within the next few days Sade had regained enough energy to write to an old friend, an abbé who had once been his wenching companion. They should meet again, he suggested, to exchange stories about their conquests and make some new ones.

It was not until their third day in Paris that Renée-Pélagie let her mother know they had arrived. Three days later Inspector Marais, who had played no part in Sade's affairs since escorting him to Pierre-Encise nine years previously, appeared at the Hôtel de Danemark to arrest him under another *lettre de cachet*. Sade was taken to Vincennes, where, at 9.30 in the evening, he was locked up.

Chapter 6

Imprisonment and Escape

Medieval fortresses made good prisons. Built with thick walls and small window-spaces to make it hard for besieging forces to break in, they were easily adapted to make it hard for prisoners to break out. The keep at Vincennes, which was started by Philippe de Valois in the fourteenth century and finished by Charles V in the sixteenth, was as solidly built as any in Europe. According to Mirabeau, who was a prisoner there later on in 1777, it still showed no signs of deterioration, and even today it shows very few. Surrounded by two huge moats, the outer walls had only one entrance containing three gates which could not be operated independently or by less than two men. The sergeant of the watch and the turn-key worked together to manœuvre them, while two sentries were on duty outside. At each corner of the building inside there was a turret, with a triple-gated entrance. The prisoners' rooms were inside the walls, sixteen foot in thickness, which connected the turrets. Each cell had three doors, which reinforced each other. The innermost was iron-clad. Each door had two locks and three bolts. Little daylight penetrated into the cells from the narrow peepholes which were protected by a dense network of iron bars, well out of the prisoners' reach.

Every night, the drawbridges were raised and the doors to the towers locked. Two sentries were positioned so that all four walls were in view of one or the other, and at half-hourly intervals a squad of guards marched round to inspect all the windows from outside.

At the end of his first month Sade wrote to Mme de Montreuil arguing that it was idiotic to shut a man up like a wild beast in order to punish or reform him. 'Any reasonable person will see that for me the only possible result of such treatment is organic disturbance.'

Renée-Pélagie did not know where he was. She assumed that he was in the Bastille, but 'the drawbridges are always up and the guards do not allow one to stop and look'. The only information she had was from the Minister, who assured her that her husband was well and had everything he could desire. Mme de Montreuil was denying responsibility for the arrest. She was incapable of such treachery, she said, but perhaps the imprisonment would be advantageous when they were pleading for the 1772 sentence to be quashed. The Keeper of the Seals had promised her that he would be helpful as soon as he could.

At the end of February Sade wrote to Renée-Pélagie: 'There are moments when I do not know myself at all ... I feel I want to turn my fury against myself and if I am not outside this place within four days, nothing is more certain than that I shall beat my head against the walls.' But his mind was also engaged with such questions as whether Mme de Montreuil might now be in possession of the papers he had left at the Hôtel de Danemark. Among them were 'things which to her would have appeared improper', especially something in his handwriting, dictated by a man he met in Italy. He would be quite willing to provide explanations of these papers, but it was important in the meantime not to let her draw any unfavourable conclusions.

In Miolans, Sade had seen a good deal of de Launay; in the cell at Vincennes he saw nothing of the prison governor until very much later. Food was served only twice a day, mostly on very dirty plates. Lunch was at 11 o'clock in the morning, dinner at 5 in the afternoon, so there was a regular stretch of eighteen hours with no food. Lunch consisted of an entrée and boiled meat; dinner of an entrée and roast meat. Each prisoner had a pound of bread and a bottle of wine every day, and two apples at one of Thursday's meals and one of Sunday's.

Writing to Gaufridy at the beginning of March, Mme de Montreuil did not hide her jubilation. 'Everything is as good as it could be, and nothing can go wrong: it was high time!' The notary must go on sending her reports of everything that happened at Lacoste, and copies of every letter her daughter wrote to him. It was quite safe, she told him. She burned all his letters as soon as she had read them. How unfortunate, though, that the Marquise was not more forthcoming with her. At least she had seemed less shattered during the last few days, although the ministers were still keeping her in ignorance of her husband's whereabouts. 'All that is as it should be.'

In prison Sade was to become more emotionally dependent on

Renée-Pélagie. 'Oh my dear love,' he wrote on 6 March, 'there is nothing to equal the horror of my fate, no way of describing everything I am suffering or of assuaging the anxieties that rack me and the agonies that devour me. Here there is nothing to speak for me except my own tears and cries, which go unheard . . . What has become of the time when my dear love shared them? Today I have no one. The whole of nature seems dead for me.' He did not even know whether she was receiving his letters: no answer to his last one had arrived. The treatment he had received at Miolans was, by comparison, luxurious. After sixty-five days in the keep, he wrote: 'I am in a tower, enclosed behind 19 doors of iron and receiving daylight only through two small windows with a score of bars on each. For ten or twelve minutes each day I have the company of a man who brings me food. The rest of the time I spend alone, and weeping.' He had been exercised only five times since his arrest, walking for an hour 'in a kind of cemetery, about 40 foot square, surrounded by walls over 50 feet high'. He was accompanied by a warder who was not allowed to speak. He implored her to visit him if she could obtain permission, to write to him, to ask for him to have more exercise, and to provide a second pair of sheets. He had not been allowed to send for his camp-bed. 'I have not slept a wink for seven nights and I have been vomiting up everything I ate during the day.'

A few days later he signed an appeal to the King for the annulment of the Aix sentence. The document had been drawn up by a lawyer and, as he said in his letter of 29 April, it all seemed quite irrelevant to his present ordeal. How could a government be so feeble as to make itself the instrument of a shrew's vengeance? Mme de Montreuil could have secured a *lettre de cachet* exiling him permanently from France, but that would not have satisfied her. In another two weeks he would have been locked up for three months, and that was as much as he could be expected to bear. His desperation would teach him how to escape for eternity from the odious confinement which had become insufferable.

Meanwhile the ineffectual M. de Montreuil had very nearly let his daughter into the secret of his wife's correspondence with Gaufridy. He was severely reprimanded and told to be more careful in future; the lawyer was reassured that care would be taken not to compromise him. Even with Sade in prison, Mme de Montreuil was devoting a good deal of her time to his affairs. She cross-examined Catherine Trillet, who revealed that another girl had been living secretly at the château. Gaufridy was instructed to remove some evidence from one of the rooms there. Apparently it might be dangerous, but Mme de Montreuil was not sure whether it consisted of papers or of mechanical aids to libertinism.

Mme de Montreuil's next objective was to obtain full power to act as agent in all her son-in-law's affairs, but Sade indignantly refused to sign the document that had been drafted. His anxiety was increased by the inference that it was not a gambit she would have attempted if he was likely to be released in the near future.

She had also been using her influence to prolong Nanon's imprisonment 'on various grounds which do not reveal the true one', as she confided to Gaufridy in a letter of 3 June 1777. She may have been nervous about the mysterious evidence at the château which had not yet been destroyed, or she may have been trying to build up a reserve of evidence for use against her son-in-law. Nanon's father had been trying to find out who was paying the costs of her imprisonment, while she had managed to contact her uncle, a priest in an Auvergne village, who persuaded the Intendant and a local nobleman to make representations to the Minister. Mme de Montreuil then sent Gaufridy to negotiate with the prisoner. Could they count on her silence? She was not finally liberated until February 1778, and then on condition she did not go within three leagues of Lyons or Vienne. She was given 320 livres in lieu of the wages she could have earned, and she promised not to talk about the past. Later, when she came back to Lacoste, she warned Sade not to trust Gaufridy, who had encouraged her to make false accusations. ' "Revenge yourself," he told me. "He's the one who had you put in prison. If you will only make a statement that the way things happened was so-and-so, we can make sure that he spends the rest of his life rotting in prison." '

Even at the beginning of June, when Renée-Pélagie had finally learned where Sade was, she was still not allowed to visit him, and letters between them were censored. 'You ask me how I am,' he wrote in one. 'But what point is there in telling you? If I do, you will not receive my letter.' During the summer, his increasing despondency produced an unpleasant physical symptom: severe piles. She told Gaufridy to inform the Abbé: the news 'will have the effect of rejuvenating him'. The joke was badly mistimed: at the end of the year the Abbé died. He was in his seventy-third year, but a Spanish woman had been living with him. One of his sisters produced a eulogy, finding pious consolation in the circumstances of his death, while another sister, who had been contesting the ownership of his china for twenty years, appropriated it.

Sade had spent almost the whole of the year in Vincennes, but Mme de Montreuil went on ignoring his appeals for mercy. On 8 December he wrote to Renée-Pélagie that everything she sent him seemed like yet another proof that there was no prospect of reprieve. But he wanted her to go on supplying him with calendars. 'Alas, it is my life: to count the days ahead, mournfully to let my mind go backwards over what no longer exists and forwards to the frightful road on which I am being led to my grave.' On 5 January 1778, appalled at the prospect of the year ahead, he used his blood as ink in another appeal to his mother-in-law. Her latest idea was to make out that he was mad. If he would connive at the pretence, she could represent him at the hearing in the Parlement. She had been evolving this plan for about six months, ostensibly as a means of obtaining the annulment from Aix. Combined with the lack of proof, she said, it would dispose of the sodomy question. Latour, who had disappeared abroad, had sworn his denial of the crime. Marguerite Coste had withdrawn her statement: Marianne's evidence could probably be discredited because she had asked for indemnification when she withdrew her charge, while Marianette, who had been looking out of the window, would not be regarded as a reliable witness.

Mme de Montreuil's determination was now pitted against that of Sade, who adamantly refused to plead insanity. Without consulting Renée-Pélagie or even confiding in her about the new stratagem, Mme de Montreuil went on preparing to appeal for the annulment. She made arrangements with the two chief Presidents of the Provençal Parlement, M. de la Tour and M. de Castillon, and in the middle of April she was briefing Gaufridy about the girls in Marseilles. He must not only sound them out and drill them in what to testify, but make sure that the police did not apply any pressure that would interfere with this. Sade was told that unless he consented to a plea of insanity, he would have to appear in person at Aix. Suspicious that the trip to Aix might be a trap, he wanted reassurance from Renée-Pélagie that it was not, but, after fifteen months in prison, he had still not been allowed to receive a single visit from her.

In May he lost his Lieutenant-Generalcy, which had been suspended since 1773, to his twenty-nine-year-old cousin, Jean-Baptiste-Joseph-David, Comte de Sade d'Eyguières, the elder brother of Véran de Sade, who was now twenty-five, and still at liberty. There is no proof that the Viscount was led astray by the Marquis or that the Count put pressure on the Aix magistrates,[1] but by 1775 the Count certainly knew about the excesses of his dissolute cousin. He had been told about the orgies at Lacoste by the no less debauched but much more reputable Bruny d'Entre-castaux. The Count's designs on the Lieutenant-Generalcy probably date at least from 1775, if not from 1772.

Meanwhile Sade was more immediately concerned about the trip to Aix, and later on in the month he received a visit from M. Bontoux, a lawyer, who appeared with a letter of recommendation from Mme de Montreuil. After failing to convince Sade about the wisdom of pleading insanity, he discussed arrangements for the journey to Aix. When he was told he would have to have a police escort, Sade asked to have no one but Inspector Marais together with Marais's servant and his own valet La Jeunesse. He also asked for suitable clothes. What he was wearing was not fit to be seen outside the prison.

The King granted letters of *ester à droit*—permission for Sade to make the appeal, although more than five years had elapsed since the sentence was passed. On 14 June 1778, after sixteen months in the prison, Sade left his cell under Marais's escort. They arrived in Aix during the evening of the 20th and stayed overnight at an inn. In the afternoon of the next day, a Sunday, he was gaoled in the Royal Prison, where he was to stay for five weeks, importuning Marais with what the policeman called 'demands for special treatment, although he had all the privileges that a man of quality can expect in prison'. He wanted to 'prove his generosity by making gifts to all the other prisoners'. He spent 72 livres at the prison canteen, and he was very persistent in pressing his attentions on a young female convict.

As soon as the letters of *ester à droit* had been accepted by the Parlement, proceedings were merely formal. Within three weeks

[1] See page 64 above.

the sentence, which could have cost him his life, had been converted into a mere admonition.

After leaving Vincennes without being allowed to see his children, Sade had still had no contact with his wife who was in Paris. Nervous that she might intervene, Mme de Montreuil had not told her that he was in Provence. She had gone on writing to him in Vincennes and worrying about his silence. Was he ill? Did he not know that she would give her life's blood for him? When the news reached Lacoste that he was now only thirty miles away, Gothon sent him flowers, fruit and jams, with an affectionate letter. She 'often wept' about his sufferings, and she had felt 'an inexpressible joy on learning of his presence in the neighbourhood'. When he asked for clothes from the château she sent him two brown dress-coats, three jackets, including one with green and white stripes, two pairs of white breeches, as well as the underwear she thought he might need, and a pot of apricot marmalade. She also offered to go out and shoot a hare, which Gaufridy could bring to Aix on Saturday.

At 8 o'clock in the morning of 30 June, Sade was taken in a sedan chair with drawn curtains to the Jacobin monastery where the Parlement held its sittings. The Marquis knelt in front of his judges until the President signalled him to rise. After speeches in his defence by the lawyer that Mme de Montreuil had engaged and by the Royal Attorney, the Parlement declared the Marseilles trial to be invalid. There had been no adequate evidence of the alleged poisoning, but the two other charges—debauchery and sodomy—should be re-investigated. Within two hours the court was adjourned. Outside the gates a crowd had gathered to see the prisoner, but again the curtains of the sedan chair were drawn. Gaufridy was then summoned into the presence of the President and the Royal Attorney, who suggested he should go to Marseilles and make sure that the girls would swear there had been no sodomy. He left the next day and dispensed generous bribes not only to the girls but to the surgeons and the apothecaries.

A week later, when the cross-examination of the girls was well under way, Mme de Montreuil again intervened. The principal magistrates were told that she wanted the terms of the final sentence to leave no stains either on the accused or on the honour of those 'to whom he belonged'. Having paid for him, the Montreuils were, in her opinion, entitled to regard him as their possession.

She was still keeping her daughter in ignorance of the proceedings at Aix. She told Gaufridy that it was on the Minister's orders and as a precaution against the Marquise's being shut up in a convent.

On 14 July 1778 the public was admitted to the final hearing of the case. Sade was cross-examined and judgement was pronounced at the bar. The court found him guilty of debauchery and inordinate libertinage. It ordered that 'Louis-Aldonse-Donatien de Sade shall be admonished behind the bench in the presence of the Attorney-General in future to conduct himself with greater decency'. He was also banned from Marseilles for three years and required to pay 50 livres for the prison and for legal costs. Once the admonition had been delivered and the fee paid, he was to be discharged from prison.

At 3 o'clock in the morning he was roused from sleep to be told by Inspector Marais that they were about to leave for Vincennes. He was incredulous and indignant to the point of stupefaction. The law had exculpated him, but he was still a prisoner of the royal pleasure: the *lettre de cachet* issued in February 1777 had not been cancelled.

With Marais were his brother and two warders. They travelled in a Berlin coach, changing horses at intervals. They detoured to avoid Avignon where Sade was known. They spent the first night of the journey in the inn at Valliguières, leaving at dawn. At half-past 9 in the evening, they arrived at a posting inn outside Valence, a walled town on the Rhône sixty miles south of Lyons. Sade was taken straight to his room. Leaning on his elbows he went on staring out of the window at the main road, while the table was laid for dinner in the room. When it was about to be served, he said he had no appetite, so the two brothers sat down without him. He paced up and down while they ate. At about 10.30 he asked to go to the lavatory. Marais's brother, Antoine-Thomas, took him along the corridor and waited for him at the top of the staircase. After five or six minutes he came out quietly, creeping up behind Antoine-Thomas. When he turned round, Sade pretended to trip. Trying to help him, Antoine-Thomas was pulled off balance. Sade got up nimbly and dodged under his arm to rush down the stone staircase which led into the yard just by the door to the street. Antoine-Thomas ran down the stairs shouting, with his brother and the two warders not far behind. Convinced that the street-door had not been opened, the four of them searched the stable and the coach-house, the cellar and the hayloft, the gardens, the roof and finally the surrounding houses. Marais's next thought was to alert the local constabulary but, as Sade must have noticed when he was looking out of the window, the inn was outside the town walls and by now the gates were shut for the night. All the inspector could do was search the roads, sending his brother in a carriage with one of the warders along the road to Montélimar while he went in another carriage with the other warder down the road to Tain.

Sade was hiding in a hut about half a mile outside the town, close to the threshing-floor used by the peasants. He talked two of them into acting as his guides. Under cover of of darkness they took him towards Montélimar, but after about two miles they had a better idea. Finding their way to the river, they walked along the bank looking for a boat. They did not find one until just before daybreak. At Vivarais a boatman was about to sail downstream and he agreed to take Sade all the way to Avignon for 20 livres.

As soon as the town gates were open, Marais called on the sergeant of the mounted constabulary to report the incident and describe the runaway. Using the dozen men he had at his disposal, the sergeant ransacked the town, the outskirts and the surrounding countryside. Horsemen were sent down all the roads that led to the river bank. Meanwhile Marais was in a panic, knowing that his future depended on recapturing his prisoner; but there was nothing he could do except report the incident to the Provost General's magistrate, who came to the inn, bringing his clerk. In the room where Sade was to have slept, the magistrate took a statement from the policeman and an inventory of everything in the room that belonged to the escaped prisoner. His trunk was then wrapped securely in canvas and put under seal.

In the papal city of Avignon Sade was outside French jurisdiction, but after supping and sleeping in a lodging-house he made ready for another overnight journey—back to Lacoste. He arrived at 9 o'clock in the morning, exhausted and famished. Gothon was overcome with astonishment, delight and fear. He took some pleasure in comforting her. She had a particularly well-shaped bottom, the loveliest, according to Sade, that had emerged from the Swiss Alps for a century.

After sixteen months in the darkness of Vincennes and five weeks of tantalizing suspense and humiliating dependence on policemen and warders, the first taste of liberty was inebriating. He wrote to Gaufridy asking for the papers and all the keys which had been deposited with him. Also some lemons. There is a longer letter to Gaufridy with the same date on it, though it must have been written a couple of days later. He has seen everybody. The priest is going out of his way to be helpful. 'I think he is in love with me.' Never before has his arrival at the château caused so much stir. 'There is too much to say: so I shall say nothing. We must certainly spend a few days together.' He is burning with impatience to stake his claim in the Abbé's estate at Saumane. Would Gaufridy be able to go with him? The letter is effervescent and intimate. He 'will have a great deal to say' about the seduction of the gamekeeper's daughter by the farmer, Chauvin, and he wants to tell Gaufridy about the girl-prisoner at Aix. He has been trying to write and to send money to her.

It was only now that the unfortunate Renée-Pélagie was allowed to learn about the expedition to Aix and the quashing of the sentence. Her indignation at having been kept in ignorance had no effect on Mme de Montreuil, who had not yet heard about the escape. Coldly she announced her intentions. Sade would be released, but not yet. As soon as she knew he was at the château, Renée-Pélagie wanted to leave Paris but her mother was 'like a lion', threatening, quite seriously, to have her locked up. She must not expose herself to renewed dangers of being reviled and compromised. She wanted to help her husband: so be it. But she must help from Paris. Knowing that her mother would appeal to the authorities if she left for Lacoste, she could do no more than send him an anonymous letter, via Gaufridy, warning him to be very careful. The letter reached him but, still in a state of euphoria, he ignored it as he ignored Nanon's warning about Gaufridy, who seems to have been helping Mme de Montreuil to build up the store of evidence that would increase her power over Sade.

Even when Sade learned about the notary's secret correspondence with her, he was irrationally reluctant to stop confiding in his old friend. As in the affair of the children, he revealed himself as being incurably addicted to self-destructive risks. When he complained to Mme de Montreuil about the way Gaufridy was betraying him to her, he asked her not to tell Gaufridy that he knew. In his own dealings with Gaufridy he treated the double-dealing as a joke, saying that if Mme de Montreuil eventually showed him the letters she had received from the lawyer, he was sure to find in them only 'the affectionate concern of friendship and the constant proofs of trustworthy sincerity'. When Gaufridy responded by protesting his innocence, Sade ironically reassured him:

> I have always appreciated your delicacy in keeping me informed about your correspondence with Mme de Montreuil ... You say you always co-operate with her in everything that will be useful and advantageous for me ... Mme de Montreuil considers it useful and advantageous that I should be imprisoned. I regard the opposite state of affairs as useful and advantageous. Are you in agreement with my opinion or with hers?

Whether he was taking pleasure in the danger or blinded to it by euphoria, Sade stayed on at Lacoste. When his wife's anonymous letter arrived, he thought it was a practical joke: 'They are no more anxious to recapture me than I am to drown myself.' But Mme de Montreuil was ominously refusing to open the letters he wrote her. She said she could not risk giving the impression of conniving at his defiance of the King's will.

On 19 August, as Sade was enjoying a stroll in his park with the priest and with Mlle Rousset, an educated but impoverished lady who had formerly been a visitor to the château and had been housekeeping and looking after him while Gothon was away, Sambuc, the gamekeeper, rushed up to warn them that suspicious characters were arriving at the village inn. Sambuc seemed rather drunk, so Mlle de Rousset went to investigate. It appeared to her that they were what they said they were—silk-merchants. But Sade was sufficiently unsettled to move into Canon Vidal's house at Oppède, briefing Mlle de Rousset to send news to him twice every day. On the 21st the news was alarming enough for him to retreat overnight to a disused barn two miles outside the village. Though the canon sent a woman to look after him, he rapidly grew tired of having nothing to do. When he said he was going back to Lacoste, the woman ran to fetch the canon who did his best to dissuade Sade. Would he not at least stay in hiding for another four days? But he was self-destructively intractable. He said afterwards it was like being pushed by a hand stronger than he was.

Two days after returning to the château, he learned that he had been relieved four months previously of his Lieutenant-Generalcy. At least, he told himself, they would not have had the heart to give him such bad news if they were about to arrest him again. He had also found two letters from Renée-Pélagie, both reassuring. But at 4 o'clock in the morning a naked Gothon ran screaming into his bedroom: 'Hide yourself!' In his night-shirt he ran out of the room, but no hiding-place had been prepared. He shut himself into another room. The door was broken down and he was dragged out to face ten men. Some pointed their swords at his chest; others held pistols to his head. It was Inspector Marais's moment of triumph. With three policemen from Paris and six men from the local constabulary, he had come to reclaim his prisoner. Now he would spend the rest of his life in a cell, Marais promised, calling Sade 'little man', and threatening him about the human bones. The sadistic inspector had Sade gagged and bound in ropes. He was then dragged out of his château. The flow of insults and threats was kept up most of the way to Valence.

This time instead of protecting him from the curiosity of the crowd, Marais exposed him to it. Bound and gagged, he was exhibited as an object of ridicule in the places where his innocence had been proclaimed only a month ago. Passing through Cavaillon, he was visible to anyone who wanted to look at him, and in Avignon he was seen by about 300 people. From Lyons he wrote to Gaufridy, asking him to spend a few days at Lacoste to make arrangements with Mlle Rousset and to write to Mme de Montreuil asking her to work for his release. Mlle Rousset also wrote to Gaufridy with the same request: would he plead Sade's cause with Mme de Montreuil. 'He is your friend,' she wrote. 'He sincerely likes you.'

Chapter 7

Victimizer as Victim

'What am I to believe?' wrote the distracted Renée-Pélagie to Mlle Rousset. 'The frustrations, the duplicity, the semblance of good faith in people holding responsible positions! They appear to be incapable of hypocrisy. I find it overwhelming, and I see no way out.' Since the news from Lacoste she had not spoken to her mother. 'I have taken an oath in writing of hatred and eternal vengeance if within three days she has not arranged for me to rejoin my husband, wherever he is, wherever she has had him moved ... For eighteen months everybody has made a fool of me, and I am exhausted. The ministers are like thick walls.'

Thrown back into a small dark cell, and into ignorance of how long his captivity would last, Sade sank into a despair as extreme as his exhilaration had been. Outrage at the brutality of the policemen on the journey merged with outrage at being in prison again after the judgement at Aix. 'What has just been done to me,' he wrote to Renée-Pélagie, 'is so absurd, so completely at odds with all the laws of good sense and justice, so patently the work of an enemy who wants only to destroy me and the children, that certainly I do not suspect your mother.' It would have been a hundred times better, he said, if 'the good folk who render me such important services, who have a favourable verdict pronounced so that I can more effectively be slandered afterwards, had simply given the order for someone to come to Lacoste and shoot me dead ... That would have been better for the honour of the family ... Behaviour like this is as damaging to my judges as to me: if I was guilty they should have condemned me; if their consciences tell them I am innocent, I should not be punished afterwards.'

Like Marais, the gaolers were being more vindictive than before. For trying to escape he must be punished. His new cell at Vincennes was even more uncomfortable than the previous one, and more airless. The ventilation ducts were blocked up and he could scarcely see anything of the sky. As before, the floor was untiled, but this cell was damper and the dust rose whenever he walked about. The combination of damp, dust and stuffiness caused migraines and bouts of dizziness. He was deprived of both paper and the right to take exercise. 'Not only shall I have no fire throughout the winter,' he wrote on 4 October, 'but I am being devoured by rats and mice who do not let me rest for a minute during the night . . . When I ask for a cat to be put into the neighbouring room, they say "Animals are prohibited". To which I reply: "You are such fools! If animals are prohibited, so should rats and mice be." ' His diet was changed for the worse, and whereas a gaoler had previously stayed with him while he ate, there were now only seven minutes in the day, he estimated, when he was not alone. He was awakened at dawn by a gaoler who asked whether he had slept well, but hardly waited for an answer. He came back three times during the day—twice to bring food, once to shave him and sweep the cell.

Beyond the boredom, the discomfort, the humiliation, the hunger and loneliness, he had the stupefying sense of existing aimlessly in a void that could not be measured. Nothing mattered, nothing was even of interest, except to know how much longer the ordeal and the waste of life would continue. Since there was no way of finding out, he invented ways. The idea of an infinite vacuum was intolerable. If the only methods of making it finite were insane, then insanity was the price he would pay. Having so little to do except read and re-read Renée-Pélagie's letters, he began to interpret them as if they were occult scriptures. Who was responsible for the crossings out? She herself? Was this a code? The unhappy schoolboy counts the days that separate him from the end of term; the only days Sade could count were the days that went past. In his previous stretches of imprisonment he had not done much counting, but now it became a mania. He would count the number of lines in her letters and the number of times particular words recurred. If his enemies were censoring his letters, then his friends must surely be inventing ways of smuggling information past the censorship. But they had no means of explaining the codes they were using. He would have to decide for himself whether the numbers were clues to the date of his release or indications of the days or weeks or months that must elapse before Renée-Pélagie would be allowed to pay him a visit or before a privilege he had forfeited would be restored. When he needed more numbers than the date and the rest of the letter provided, he could count lines, words, syllables and even letters: 'This letter has 72 syllables which are the 72 weeks still to go. It has 7 lines plus 7 syllables, which are exactly the 7 months and 7 days there are from 17 April to 22 January 1780. It has 191 letters and 49 words . . .'

His impatient mind was focused so hungrily on the question of how long he would have to stay in the prison that he refused to believe Renée-Pélagie did not know. 'Do not go on telling me such lies, in the name of God! Do not continue with it. It makes my blood boil. I will prove to you in the most arithmetical fashion you can imagine that since 14 February 1777 you knew that my case would come up for trial on 14 June 1778. Now, if you knew about this first part of my confinement, how can you hope to persuade me that you do not know about the second? But what am I saying? Alas, you are not refusing to tell me, and you are saying it so loudly and expressively that you have indicated the sixteen months with your number 22. Nothing could be clearer than "Saturday 22 February, No. 3 finally." To doubt, after this, that I will be released on 22 February 1780 would be a fatal illusion. But, for fear that I might not be quite convinced, you had the goodness to send me, very shortly afterwards, three blank pages for signature, confirming that it would be for three years.' Six years later he had still not freed himself from his obsession with figures, though by then irony enabled him to hold it at a distance. In February 1774 he wrote: 'Your mother must be drunk or raving mad to risk her daughter's life to form a 19 and/or 16 and 9, not to become tired of all that for twelve years. She must have suffered badly from indigestion with digits, the foul woman. If she died before the explosion and she were opened up, millions of numbers would have come pouring out of her guts.'

Renée-Pélagie did her best to cheer him up, but he submitted her efforts to the harshest of criticism, quoting her own phrases back at her in ridicule. Her behaviour was 'horrible', 'execrable'. He would never forgive her. 'I used to dissimulate, because I have been taught to be false, but I have always regarded you as a heartless and feelingless woman, *who bows to every wind and collapses at the slightest of shocks*. In a word, you are like a ball of wax. Whoever comes along can remould you.' Unless she tells him when he is due to be released he will curse her 'as the last creature on earth' and regard her 'as a monster I will never see again as long as I live'.

She filled her letters with news about the children, who were being brought up by the Montreuils. The older boy was now twelve and the girl, whom he had never seen, seven. In Sade's enforced idleness, they occupied his thoughts more than ever before. There was never a night, he said, when he did not dream about them, and he was liable to shed tears when he wrote to her about them. But grief at the separation was mixed with self-pity. In October she told him that they had gone away for two years but that she had promised them they would see him again when they came back. This he took to mean that he would have to wait two years for his release.

In November Milli Rousset (as Sade called her) arrived in Paris, where she stayed at the convent with Renée-Pélagie in the rooms that had been the Dowager Countess's. Writing to Gaufridy, she described her first meeting with Mme de Montreuil.

Imagine two cats about to have a fight, the aggressor drawing in its claws and then showing them to rouse its enemy . . . In the heat of combat I saw quite positively that she loved the Marquis de Sade and was at heart embarrassed at having him where he is . . . After a recital of the reasons he has to be grateful to her—and indeed they are considerable—came the grievances. 'He acknowledges them,' I told her, 'but he can make no amends where he is.'

'Oh Mademoiselle, if you only knew the promises he used to make! The oaths he has sworn in this very room!'

'I can believe it, and he genuinely intended to keep his promises. But men are feeble, Madame, as you are well aware. Age and wretchedness have changed him considerably.'

'I hope so. But tell me, Mademoiselle, would you accept responsibility for him?'

Oh, M. Gaufridy, fortunately I had expected that question. Without either too much eagerness or too much reluctance I answered modestly 'Yes, Madame'.

If Milli Rousset was right about Mme de Montreuil's love for Sade, she failed to see how sour it had turned: 'I have seen the high priestess,' she reported, 'and shall see her again. I am not displeased, but to hurry the affair would be to spoil everything. There is still much prejudice, but with moderation and good reasoning we will win, and our confinement will at worst be over by the end of the spring.'

A far better letter-writer than Renée-Pélagie, she found it easier to respond cheerfully to his letters of gloomy recrimination, and developed a technique of long-range badinage, well calculated to ginger him out of his despondency: 'Women must be mad to become involved with a cross-patch like you!' If he does not like the blanket, he can send it back. 'I will use it myself.' The Marquise has told her she must write something cheerful, but today she cannot. 'Your beastly letter has made me sad.' Anyway, what is there to say? She still believes that the Montreuils are making efforts on his behalf. Perhaps he will not have to wait very much longer for good news. She even attempts a little flirtatiousness. Since he appears to have a jealous disposition, heaven preserve him from ever feeling anything for her or he will suffer the torments of the damned. 'I invite you to adopt a defensive posture. Ugly women are much slyer than beauties.' In December he was cheerful enough to adopt an equally teasing tone. He complimented her in verse and began to address her as Saint Rousset.

On New Year's Day 1779, Renée-Pélagie wrote: 'Since I cannot begin the year with you, I must make up for it with a little chat, not in verse, but I will tell you in good French my premonition that they will not be such barbarians as to stop us from ending the year together ... We are the victims of other people's bizarre habits of thought. They think that after spending so much time there you will emerge as well-behaved as a lap-dog. They do not understand how much harm it is doing to you, as well as to your affairs and your children. The silly answers they give me make me angry enough to bang their heads against a wall until they change their way of thinking. You see, I am not so gentle as you are in the tortures I dream up for them!'

With more skill in disguising her paraphrases of his own opinions, she might have been better at consoling him. He had written before and was to write again, many times and at great length, about the ineffectuality of imprisonment as a means of improving the character. It was like prescribing the same pills for every illness. 'What good has Pierre-Encise done me? What good did Miolans do? The first confinement in Vincennes? Damaged my intelligence and my humour, embittered me, confirmed me in my old ways. With my perverse disposition the only effect punishment can have is to make me worse.' Or as he said in another letter, his personality 'has not changed since childhood—Amblet, who brought me up can tell you—and it is not going to change . . . In 20 years from now my mind will be no more mature than it is today.'

The one infallible effect of imprisonment was physical damage. He had been right to expect no fire for the winter. 'If I die, so much the better: they will have got me out of the way, and I am convinced that except for the sake of appearance, they would not be angry.' Apart from his month of freedom, he had now been living in prison cells for two years. 'I feel a thousand times worse than when I came here, my temper has turned sour, cantankerous, my blood is a thousand times hotter, my head a thousand times worse. In short I will have to live like a hermit when I come out. I will be unfit for human society.' He was still suffering continually from headaches and dizziness, and sometimes he would go for two weeks without any continuous sleep, but he was not ill enough to qualify for medical attention.

By the end of January 1779 Milli Rousset was cured of illusions about Mme de Montreuil. To have her son-in-law at liberty again would make it harder for her to marry off her other daughters. Her youngest was now eighteen. But Milli Rousset, like a doctor nervous of telling her patient the truth, did not communicate her pessimism to Sade.

He was too unsettled to make good use of the time, being still unresigned to the prospect of indefinite imprisonment. But he sometimes took pleasure in reading Petrarch, together with the book on him by the Abbé, and in February he had a very vivid dream about Laura. 'Her eyes still had as much fire as when Petrarch celebrated them . . . "Why stay groaning on the earth?" she said. "Come to me. No more evil, no more vexation, no more trouble in the boundless space I inhabit. Have the courage to follow me." '

The Governor of the prison had not visited Sade's cell until January, and after that he did not return until the end of March. Like many officials who had power over other men's lives, Charles-Joseph de Rougemont had bought himself a lucrative position. The illegitimate son of a French nobleman and his English mistress, he was now fifty-nine, fat and self-important— 'a balloon filled with air', Sade called him. He wore an apple-green coat, and had his hair done in six tiers of curls. 'In the cells he is an absolute despot, never happier than when he can discover a hiding-place, order a prisoner into chains, rule with a rod of iron. Do not mistake the smoothness of his talk for gentleness ... if you once show weakness he will be on top of you, and once he has you in his clutches, you will be suffocated.' In addition to his annual income of 18,000 livres from fees paid by the families of prisoners, he made an illegitimate profit on the catering. According to Mirabeau, this must have amounted to 15,400 livres a year.

This profiteering was characteristic of the malpractice that mushroomed in the dark spaces left by the regime's administrative inefficiency and its chaotic judicial system. The underlying theory was that all crime was an offence against the personal sovereignty of the monarch, whose duty must then be to demonstrate his overwhelming power by crushing the miscreant. No one was more scathingly articulate than Sade about the anomalies. In his *Etrennes philosophiques* (1782) he complained:

> that a man who takes vengeance on his enemy has to be broken on the wheel, while those who murder the King's enemies are heaped with honours; that a man who steals a livre from you has to be destroyed while you are loaded with rewards, you who consider yourself entitled to exterminate in the name of your laws the man who has done no other wrong than submit to those of nature.

Long prison sentences were served by innocent victims or rivals of royal favourites. The King's mistresses were well placed for making false accusations. For threatening Mme de Pompadour with scandalous revelations, the Marquis de Fratteaux was imprisoned in the Bastille for twenty-five years under pretext of insanity, and then kept in solitary confinement for another fifteen years by order of his brother, a government minister, and of his nephew, the governor of the Bastille.

Patriarchalism permeated the system. It is equally visible in the wording used for pronouncing judgement and for appealing against it. In April 1779, at the instigation of Renée-Pélagie, a petition was submitted to the Provençal Intendant by the priests, clerics and mayors-consul of Lacoste. Drafted by Gaufridy, it testified to Sade's good behaviour during his last stay at the château, and it culminated in a promise from the local dignitaries that if their request was granted, their hearts 'blighted with trouble and bitterness, will bless the hand which will have restored to them their lord, their father and their protector'. The statement corresponded neither to their real attitude nor to his. Two years later he received a letter about the wretched state of the paupers in the community: would he at least pay the arrears of the money he owed? The next year, 1782, the poor were described as 'covered with vermin' and 'dying of hunger'. When Sade failed to answer the letter, the seigneurial representative was excluded from meetings of the *bureau des pauvres*.[1]

In the prison the commandant was sovereign, but Sade was too proud to flatter him, or even to observe the protocol. In October 1779, he wrote to tell Mme de Montreuil that he was spitting blood and worrying whether his chest would stand up to another winter in an unheated cell. At the end of November his cough suddenly became worse. He sent a note to the surgeon on the evening of 1 December, asking for a new medicine. In the morning the gaoler brought back his note. It should have been addressed to the commandant. The consultation was only delayed, not prevented, but he was unable to get himself transferred to a better cell, despite his earlier successes in wringing concessions over walks out of de Rougemont: in May his weekly ration had been increased from three to four and in July to five. In April 1780, after receiving a visit from M. Le Noir, he was allowed a walk every day. But the Police Chief also promised that the Marquise would soon be allowed to come, and she was not.

Sade's playwriting seems to have begun in about April 1779. In a letter written in either March or April he was still complaining to Renée-Pélagie that he could have used the time more profitably if only he knew how long his imprisonment would last. But by May he was pressing her for reactions to the dialogue in his scripts. She was to keep the manuscripts in her possession. He had

[1] Michelle Vovelle, 'Sade seigneur de village' in the Centre Aixois's *Marquis de Sade*.

been influenced, he told her, by the comedies of Destouches and by his Preface to *Le Dissipateur*, which formulated principles that had served Sade as rules. But by the end of 1780, expressing pleasure at her reaction to his plays, he claimed:

> In them I can tell you, there is a constant truth and what I believe to be a new theatrical principle ... I madly love to see your handwriting ... I will always remember that when I was in Italy you started to copy out passages of *Le Célibataire* because you thought I would like them ... How I would love to have a complete copy of my verse play with notes by you in the margin, awarding praise and blame.

Later he would ask her to let Mlle Rousset and Abbé Amblet see his manuscripts, but no one else.

On 2 June 1780 Sade was forty. At the end of July, in another letter to Renée-Pélagie, he described himself as 'up to my neck in filth and muck, eaten alive by bugs, lice, mice and spiders, and served no better than a pig. As soon as they have brought my meals in, they escape from my room with such exaggerated haste I never have time to ask for what I want, and our landlord's three errand-boys are always standing there, ready to shoot, when the cell door is opened ... I do not mention my hair, which has absolutely been falling out ... It is beyond remedy and I am beyond vanity, thank God. When I come out I shall wear a wig. It is a good decision. Well there you are, my dear, I am old enough, am I not? No more illusions. I have had them for forty delightful years, when I was always promising to mend my way of life. I am well rid of them, and it is time to begin, little by little, taking on the right colour for the coffin. Then death is less of a surprise. It can come when it pleases. I am waiting with neither desire nor fear.'

He thought about death a great deal. After three years in 'this execrable place,' he wrote, 'for seven months I have eaten absolutely nothing through lack of exercise, and because of the pain in my chest ... and yet I cannot take even an eighth part of the care of myself that is necessary. The result is that in addition to the pain in my chest, I have such violent giddiness and such profuse bleeding of the nose that you can expect me to be found one of these mornings choked in my own blood.'

At the end of June, there was another abrupt outburst of violence like the one at Miolans. When a gaoler was impertinent, Sade raised his arm to strike the man and then fainted. He was unconscious for some time, and he went on spitting blood all night. When the Captain of the Guard told him that he had forfeited his right to take walks, he went berserk, swearing at the old soldier and shouting through the door and the window to the other prisoners, including Mirabeau who was in the garden. Sade accused him of kissing the arse of his protector for the privilege of walking there. 'Tell me your name if you dare,' said Mirabeau, 'and I will cut your ears off when I am outside.' De Rougemont afterwards complained to the Chief of Police that it was not the first time Sade had behaved subversively. Once, when another prisoner had passed his door, he had warned him: 'Comrade, be careful about what you eat: they are trying to poison us.'

In July 1780 Mlle Rousset proved herself to be more efficacious than Renée-Pélagie in pressing for justice. The Ministers received a petition that 'either the prisoner should be released or valid reasons should be given for detaining him'. It was accompanied by letters of recommendation: several of the princesses were appealing to Maurepas for justice. Later on in the month he ordered a junior minister to look into the case and present him with the facts. It was not until late October that Milli Rousset received an answer. Writing to Gaufridy on the 21st, she said that Mme de Montreuil was 'less to blame than we believed. More powerful enemies have justifiably felt provoked. Unless some die and others forget, we have no hope.' Almost certainly the Comte de Sade-Eyguières was one of them. Having now ousted his cousin from the Lieutenant-Generalcy, he would not be eager to have him at liberty again. As well as not wanting the family name to be sullied by fresh scandals, he may have been nervous that Sade would try to revenge himself.

Two days later, Milli Rousset wrote: 'The various police officers who have been to the château have made abominable reports. These men are very coarse. M. de Sade's whole life is written up in a dossier. Never mind the title. The man is for hanging! I had thought that very few people were in possession of certain facts which are now common knowledge, together with many other things—good God!—which call for the deepest of silences. I believe the confinement will be a long one.'

On 14 December Sade wrote to Renée-Pélagie that it was 'the 1,400th day, the 200th week and the end of the 46th month since we last saw each other'. Since being in this cell he had received from her 68 fortnightly payments and 100 letters. This was his 114th letter to her. But when she sent her good wishes for the New Year, he wrote a savage reply: 'May you and your execrable family and its scurvy valets be all put in a sack and thrown to the bottom of the sea. The moment I hear that has happened will be the happiest of my life.'

In the early months of 1781 his mind was much taken up with the idea of offering his enemies an alternative satisfaction. What if he volunteered to spend the rest of his life in exile? Or shut himself up at Lacoste on parole? On 20 February, temporarily well supplied with paper, he wrote the longest of all his letters to Renée-Pélagie, running to over six thousand words, mainly in an elaborate attempt at self-justification. 'Yes, I am a libertine, I admit it: I have imagined everything of that kind which can be imagined, but I certainly have not done all that I have imagined, and I certainly never shall. I am a libertine, but I am neither a criminal nor a murderer.' The letter goes on to enumerate several good deeds. Three indigent families have lived for five years on his charity; he saved the life of a deserter who had been abandoned by his regiment; he risked his life to rescue a child who would have been crushed under the wheels of a cart drawn by two runaway horses. Searching his memory for virtuous actions, he was writing as if he had never mentioned them to her. This is characteristic of his letters: they do not so much continue his relationship with her as forge a new one.

At the end of March 1781, Sade learned that the King had given permission for him to be transferred to the fortress at Montélimar so that he would be closer to his estate. Believing the decision to be the result of Mme de Montreuil's machinations, Sade refused to be moved into that 'abominable cesspool where the light of day is scarcely to be seen'. In fact the initiative had been taken by Renée-Pélagie, with the support of the Marquise de Sorans, cousin of Sade's mother.

In April, still assuming he was in a position to negotiate, he wrote twice to M. Le Noir, proposing that Mme de Montreuil should have complete control over the children, and stipulating conditions he would find acceptable for his exile or his subsequent imprisonment. Compulsively, he went into an elaborate display of reasonableness, doing his best to camouflage his desperation. But his enemies were under no obligation either to reason with him or to behave reasonably.

They gained gratification, perhaps, if nothing else, from making it impossible for Renée-Pélagie to visit him until 13 July, four years and five months since they had last seen each other. They were not allowed to be alone together: under the eye of a policeman, they talked in the Council chamber. But the main effect of the meeting was to throw Sade into a fever of jealousy as he began to torment himself with suspicion that she was being unfaithful to him, possibly with Lefèvre, the boy who had been their so-called secretary ten years ago, and possibly with the Marquise de Villette, a beautiful woman of twenty-three married to a forty-three-year-old homosexual. According to Sade she was 'a great fucker'. Lefèvre had bought some books for Renée-Pélagie; the Marquise had invited her to stay. If she accepted the invitation, she would also meet other men.

From Sade's point of view, a woman's infidelity to a man was generically different from a man's to a woman. 'The consequences are so grim and deadly that I have never been able to bear it.' In his whirlwind of reproaches he forgot his history of complaisancy towards actresses and dancers: 'I have never had anything more to do with a woman once I have suspected her of being unfaithful to me.' Nor did his history of intimate relationships with valets diminish his outrage about Lefèvre's humble birth. 'So you are betraying me with an oaf like that, a little peasant from my estates, a good-for-nothing who went rotten in the filth at Aix.' Writing to him on 5 August 1781, she tried to reassure him, but the letter now has bloodstains and scrawled obscenities all over it. As violent to himself as he had once been to prostitutes, he had worked himself up into a fury. He applied his mad numerology to make inferences about the dimensions of Lefèvre's penis, measuring circumference and length in inches. After her words 'I who adore you' he has interpolated 'my dear Lefèvre', and her sentence about having to pay nine months' rent on taking the furniture out of her rooms is construed in his annotations as an allusion to pregnancy.

He had objected to her clothes, and when she defended herself, he ordered her to dress like a woman of sixty. 'If you are a respectable woman, it is only me you should want to please, and that you will do only with the appearance and the *reality* of great propriety and modesty.' Next time she comes to see him she must be in 'what you women call a wrapper, wearing a very large bonnet, with your hair combed simply and no elaborate coiffure. Not the least sign of false curls—a chignon and no tresses. No sign of your figure, and no indecent décolleté like last time.' He went further still, celebrating his jealousy with a ritual destruction of Lefèvre in effigy. Milli Rousset had done a sketch of the young man in pencil. He had a full face, thick eyebrows and a small round nose. There are now thirteen knife gashes in the drawing, all on the face, and eight of them are edged with dried blood. In the right-hand margin, Sade has written a denunciation of the woman who, from physical desire or lust for vengeance, gives herself 'shamelessly to a valet, a peasant of the coarsest kind, whose father received charity from her husband'. Renée-Pélagie faced these onslaughts of vituperation with the unflinching docility that had survived the orgies of flagellation at Lacoste: 'I need you to be happy and satisfied. I prefer you to express your suspicions and anxieties than to keep them to yourself, because it is very easy for me to justify myself.' At least she now had the satisfaction of knowing herself to be more important to her demanding husband than any other woman. To appease his unreasoning jealousy she turned down the invitation from the Marquise de Villette, and moved into the convent where his mother had been living. But her self-denial was more appeasing to her own masochism than to his jealousy.

To accompany the physical pleasure he could now take only from himself, he needed mental excitement: this he could derive from his fantasy about Renée-Pélagie and Lefèvre. Later, in stories about infidelity, he would draw on memories of the experience he was now whipping up for himself. His need to be jealous was so urgent that long before her visit he began to have a recurring dream: 'I see you much older than when I left you, always with a secret to tell me but never willing to tell it, and always unfaithful, in the full meaning of the word, and at your mother's instigation . . . I have had this dream perhaps 500 times.' Both in flagellation and in sodomy he had enjoyed exchanging roles with his partner; the games he had played with Latour involved role-reversal in the master-servant relationship. Perhaps unconsciously, he was now taking masochistic pleasure in the humbleness of

Lefèvre's origin, and in destroying the man's effigy he was repeating what the Provençal Parlement had done to him and Latour.

Bisexuality increases a man's ability to imagine the pleasure a woman has in making love, and Sade, unlike Renée-Pélagie, was now cut off from any possibility of contact with another man's penis. She had taken part in the orgies voluntarily; now she was being his involuntary accomplice, giving him, however innocently, a pretext for thinking with a mixture of love and hate, about a low-born rival with an outsize penis. He even wrote obscene verses to her, celebrating the sensual pleasure she took. Her naïve placidity was the perfect complement to his aggressive suspiciousness; her provocations were all the more effective for being unintentional. When she began to put on weight, she was glad to think herself less attractive: now he would suffer less from jealousy. 'I am pleased to tell you,' she wrote, 'that I am becoming so fat I am mortally afraid of becoming a great sow. When you see me you will have a surprise.' It was she who had the surprise when she read his next letter: 'As result of letting yourself be served? Great? What does that word mean?' His shouts of abuse as he read her letter were so violent that the gaolers reported them to M. Le Noir, who warned the Marquise that her husband was making no secret of his suspicions. If she persisted in wanting to go on visiting him, the Minister would have to be informed of the full circumstances.

Jealousy was rousing Sade out of the acquiescence that for nearly five years had stifled all but a very few explosions of indignation at the humiliations inflicted by the gaolers and the prison routine. At the end of October, the gaoler had his ears boxed. (At least he said he did; according to Sade he had made only a threatening gesture.) Sade was punished by having to go without his daily shave, while his cell went without its daily sweep. 'These are two things essential to health and hygiene ... I demand not to be treated worse than beasts in a menagerie.' Asking Renée-Pélagie to see M. Le Noir and complain, he conceded that his reactions and judgements must have been unbalanced by the persecution de Rougemont had been inflicting through petty domestic tyrannies: 'Do not judge my behaviour either by my conduct or by my comments. I am submitted to provocations and horrors, that are renewed week by week, one torment after another; and I am expected not to take the revenge that I can. I am not made of wood,

though they are working very hard to render me insensitive, to
destroy the root of all good qualities in me.' He was not allowed
to see Renée-Pélagie again, in spite of all her efforts to convince
M. Le Noir that by harshness and deprivation he would not succeed in pressuring Sade back to his former level of good behaviour.
Nor would Le Noir agree to let the Abbé Amblet visit his former
pupil. All Renée-Pélagie could do was write soothing letters, urg-
ing him not to go on making matters worse by tearing up the
books she sent.

Though his playwriting had been influenced by plays he read,
it was not until the sixth year of his imprisonment that his reading
began to interact fruitfully with his writing. Sometimes reading
would make him so excited that he would break off to scribble on
a scrap of paper:

> last line page 143
> outrages—a *lettre de cachet*! The most solid proof of stupidity
> and the best weapon of tyranny. A man who could have emi-
> grated has been made to rot in a cell by the finest invention of
> despotism . . . *O tempora, o mores!*

or

> they will never be released. It is the characteristic of stupidity
> and absurdity to use torture instead of reasonable persuasion
> in the attempt to convince. Persecution proves nothing but
> despotism; a good cause does not torture; it reasons
> bottom of page 117
> end of note

In the interpolations he scribbled into Renée-Pélagie's letter of 5
August 1781, he was merely venting spleen; in these he was visi-
bly making himself into a professional man of letters, thinking
directly on to the paper, and assuming that latent in the written
word was the power to make his persecutors recognize themselves for what they were:

> Read with some care, I beg you, the first 11 lines of page 200,
> and then you pack of brutes, you indefensible bunch of gossips,
> look at yourselves in a mirror and say There we are.
> 16 January, evening.

Full of righteous indignation, the notes he wrote for himself are a bridge between his letters to Renée-Pélagie and his more extended pieces of writing. For five years he had funnelled tremendous quantities of energy into letter-writing. The one activity and the one form of self-expression he was allowed, writing also provided him with a means of deepening and disciplining his thinking. In the calculations based on counting, he had found relief by putting his mind at the disposal of his compulsions; he was now finding a new balance between self-indulgence and self-control, relaxation and alertness, complaint and creativity, passivity and action. His powerlessness did not preclude the possibility of writing powerful prose. And he was aware that Renée-Pélagie's visits gave less impetus to his literary activity than solitude did.

Let me know, then, whether it is true that you are going . . . so long without seeing me . . . If it is true and if you will not be coming for a long time yet, I am going to begin a delicious little poem, a little dialogue. I know of nothing more interesting than to sing to you. And Magdalene of Montreuil—the more I am plagued, the more I need my brain to be distracted, and it plagues me to be prevented from seeing you.

The ambivalence is scarcely concealed: would he not prefer singing about her to seeing her? The situation is oddly similar to the one Kafka created for himself at the end of 1912: after three months of receiving voluminous letters from him, Felice Bauer suggested they should meet for Christmas in the 'external reality' of Berlin. He demurred, saying he needed a few free days for writing, and then spent much of the time writing to her. Sade was in a situation that gave him few options. He had to rely on surrogate satisfactions, but in developing the art of providing himself with them, he also became addicted to them, and in becoming aware of the syndrome he was caught in, he found himself thinking more dialectically. Without knowing what he was doing, he had equipped his mind to accommodate both halves of any contradiction that presented itself.

For five years he had suffered from having nothing to distract him from himself. Confinement in a small space forcibly concentrated his attention on his body, its needs, its smells, its noticeable deterioration. He could also distract his attention from it by using his brain, but he was aware that reasoning had led him into un-reason. Without abandoning his numerological calculations, he knew they were irrational; without abandoning his attempts to reason with his persecutors, he had lost faith in the power of rational discourse. What he would develop in his fiction was the logic of unreason. If his enemies used moralizing argument as a weapon, there must be a way of either turning it against them or discrediting it. Like a wrestler, he must take advantage of the muscular pressure being exerted against him. The image in his mind was that of the wine-press: he had been submitted to '59 months of pressurage' in Vincennes. Philippe Roger explains[1]

Pressurage(1296): operation by which a substance is compressed in a wine-press. Feudal right.

As Sade put it in a letter to Milli Rousset: 'It is a little bit like the juice of sour grapes, is it not, my reasoning? What can you do? *Fructus belli.*'

The first fruit of his paradoxical reasoning grew out of postulat-ing something he totally disbelieved in—the existence of God. After five years of self-absorption and fantasy about revenge, he had reached the point of needing to envisage an antithesis to the constriction and impotence he was suffering. He evolved a sup-reme fiction, hypothesized a character free of all limits. Like Laura in his dream, the God he visualized was unconfined by space or time. Without having come any closer to satisfying his hunger for revenge against Mme de Montreuil, he was at last able to bring his sense of humour into play, picturing 'the executioner of my life taken into the presence of the God she has outraged'. She would say: 'I am just like the deity, because I punish in the same way.' His answer would be: 'Horrible flea of nature! You dare to carry blasphemy so far?'

This letter was written in April 1782, the same month as Sade's 'Prière du soir': 'Put my destiny, oh my God, into the hands of virtue. It is your image on earth and those with no respect for it should not concern themselves with the reform of vice. Oh, best of beings, do not put me into the power of a monopolist, one who steals from the poor, a bankrupt, a sodomite, a buccaneer, an officer of the Inquisition, an unfrocked Jesuit and a procuress.'

[1] *Sade: La philosophie dans le pressoir.*

Again and again in his novels, innocent victims will suffer at the hands of omnipotent libertines. While the image picks up from sadistic experiences he had enjoyed, it gave him enjoyment in the present by inverting the situation of the impotent libertine dominated by the ruthless mother-in-law. After inflicting imaginary tortures on her in letters to Renée-Pélagie and in notes on scraps of paper, he arrived at moments of greater relaxation when he could enjoy empathizing ironically with Mme de Montreuil in plotting against him. This is a literary co-efficient of the physical reflex that had made him want to exchange roles with the victim of his flagellation. Here, with macabre relish, he is identifying with the woman who is victimizing him. There is one note on a scrap of paper which starts in the middle of an argument:

I say unction because how could Madame la Présidente's bidet sponge fail to be very oily? Tell her that I ask her, the next time she sees the *buccaneer* or the *freebooter* Sartinus to be sure and tell him: 'Monseigneur, we thank you for your advice. Nothing does so much good as prison. Our son-in-law proves it. He is unrecognizable since he has been there. Oh, what wise advice you give, Monseigneur. Oh, what a great man you are, Monseigneur.'

Chapter 8

Birth of a Middle-Aged Writer

Sade now found himself wanting to construct a mirror that would throw back a reproachful image of contemporary absurdities. If his opinions counted for nothing in the world outside the cell, what he needed was an alternative reality, a literary space, where he would be omnipotent. Tired of being the system's victim, he appointed himself its ribald judge.

Apart from his letters, his first important work was an atheistic credo, *Dialogue entre un prêtre et un moribond*, which he completed on 12 July 1782. It represented the next step in the development of his dialectical thinking after his 'Prière du soir' and his fantasy about Mme de Montreuil's confrontation with 'the God she had outraged'. Paradox had become Sade's favourite plaything. If there was no circuit of communication by which he could prove his innocence, at least he could have fun by short-circuiting the line of argument.

That he found relief by writing is unremarkable. In his situation, nothing could have been more natural than the urge to pour words over every available scrap of paper. But if what he wrote had not been important, it would not be disturbing 200 years later. He did not choose to turn his attention inwards: he had no option. His achievement is that before the Romantic movement had been launched, he succeeded in making solipsism look like omniscience.

His *Dialogue* is the story of a death-bed conversion, but it is the priest who is converted. When the dying man is asked whether he regrets the sins to which human frailty has led him, he says it was religion that led him into sin, by teaching him to resist the desires that nature had implanted. If only he had had the good sense to acknowledge Nature's omnipotence, he would have yielded to them completely and had a more enjoyable life.

The priest is unable to explain why God, after creating a corrupted nature, should have wanted to test humanity by giving it freedom of choice. He must have been able to see into the future, and if he wanted us to resist temptation, why did he choose not to make us stronger? As it is, we are all driven by irresistible forces, victims of our own inclinations. Our virtues and our vices are equally necessary to Nature, who skilfully holds the balance between them. The best incentive to virtuous behaviour is not intimidation but reason. Ethics depend entirely on the principle of trying to make other people as happy as we wish to be ourselves. The dying man would therefore like to make the priest as happy as he intends to be himself in his final minutes. In the neighbouring room are the six lovely women he has been saving for this occasion. He offers to share them with the priest, who is promptly converted.

The priest's change of heart is totally unrealistic, and so is the vigour the dying man displays in arguing and in making love. But the dialogue belongs to the convention by which literature—obliged, in self-defence, to prove itself morally useful—had been combining the arts of oratory and fable. There was still nothing to divide fiction from philosophy or philosophy from science. As a literary form, dialogue derives from the work of Herodotus and Thucydides in the fifth century BC. The earliest Socratic dialogues were probably based on notes taken during conversations, but the best of Plato's dialogues show that he had also been influenced by the dramatists. The *philosophes* of the Enlightenment followed the same principle of mixing seriousness with playfulness, putting forward challenging ideas in an entertaining way, exploiting the dramatic potential of both internal conflict and conflict between contrasted characters; while progress towards a revelation of the truth can itself be intrinsically dramatic. Voltaire's dialogues are less successful than his philosophical *contes*, such as *Candide* and *Zadig*, but Diderot's dialogues are among his best work.

The first sparks of Sade's originality as an immoralist are visible in his *Dialogue*, but it also owes a great deal to Diderot's *Lettre sur les aveugles*, which had been written in 1749. This contains a death-bed conversation between a blind mathematician (Saunderson) and a priest (Holmes) who is asked for proof of God's existence. He tells the dying man to touch himself and to recognize divinity in the perfection of his own physique. But to Saunderson the existence of blindness suggests that the world may be no more than an episode of limited duration in the life of a chaotic universe, which was not created by an omnipotent and omniscient God.

This was the argument that had cost Diderot three months of incarceration at Vincennes, despite his caution in refusing to side unequivocally with either of his spokesmen.

Sade's debt to Diderot was mainly formal; as a source of materialistic ideas, Holbach was more important. He had pointed to the wide gap between the laws of Nature and the laws of religion, attacking the priests for swathing their theology in a fog of mystification. Since reading *Le Système de la nature* about seven years earlier, Sade had not had the opportunity to re-read it, though it is clear from two letters he sent to Renée-Pélagie in November 1783 that he had been thinking about it. 'It is absolutely impossible,' he complained in the first, 'for me to enjoy the refutation of the *Système de la nature* if you do not send the *Système*.' In the second letter, written at the end of the month, he called it 'truly and quite incontestably the basis of all my philosophy . . . I am its devotee to the point of martyrdom if necessary.' The impact it had made on him had been disconnected from any action he could take, but in obviating all activities except reading, writing and thinking, imprisonment had brought the three of them into a closer and more reciprocal relationship.

Sade was making himself into a professional writer, and though the development had been too gradual for us to give it a date, the letters of 1782–3 are incomparably better written than the earlier ones. He had always been capable of irony, but it had taken a long time to convert outrage at his immobilization into a powerhouse of righteous indignation. After five years of screaming out about the injustice of his punishment, he was able to take it for granted that justice was unavailable. If the letters to Renée-Pélagie had served no other purpose, they had at least apprenticed him to the craft of arranging words in sentences, and now, if he could keep his mind calm, he could pick up threads from several earlier phases of his life—the study of rhetoric with the Jesuits, the philosophical reading he had done in the early '70s, the sensual and sacrilegious experiences of his libertine adventures. But there is nothing blasphemous in his *Dialogue*: the solitude he would never have experienced—given freedom of choice—had brought him to a cool-headed synthesis he could never otherwise have achieved.

From 1782 onwards, the letters to Renée-Pélagie are illuminated with shafts of literary brilliance that reach a long way beyond the private suffering. It did not matter that she was incapable of appreciating the nuances of his satire, or answering on the same intellectual level. Prison had taught him to be self-sufficient. He would have written neither the letters nor the plays without having someone to read them, but his dependence on her reactions was superficial and sometimes sadistic: he took pleasure in knowing she would be totally nonplussed by such Swift-like sallies as the one in his letter of July 1783. Was there any truth, he enquired, in the rumours that after his arrest in the Hôtel de Danemark, Mme de Montreuil wanted an expert to confirm whether M. de Sade had 'outraged' his wife's buttocks? He has been told, he says,

that you then tucked up your petticoat. The magistrate Le Noir, put on his spectacles, Albaret held the candle, the officers of the Inquisition took notes. And an inventory of fixtures was written in these terms: Item . . . we avouch the said Pélagie du Chauffour to be well and duly equipped with two very white buttocks, very beautiful and intact. We approached the said member and had our bailiffs approach as closely as ourselves. At their risk and peril they did half-open, part, sniff and study thoroughly, and having, like ourselves, observed nothing but health in those parts, we have delivered the present act, for use in conformity with the law.

Everything he wrote was subject to inspection, and within a few weeks of his filling the exercise book that contained the *Dialogue*, all the books he had been reading were taken away. They overheated his brain, he was told, and induced improprieties. 'I am in despair,' Renée-Pélagie wrote, 'at seeing you reduced to having nothing to do . . . I beg you to restrain yourself in your writings. You are doing yourself infinite harm. Make reparations by thinking in accordance with the decency which is there at the bottom of your heart.'

The confiscation of his books upset the precarious equilibrium he had achieved. In a June letter that ended 'I have begun my 210th week of imprisonment', he had come close to apologizing for his suspicions of infidelity: 'Six visits from you were enough to awaken me from my nightmare, which was an insult to you. I shall never have it again. I know better how to value what I love.' But at the end of July he had another violent quarrel with his gaoler. Whether the man was hit, or only threatened, Sade again forfeited the right to take walks, even in the corridor. In August, with no books and no exercise, he must have been extremely depressed, and it was about this time that he began working on *Les 120 journées de Sodome.*

Two years earlier he had ended a letter to his wife with the phrase: 'My brain will never ripen in the shade.' What he now felt, justifiably, was that it had ripened. 'In 1777,' he wrote on 19 August 1782,

> I was still fairly young . . . My soul had not yet hardened. It was not yet inaccessible, as you have carefully made it, to kindly sentiments. Different methods could have produced consider- able results, but you did not want them and I am grateful. All I have to do is chase your figures out of my head, which is better than having to dismiss an infinity of things and details which I find very delicious. They relieve my unhappiness when I let my imagination wander. It can be said that you have been given the wrong advice but, in all conscience, I am very glad things turned out the way they have.

What was saving him from despair were the mental habits he had formed. As he said in the same letter to Renée-Pélagie, 'Habits are so prodigiously bound up with a man's constitution that ten thousand years of prison and five hundred pounds of chains could do nothing but give them more force. I would greatly surprise you if I told you that the memory of all these things is what I call to my aid when I want to blunt the pain of my situation.'

His novels are not generically different from his *Dialogue.* The ratio of action to argument may be higher, but argument bulks large in all his fiction, and it is obvious that the excitement of writing it was not merely intellectual. Just as a sense of wrong- doing had been integral to his sexual pleasure—he preferred the anal position for moral as much as sensual reasons—the pleasure he took in immoralism was almost physical. The *Dialogue* contains the seeds of all his subsequent fiction. The crucial experience, I suspect, was the discovery of how much pleasure was to be had from writing out his fantasy about an orgy involving a priest, a dying man and six beautiful women. Erotic daydream draws freely, if tenuously, on memories of physical contact; the act of writing, the appearance of words on paper, not only stabilizes the imaginary action but helps to elaborate it. In becoming less cerebral, the experience becomes more orderly. Even if the words will never be read, they are hostages to space outside the mind. They have a tangible, if two-dimensional existence, and they systematize the action, discipline it, commit it tidily to a sequence or a scheme. A description of a woman's body, for instance, may be based on a merging of memory with desire, anthologizing any number of appetizing features, but it must be self-consistent. In fantasy she can be a redhead one minute and blonde the next; in eighteenth-century prose she cannot:

> The elegance of her figure did not detract from her freshness. It did not stop her from being plump and rounded. The most delicious curves, offering themselves under a skin whiter than lilies, gave the impression that love itself had carefully formed her. Her face was slightly long, the features extraordinarily noble, with more majesty than prettiness, more grandeur than delicacy. Her eyes were big, black and full of fire; her mouth extremely small and decorated with the most beautiful teeth that could be imagined. Her tongue was thin and narrow, of a beautiful rosy pinkness and her breath was even sweeter than the smell of a rose. Her throat was full, very round, as white and firm as alabaster. The most extraordinary curves led down deliciously from the small of her back to the most precisely and artistically sculpted bottom that nature had produced for a very long time. Its roundness was exact. It was not very big but firm, white, curved and half opening only to offer the most seemly, most enchanting and most delicate little hole. This bottom, charming refuge of lubricity's sweetest pleasures, was delicately coloured with a hint of pink. But, good God! These attractions did not last long. Four or five assaults from the Duke soon withered all their gracefulness.

But what is the real function of the last three sentences? Ostensibly an account of damage inflicted by a large male organ, they have a secret connection with the way that masturbation fantasy dissolves into vagueness as the sensation recedes. As Sartre says in *Saint Genet*, the characters melt, the onanistic activity produces only a caricature of love. The masturbator evokes the notion of a couple without ever believing himself to be one. The other person is not there. But the pleasure is real, and, as it fades, the feeling of guilt needs to be counter-weighted by a defiant satisfaction. 'The failure of the pleasure is an acid pleasure in failure.'

Masturbation is a strategy for coping with a situation in which contact is being made with no other bodies; literature resembles it in so far as the act of writing yields a pleasure in which no one else can participate, however much pleasure the results yield later. Writers vary in the extent to which they think of impact on the reader. *Les 120 journées de Sodome* is like Genet's *Notre-Dame des Fleurs* in setting up a dangerously intimate relationship in spite of —or because of—the improbability that either book would ever reach any readers. *Notre-Dame des Fleurs* was written in pencil on brown paper that should have been used for making bags; one incomplete draft was found by a warder and burnt. Sade wrote in constant fear that his manuscript would be confiscated and destroyed.

Sartre has said that Genet's book seems to be about fatality. 'The characters are fate's puppets; but it quickly becomes clear that this pitiless Providence is the obverse side of a supreme, divine freedom—the author's. No book is more pessimistic: with maniac scrupulousness, it leads human creatures downhill towards death. Yet, in its strange language, it presents their downfall as a triumph: all the miserable creatures he describes emerge as heroes, the elect.'[1] The same could be said of *120 journées*. The structure of the book leads the four libertines, their acolytes and their victims ineluctably downhill from the simple passions of Part One through the 'double' and 'criminal' passions of the second and third parts to the 'murderous' passions of the fourth. Had Sade completed the book, only sixteen of his forty-six characters would have survived. Thirty of them would have been wiped out in a tidal wave of aggression that would not have seemed to have its source either in fate or in the dominant characters. Like Genet's *personae*, they are not fortified with the semblance of autonomy. Genet told Sartre: 'My books are not novels because none of my characters takes his own decisions.'[2] 'That,' says Sartre, 'explains the desolation of the book. It is like a desert. Hope could have been prompted only by active, free characters. Genet is concerned only to

[1] *Saint Genet* (p. 417), Paris: Gallimard, 1952.
[2] Ibid., p. 421.

indulge his cruelty . . . a savage God who gets drunk on human blood.'

The relationship of writers to their characters is like that of parents to a child: they cannot give what they themselves lack, and if the emotional lack is chronic, they will try to take. Sade and Genet both achieved freedom by squeezing it out of their characters. If Apollinaire was right to describe Sade, who spent more than half his adult life in prison, as 'the most free spirit that ever lived', this is how he achieved freedom.

But is this freedom real or imaginary, sane or schizoid? It is worth comparing both the real isolation of Sade and the isolation he imagined for his libertine heroes with schizoid isolation as R. D. Laing describes it.[1] The individual

> in one sense is trying to be omnipotent by enclosing within his own being, without recourse to a creative relationship with others, modes of relationship that require the effective presence to him of other people and of the outer world. He would appear to be, in an unreal, impossible way, all persons and things to himself. The imagined advantages are safety for the true self, isolation and hence freedom from others, self-sufficiency, and control.

When Sade, before his imprisonment, had had opportunities for making creative relationships with other people, he had been unable to take advantage of them. There had been no rapport in any of his relationships. Freed, forcibly, from the compulsion to take sadistic pleasure from other people's bodies, he had to be self-sufficient—to find a way of being all persons and all things to himself. The only real, possible way was to create an unreal or fictional world.

120 journées is not a healthy, wholesome or balanced book, but if Sade is recognized as the patriarch of modern nihilism, it must also be acknowledged that it was not mere *ennui* that was alienating him. It could be said of all his decadent descendants that their aggressions against humanity were, in origin, defensive, and that they were defending themselves against pain, psychological or physical or both. It seems that Sade did much of the preliminary work for *120 journées* when he was in both kinds of pain.

[1] *The Divided Self.*

In the summer of 1782 he was still receiving occasional visits
from Renée-Pélagie, as he had been since the beginning of the
year. Deprived of both books and exercise, he could at least
look forward to seeing her, and, as his letters show, the moral
pressure she exerted had a negative effect: it provided something
to resist.

> As to what concerns me, me personally, I promise you nothing.
> The beast is too old. Believe me: you must give up trying to
> educate him ... Our habits do not depend on us but on our
> constitution, our system ... One cannot make virtues for one-
> self, and one does not have the power to adopt a particular
> taste in those matters any more than one has the power to
> straighten one's spine if it is born crooked.

But in September 1782, to punish him for behaving badly, her
visits were once again stopped. She appealed against the decision,
but unsuccessfully. During the depression that ensued, he became
increasingly convinced that de Rougemont was poisoning him.
He complained of pains worse than those suffered by a criminal
broken on the wheel and he begged to be transferred to another
prison. In the middle of December, after about twenty weeks with
no exercise, he was given permission to walk up and down the
corridor. Early in 1783 he began to have trouble with one eye—a
corneal opacity. By 4 February, he was complaining that he could
not see out of it at all, and asking for an oculist. The handwriting
in the letters sent between February and April is much larger and
shakier than usual. 'Since I can no longer either read or write,' he
said in a letter of about 10 February, 'here is the one hundred and
eleventh torture I am inventing for her. This morning, in great
pain, I saw her, the whore, I saw her skinned alive, dragged over
thistles and then thrown into a barrel of vinegar.'

In the notes he prepared for Parts Two to Four of the book, it
is not only the days that are numbered, but the atrocities, and the
102nd in Part Four involves dragging the victim over red-hot
spikes and throwing her into a brazier. A reader ignorant of what
Sade was suffering might find his malice incomprehensible; his
need to torture his characters was like Genet's when he wrote,
'It's time for this pimp, cocky and so beautiful, to experience the
torments reserved for the feeble.' Later on, during the revolution,

Sade would have a real opportunity to revenge himself on Mme de Montreuil. But having vented his hatred in fiction, he would have the strength to spare her life. At the moment of venting it, he was feeble.

120 journées is a diabolically ingenious machine which simultaneously inverts the reality of Sade's situation and subverts the morality that justified it. He described his four debauched heroes as 'champions'; they were for him what Beckett calls 'vice-existers'. They even gave him a flattering mirror-image of his own isolation. To enjoy flagellation, perversion and sexual excess, they imprison their victims in a Gothic castle which is remote and inaccessible enough to guarantee freedom from society's interference. What Sade accepted involuntarily they chose.

Realistic criteria are almost as irrelevant as they were to the *Dialogue*. Having total power over their victims, the libertines would not need to explain anything, but the narrative is replete with explanations. Subtitled *L'Ecole de libertinage*, the novel reverses the tradition of the moral fable, while illustrating Sade's dictum that to be erotic it is essential to articulate crime in language. It is not merely that words were his only means of representing actions: what was revolutionary about the book was its uninhibited exploration of the space between sensation and formulation. Unlike animals, we seldom enjoy a sensation without describing it to ourselves. Awareness of pleasure or pain is always impure, contaminated by words, even when they remain unspoken. At the same time, verbalization extends the pleasure or the pain. Once words have been let in, the imagination cannot be kept out. The idea of using narrative to spice and protract sensual pleasure is at least as old as the *Arabian Nights' Entertainments*; but Sade was sensualizing language in a different kind of assault on the *'ami lecteur'*, who is addressed in the second person singular with the insolent promise of

the impurest story ever told since the beginning of the world . . . No doubt you will dislike a great deal in all the misdeeds described—one is aware of that—but some of them will warm you up so much it will cost you sperm, and that is all we have to do; without telling you everything, analysing everything, how could we have found out what appeals to you?

A play-within-a-play tends to focus attention on the relationship between action and audience by offering an onstage simulacrum of it; stories-within-a-story can question the relationship between fiction and reader in a similarly provocative way. Sade's four libertines have recruited four experienced ex-prostitutes to reminisce about unsavoury episodes. The function of these stories is to revive the libertines' appetite for new orgies.

Without any grounds for expecting the book to be published, Sade was visualizing a male reader, and writing with one eye on his erectile tissue. We are obviously intended to follow the example of the libertines, who continually interrupt the story-telling in order to act out something that has been directly or indirectly suggested. Even if we do not follow suit, the deft alternation between the two levels of narrative not only reminds us of the medium but forces us to re-examine the connection between word and sensation, image and action.

One of the stock arguments against describing the sexual act is that it is always the same. Sade's structure is based on the conviction that it is not: an enormously extended set of variations moves progressively away from the original theme. This was not merely a stratagem for avoiding repetition: it was a logical development from the assumption that to the connoisseur of sexual pleasure, diversification is essential. For the libertine who has the means of gratifying every desire, the problem is how to save the appetite from becoming jaded.

The scheme of the book follows the plan agreed by the libertines:

> The idea was to hear stories, told systematically and in great detail, about all the different perversions, all the variations and adjuncts, or, in libertine parlance, all the passions. When a man's imagination is inflamed, he diversifies them to an incredible degree. If men differ exceedingly in all their other manias and tastes, the difference is even greater in this one. If it were possible to pin down these perversions in a detailed catalogue, it would perhaps constitute one of the finest works about manners, and perhaps one of the most interesting.

This serves as a justification for the stories-within-the-story, but it is also a rationale for perversion. Sade's narrative method was

wedded to his immoralism. Analysis and classification lead naturally to diversification, which will inevitably carry us further and
further from the norms. One of his deadliest insights is expressed
in one of his pithiest epigrams: 'The true way of enlarging and
multiplying one's desires is to wish to impose limits on them.'
This also explains the principle by which the book was written.
He imposed a rigidly schematic structure on the action, planning
an organized progression through the 120 days and arranging his
characters mathematically in groups: the four libertines, their four
women, eight young men, each with an outsize penis, eight boys,
eight girls, four story-tellers, four old women chosen for their
vileness, and six cooks.

He also did well to make the libertines formulate strict rules for
themselves and their victims. The subject matter is potentially
anarchic. The sexual excesses and the coprophilia break down all
the barriers erected by hygiene and by civilization. Some of the
libertines' rules go directly against the old rules. Religious piety
is severely punished. The boys and girls have to leave their bodies
unwashed and their bottoms unwiped for stipulated periods.
Farting, defecation and perverted sexual intercourse are made into
spectator sports. Semen, urine and excrement are consumed in
prodigious quantities. But there are strict rules governing property, privacy and the preservation of virginity—rules which are
made by the novelist only to be broken by the characters. They
are like a grid made of ropes. The subject-matter can burst its
bonds, while the anarchy can be measured against a scale.

But if Sade had finished the novel, he might have found himself
needing to modify his style, as if he were progressively introducing discord into a classical symphony. The 120 days are spread
over four winter months, November to February, and each of the
story-tellers is on duty for a month. We know that the criminality
will increase steadily, both in the main narrative and in the story-
tellers' stories, so the mounting disorderliness of the behaviour
creates a disturbing, almost disrupting, pressure within the geo-
metrically orderly framework. Between bouts of progressively
outrageous self-indulgence, the libertines are mouthpieces for
Sade's philosophizing. The main source of ideas was not Holbach
but the author of *L'homme machine* (1748), Julien de la Mettrie,
who was much more radical, more indulgent towards evil impulses and towards the cruelty that appeared to fulfil Nature's

intentions. 'We are in her hands, as a pendulum is in those of the clock-maker ... So we are no more criminal in following the impetus of the primitive movements which govern us than the Nile is in its flooding or the sea in its destruction.' He refused to believe that men were subject to different laws from animals: 'man is not fashioned from a more precious clay. Nature has used the same dough, varying only the leaven.' Unlike Hume, he did not believe in innate benevolence. Man is congenitally vicious, posing as virtuous only when it is expedient. 'Many animals with a human face have become heroes.' And he argued that 'if the joys derived from Nature and reason are crimes, human happiness lies in criminality ... The man who is without remorse, who is sufficiently familiar with crime for vices to become virtues, will be happier than the other man who performs a good deed, which he then regrets.'

La Mettrie's mechanistic viewpoint is visible in the explanations of human pleasure offered in Sade's novel. The Duc de Blangis regards man as a machine in the hands of nature, and he boasts that he has been faithful to the principles he formed in his youth. 'They taught me that virtue was empty, a nothing ... only vice was made so that man could experience that moral and physical vibration, source of the most exquisite pleasures ... So I have nothing to hold me back except the laws ... My money and my credit put me above the vulgar plagues which should attack only the people.' Properly regarded, the laws are valuable because they stand between desire and its attainment, and there is no satisfaction to be had if desires are attained too easily. As Sade makes Durcet, the financier, put it: 'Happiness consists not in consummation but in desire, in shattering the restrictions imposed as obstacles to it.' Living at the opposite pole of deprivation from his characters—having unlimited opportunities for desire and none for consummation—Sade led them to conclusions from which he could take comfort. They find it very frustrating to have pleasure so readily available. 'I swear,' says Durcet on the eighth day, 'that ever since I have been here, my sperm has not flowed for what is here. It is things which are not here that make me come.' The principle of negation had never been stated more simply or more powerfully. Here is a rationale for rejecting reality in favour of the imaginary alternative, denying what is present for the sake of what is not. Sade is squashing his characters into incapacity for enjoyment of immediate action. Implicitly sexual activity is being negated and fantasy invested with the energy taken from it, as if thought and language were the only valid components in the experience of sex. As Gilles Deleuze has said: 'Sadism moves from the negative to negation: from the negative as a partial process of destruction, constantly reiterated, to negation as an all-embracing concept of reason . . . At the heart of sadism is the project of sexualizing thought, sexualizing the speculative process as such, in so far as it depends on the super-ego.'[1]

At the same time, what Sade was writing was relevant to his own situation: he was making his sperm flow for things which were not there. If his gaolers had been genuinely campaigning for his moral restitution, they might have done better to apply his own logic of inversion. Referring to himself by the number of his cell, he suggested in a letter of July 1783 that

Monsieur No. 6 should have been shut up not with cannibals but with girls . . . I would have provided him with so many of them that the devil take me if during the seven years he has been there he would not have used up all the oil in his lamp . . . No more of these *philosophical subterfuges*, of these researches disowned by nature (as if nature concerned herself with all that), of these *dangerous* deviations of an imagination which is too ardent, always chasing after happiness without ever finding it, ending up by replacing reality with fantasies, honest orgasms with *dishonest deviations* . . . Put in the middle of a seraglio, Monsieur No. 6 would have become the *friend of women*. He would have acknowledged and *felt* that nothing is *greater* or more beautiful than sex and that there is no other salvation. Occupied exclusively with serving the ladies and satisfying their delicate desires, Monsieur No. 6 would have sacrificed all his own.

Like the idea of a priest sharing six beautiful women with a dying man, this is one of the fantasies that afforded Sade all the more pleasure for being committed to paper.

For the sadist, one of the greatest disadvantages of solitude is that he cannot feel superior to anyone else. Sade put his dissatisfaction into the mouth of Durcet: 'What we are lacking is

[1] *Présentation de Sacher-Masoch,* Editions de Minuit, 1967.

comparison . . . I need the satisfaction of seeing someone who is suffering from not having what I have . . . Happiness will never exist without inequality. It is like the man who does not understand the value of health until he is ill. The greatest sensual pleasure in the world is watching the tears of those overwhelmed with misery.' This principle of *Schadenfreude* had been formulated very much earlier by Lucretius when he wrote: 'It is pleasant to watch from the shore while the wretched sailor is struggling with death . . . it is comforting to view evils we are not experiencing.'[1] One of the reasons Sade needed his fiction was that it enabled him to feel superior to his characters. He also used them as a device for remodelling his memories of earlier experiences. On the twenty-third day, playing idly with the buttocks of Fanchon who is one of the old women, Curval, a President of a law-court, is talking about cynicism. It is well known, he says, that punishment breeds enthusiasm, that disgrace can cause an erection. 'Everyone knows the story of the Marquis de . . . The moment he was told that he had been sentenced to be burned in effigy, he pulled his cock out of his breeches and shouted: "Cock's body! There I am, exactly where I wanted to be. There I am covered with shame and infamy! Leave me, leave me. I need to discharge!" And he did so instantly.'

Writing over ten years after the event, Sade is imputing to his former self a contemptuous detachment he had only afterwards learned to cultivate. This was a long time before the word 'alienation' acquired its modern sense, but Curval's comment comes close to defining what we mean by it: 'In every other case shame would serve as a counterweight to the vices his spirit would try to release him from . . . but this man is the first to be exiled from his spirit, and it is exactly one step from the state of never blushing to that of loving everything which causes blushes.'

The remarks in Sade's letters about taking on the right colour for the coffin and waiting indifferently for death had been indications of his development. In *120 journées* he makes one of the story-tellers talk about a libertine whose ambition was to go on kissing arses until he was on his deathbed. In the brothel he liked to play-act at dying. The prostitute had to nail him into the coffin that was waiting, and the sound of the hammer would bring him to orgasm. Curval's theory is that the man wanted to familiarize himself with death through a libertine idea. The Duke's inter-

[1] *De rerum naturae*, Book II.

pretation is much the same: 'This is a man who mocks at everything and wants to condition himself to think and to act the same way in his last moments.' Sade's sour joke emerged out of his need to live with the possibility that he might die without ever again seeing the world outside the prison. On one level he was talking to himself at the beginning of the story when he made his Duc de Blangis address the victims collected at the isolated château:

Here you are, outside France, in the heart of an uninhabitable forest, beyond precipitous mountains in which the passages were blocked immediately after you came through them. You are prisoners in an impenetrable citadel, and nobody knows you are here. You are beyond the reach of your friends, your parents. You are already dead to the world and alive only for our pleasure.

Though Sade was still in the process of schooling himself in detachment, his moods were liable to vary as much as the handwriting in his letters. Occasionally, full of exuberance, he would express himself straightforwardly. In the morning of 3 July 1783, he wrote to Renée-Pélagie: 'I embrace you with all my heart, my dear friend, and write to you quite simply from gaiety of spirit and to tell you that I am feeling well and to ask you to come soon to see me because it is tiresome to go so long without embracing you.' (This is one of the few letters in which he did not completely fill three sides of the folded sheet. The fourth he always left free for the address: A Madame/Madame de Sade/A Paris.) Frequently, plunged in gloom, he would grindingly reiterate demands for clean linen, candles and meringues.

He seems sometimes to have felt ambivalent about whether he had the right to find refuge in fantasy. In September he was making a frantic bid to check himself. Muzzling both his pride and his ironic creativity, he addressed himself once again to Mme de Montreuil, entreating her to let him make amends to her daughter:

No, Madame, nothing in the whole universe will be able to keep me away from her, and I will adore her even in the vengeance she takes on me . . . Do not let me die in desperation without being able to make her forget all the wrongs I have done. Love, esteem, tenderness, gratitude, respect, all the sentiments the soul can generate, combine in me towards her . . . I do not ask you to believe what I say. I want to be put to the test. Reunite us, under whatever supervision you like, and in whatever country . . . If I do her then the slightest wrong, may I never see her again and may I lose my liberty again and, if it is required, my life. I consent to everything . . . If you set your heart on seeing me at the ultimate point of humiliation, despair and unhappiness that is possible for a man, rejoice, madame, rejoice, for you have achieved your object . . . Religion and nature both forbid you to pursue your vengeance to the grave or to repulse my wish to make amends. To this ardent prayer I would add the entreaty that you do not let me out of prison if you do not wish to reunite me with my wife . . . Deign to let me see her as soon as possible, and alone, I implore you.

Humility, of course, had no effect on her, and at the beginning of January 1784 he discarded it in his masterfully obdurate attempt to intervene in the military career of his elder son, whose fate, since early boyhood, had been entirely in the hands of his grandmother. Sade was determined that Louis-Marie should serve in the Carbine Regiment. 'As soon as his eyes were open, this is what I had in mind for him and I shall certainly not change my mind. Whether 20 or 40 thousand livres are needed, I am prepared to give the money . . . I am ready to have everything sold or mortgaged, borrow money, do whatever is necessary.' And to the unfortunate boy he wrote: 'No son of mine can defy me by joining a regiment I do not wish him to serve in. He may be the son of Mme de Montreuil but he is not mine.' Throughout the sixteen years of his life, Louis-Marie had hardly ever heard from his father, but this letter was rapidly followed by another: 'If you are feeble enough to obey relations on whom you are in no way dependent while you have a father, you can bid me an eternal farewell, for I will never see you again in my lifetime.' This letter is signed 'The Comte de Sade, your father'.

If he asserted himself at all in the few threadbare contacts he had with people outside the prison, he was likely to be unreasonable. Unable to believe himself deprived of all power over the lives of his children, he compulsively issued ineffectual instructions. None of them was to leave school or home before spending a year under his personal supervision. Louis-Marie must not be married until he is twenty-five and then it must be to a girl from either Avignon or Lyons. 'You may be sure,' Sade wrote to Renée-Pélagie, 'that you, the King, the Parlement and all the laws of the Kingdom will be unable to prevent me, either in advance or retrospectively, from reducing the income from my four estates in Provence to 1,000 livres, and I can do that without selling an inch of land.' This is what he will do if she lets his son disobey him. 'I will also, Madame, inspire in him feelings towards you equal to those you have given him for me.'

The volatility of the letters is phenomenal. Sometimes the mood changes within the space of a few lines, and such was his power of irony that he could sustain two dissonant moods throughout several pages of prose. In the letter of 23–24 November 1783, there is a pungent mixture of teasing tenderness and scathing contempt. The letter is seasoned with endearments all underlined —some bland, some peppery: *my angel, my lolly, my little bow-wow, dear turtle-dove, my little mother, heavenly cat, violet from the Garden of Eden* and *fresh pork of my thoughts*. He adds a note explaining that he was fond of pork and ate very little of it in prison.

He promises to gratify her request for his dirty linen and repeats his own request for clean linen. He peremptorily reiterates his demand for a box of a certain size to contain the drawings she has been sending him. He jokes about the one of a beautiful boy, which prompts him to write out an anecdote about a Cardinal who customarily receives a fresh virgin in his chamber each morning before starting on the day's work. One day the matron who supplies them sends up a beautiful boy in girl's clothes. The gentleman of the chamber is outraged, but, after putting on his spectacles, the Cardinal smiles beneficently: 'Peace, peace, my friend. We shall deceive her in her turn. She will think that I have been deceived.'

Chapter 9

Bastille

At 9 o'clock in the evening of 29 February 1784, de Rougemont came into Sade's cell with a police officer who was to escort him to the Bastille. He had not been warned that he was to be moved; he was allowed to take nothing with him. When he picked up his pillow—the specially large one he needed to avoid dizziness and nosebleed during the night—it was snatched out of his hands. Things of that kind were never tolerated, he was told. The journey was soon over: it is only three miles from Vincennes to the Place de la Bastille. He was led into one of the eight round towers and taken up to an octagonal cell on the second floor. It was about fifteen feet in diameter—half the size of his cell at Vincennes. Humbly he asked for four boards to put under his head. The officials who were brought into the cell agreed that the sleeping arrangements were uncomfortable, but the practice there, they said, was not to make exceptions.

The tower dated from the thirteenth century, and there was only one cell on each level. The floor was of brick, the walls whitewashed. Three steps led up to a window with three rows of bars, and there were bars inside the chimney, making it impossible to climb. The walls were very thick, and so was the door which had three locks.

There were only twelve other prisoners, with fifteen warders to supervise them. Three meals were served each day—at 7 and 11 in the morning and at 6 in the evening. The catering was more generous, both quantitatively and qualitatively, than at Vincennes but prisoners were served according to their rank. It was on this that the Governor's allowance depended. He was paid 3 livres a day for each worker, 5 livres for a bourgeois, 10 livres for a financier, a judge or a man of letters, with higher rates going up to 36 livres for a Marshal of France. But for those detained by *lettres de cachet* issued to please their families, the government paid nothing. For Sade the Montreuils had to make quarterly payments of 800 livres, so, he could eat better than a bourgeois, but not so well as a man of letters.

He had been in the Bastille for just over a week when he wrote to Renée-Pélagie. He was a thousand times worse off than before, he said. His cell was too small for him to turn round, and he was allowed out of it only rarely

> to walk for a few minutes in a narrow courtyard where one smells the guards' bodies and the cooking. They order me about at the end of a rifle as if I had tried to dethrone Louis XVI! . . . I am told that I must make my bed and sweep my room. I am glad to do the former because it was done for me very badly and it amuses me. But I am no good at the latter. It is the fault of my parents who neglected to have that talent educated in me . . . For seven years at Vincennes I had the use of knives and scissors without any harm coming of it. I am well aware that I am no better than I was at the beginning of those seven years, but I am no worse. Would you not be able to have the complete use of those two utensils restored to me? I am naked, thank God, and soon I shall be as I was when I came out of my mother's stomach. They would not let me bring anything at all. A shirt or a nightcap would have made the policeman swear and de Rougemont shout his lungs out.

The letter goes on to specify what Renée-Pélagie should bring on her first visit: two shirts, three pairs of slippers, four pairs of cotton stockings, three nightcaps—two of cotton and one of taffeta, two headbands, two muslin cravats, four small cloths, five inches square, for bathing his eyes, six pots of jam, six pounds of candles and a pint of *eau de cologne* better than the last bottle, which was no good at all.

At least she was now able to see him regularly. A permit issued on 16 March gave her the right to pay two visits every month, and she arrived at the Bastille at 4 in the afternoon of the same day. She stayed for three hours, and arranged to come back on the 27th. In a letter to Gaufridy written at the beginning of May, she reported that he was fairly well but still complaining about his eye. It was not until the middle of July that M. Le Noir gave permission for the oculist Grandjean to attend him again.

Much of his writing seems to have been done in considerable

discomfort, the fantasies of pleasure counterbalancing the actual pain. Renée-Pélagie supplied his basic material needs: on 24 May she brought nineteen exercise books, a bottle of ink, a box of chocolates, a half-pound of marshmallows and a pair of sheets. On her next visit, a fortnight later, she brought six large quill pens, six small ones and twenty-one exercise books. His books had been sent on from Vincennes at the end of April, and she brought some others, including plays and travellers' accounts of their adventures. That he recovered the manuscript of *120 journées* was due not to tolerance but to the inefficiency of the censorship.

Seeing Renée-Pélagie more often, he wrote to her less, but the discovery that she had been walking to the Bastille provoked an outburst of fury which lasted long after she had left.

So it is revealed at last, the reason for that excessive heat, the frightful state you are in, each time you come to see me: it is because you come on foot, like an orange-seller, like a street-walker . . . and your parents put up with it, and your rascally servants raise no objection! How degrading! How infamous! . . . Listen, I promise to calm down, to write with all the self-control I can muster . . . So I have only one word to say to you. It is that if you ever again arrive to see me in that state, I swear to you on everything I hold most sacred, I will not see you, I will go straight back to my room and never in my life will I come down again for you . . . A woman alone, on foot, in the streets? One drunkard . . . one stone thrown by an urchin . . . a falling tile . . . the shaft of a carriage . . . a riot . . . No excuses, no evasions, saying 'My lodgings are only a few paces away'. Even if they are under the ramparts of the Bastille, I forbid you to come on foot.

The splenetic energy that went into *120 journées* was generated partly from scorn for the system that made it so easy for evil-doers to make the law and logic into weapons. His letter to Renée-Pélagie dated 4 September contains a satirical offshoot from the novel—an imaginary conversation between his mother-in-law and M. de Losme, a high-ranking official of the prison:

Mme de MONTREUIL: There now! Six months have gone by and my son-in-law has only been vexed with trifles. He has been blinded in one eye and he is not told the truth or allowed any fresh air except occasionally, but all that is nothing. I am not enjoying myself. My stomach is swollen. My digestion has been ruined. My nights are restless. You! Hangman! Come here. Be good enough to torture my son-in-law a little better.

Ex-bodyguard de LOSME: But Madame his behaviour is angelic. What the devil do you want done to him?

Mme de MONTREUIL: You scoundrel! Am I paying you to sing his praises? What does it matter to me whether he behaves well or badly? If you cannot call him to account for doing wrong, punish him for his virtues. Are you ignorant of the art of causing trouble, laying traps? What else are you being hired for?

The ironical pattern that runs through *120 journées* is based on the same assumption that virtue is punished and vice rewarded. To be happy in this world, the Duke maintains, a man must not only abandon himself to all the vices but deny himself any of the virtues. It is not enough to do evil when one feels like it: one must do it all the time. He had begun by killing his mother and his sister. 'Nothing is more encouraging than a first crime committed with impunity ... From murders that were necessary to him he soon progressed to murders that were merely pleasurable.'

In March 1785 it was over eight years since Sade had been taken to Vincennes but, as Mme de Montreuil said in a letter to Gaufridy, she had not changed her mind about the need to keep him behind bars. 'The effervescence of his character' was unchanged, she maintained, and to release him would be to invite a new succession of scandals. 'I believe that henceforth I should not intervene in this affair, having so often done so, and having procured it—his freedom—out of consideration for his wife, who has had only too many reasons for regretting it. You know what you know, Monsieur, and as to that there is nothing more to be said, and nothing more to be done towards making the best of things.'

In September 1784, after Renée-Pélagie had been turned out of her room in the convent, she had no help from her mother. The nuns had given her the use of a garret, which she described as a 'hole'. But there was no question of moving to Lacoste, and she professed her willingness to put up with ten thousand absurdities of this kind if only she could obtain justice for her husband. She was also spending money on the protracted illness of La Jeunesse. The doctors said it was necessary to cut his palate, which they did, and at the beginning of May he seemed to be recovering, but by the end of the month he was dead.

Six months previously Sade's ex-mistress, Beauvoisin, had died at the age of forty. The latest in her succession of rich lovers had been the Naval Paymaster, and the sale of her furniture and effects, which was spread over six days, attracted the *beau monde*. There were 200 superb rings, enormous unmounted diamonds, scores of gorgeous dresses and 'brocades 32 ells in width such as not even the Queen possesses'.

Sade was meanwhile dependent on masturbation. He had taken Renée-Pélagie into his confidence about it, and towards the end of 1784 he found a way of writing in great detail about his auto-erotic habits. *Manilla*—he underlined the word—signifies masturbation, while ejaculation of semen is symbolized by the flight of the arrow from the bow:

Once the habit is formed, no one is inconvenienced ... After this no one can say I have gained nothing from Vincennes ... Sometimes three months have gone by and it is not that the bow has not been pulled tight—oh do not be angry: you will be able to find reason for being pleased—but the arrow does not want to be released—and that is what kills—because I want it to go—the mind goes instead of the thing—and that does not help —and that is why I tell you prison is bad, because solitude fortifies fantasy. The derangement that ensues becomes swifter and more deadly.

But I have absolutely understood the obstinacy of this arrow in not wanting to go, especially when it does so much to cut through the air—it is really an epileptic attack—and without tiresome precautions, I am certain my neighbours would not believe this—and convulsions and spasms and pain—you have seen examples at Lacoste—it is now only twice as bad. With everything combined, there is more harm than good in it. I prefer *manilla*, which is gentle and involves none of all that. I wanted to analyse the cause of this swooning, and I believe I have found it in the *extreme thickness*—as if one wanted to squeeze cream through the narrow neck of a bottle—This *thickness* distends the ducts and lacerates them. To that one replies—the arrow should be shot more often—I am well aware that it should—but it does not want to be—and to force it against its will destroys me with vapours. . . . If I had at my disposal *those other means* I employ when I am at liberty—the arrow becomes less obstinate and departing more often—the crisis of departure would be neither so violent nor so dangerous—for the difficulty explains the danger. A door which opens easily does not require to be forced; less effort would be needed if the arrow, *more fluid*, departed more frequently. Accordingly, fewer episodes. On the other hand, *terrible episodes violent efforts* if the arrow, overfed by its overlong sojourn, is obliged to lacerate the quiver in passing through it. Imagine a cannon loaded with a ball that grows bigger as it stays inside. Fire the cannon after two days and you will have only a small explosion, but if you let the ball grow, you will destroy the cannon when you fire it.

If you have a trustworthy doctor, I would like you to discuss all this with him because I am convinced that no one else in the world has the experience that I do in this crisis. My intention is to consult a doctor when I am released. There is no doubt that I have a constitutional defect of a sort which is less apparent during youth but likely to become more troublesome with advancing age ... Deliberately released, finally, from all its moorings and kept adrift for as long as possible, the mind would involuntarily go to the devil as soon as the arrow was released, and stay there all the longer, after a very prolonged crisis with indescribable movements and convulsions which last just as long. It is not mental excitement which causes all that. On the contrary, it holds the arrow back—and that is what you have seen and must remember. The longer the arrow stays, the more mental excitement . . . If one forces it to depart, *horrible vapours*; if one succeeds, *terrible crisis*; if one fails, *head to the devil*. Judge whether I need a doctor and above all whether I need to take baths, which I am convinced ought to give me relief.[1]

[1] Lely corrected the error by which this letter had been attributed to the previous year, but he should not have assumed that nothing had changed since the Rose Keller incident; that Sade's orgasms were always dependent on an act of sadism or masochism; and that the phrases *head to the devil, deliberately released from its mooring, horrible vapours* and *terrible crisis* all refer to the imaginative activity which, in the absence of a partner, was Sade's only means of working himself up sufficiently for an emission.

Sade's accounts of sexual experience in *120 journées* were conditioned by the abnormality of his own experience. How could he even have formed an impression of what normal experience was like? He had started his narrative with detailed physical descriptions of his four vice-existers, and it could be said that the drift away from the norms had already started. He endowed the Duc de Blangis with 'the strength of a horse and the member of a veritable mule, astonishingly hairy, even at the age of fifty, and an almost constant erection in this member, whose dimensions were exactly eight inches in diameter and twelve in length.' Most of his principal male characters have unusually large penises, but Durcet's is only four inches by two inches. His emissions are 'rare and very painful, not abundant and always preceded by spasms that throw him into a kind of fury, which transports him to crime'. Curval, who is nearly sixty, has a skeletal body, exhausted by debauchery, but 'in a forest of hairs one saw an organ which, in a state of erection, would be about eight inches long and seven inches in circumference; but this state now occurred very rarely and only as a result of a furious sequence of things. However it still happened at least two or three times a week.' When he achieves orgasm he is liable to roar and howl so loudly that even the Duke is surprised at his violence. Curval attributes it to the extreme sensitivity of his constitution. 'The objects of our passions create such a lively commotion in the electric fluid that flows through our nerves. So violent is the shock received by the animal spirits which compose this fluid that the whole machine is shaken.' La Mettrie's influence is noticeable in the phrasing, and in Sade's next novel, *Aline et Valcour*, there will be a footnote about this 'electric fluid which circulates through the cavities of our nerves ... it is the conductor of pain and pleasure. In a word it is the only soul that modern philosophers acknowledge.'

The abnormality of the fourth libertine, the Bishop, is that he is fastidiously homosexual. He has had frontal intercourse with a woman only once in his life, and that was to impregnate his brother's wife in order to have a child he would eventually be able to bugger.

Among the descriptions of orgasms in *120 journées*, the one that most resembles Sade's accounts of his own occurs in a story told by Mme Duclos. On the twentieth day she is reminiscing about a man who rarely achieves an orgasm. The brothel caters for him by enlisting a toothless woman of seventy with ulcers and a diffused inflammation of the skin. He watches with great excitement while she excretes, only to hesitate, trembling, on the point of eating her faeces. A young prostitute encourages him by threatening to burn his buttocks. After pulling down his breeches to reveal a bottom scarred all over by similar manœuvres, she singes him lightly with a coal-scoop which has been in the fire. He swears at her. A deep burn forces him to swallow a mouthful of excrement. She continues until he has eaten all of it. The ensuing orgasm is so violent that he rolls on the ground, frantic.

The earliest physicians characterized the sexual climax as a minor epilepsy, which means, as Freud says, that they 'recognized in the sexual act a mitigation and adaptation of the epileptic method of discharging stimuli'.[1] The affinities between Sade and Dostoevsky could be analysed in terms of epilepsy, 'the uncanny disease with its incalculable, apparently unprovoked convulsive attacks, its changing of the character into irritability and aggressiveness, and its progressive lowering of all the mental faculties'. Freud was probably right to regard Dostoevsky's epilepsy as no more than a symptom of his neurosis. The boyhood onset of the disturbance came in the form of severe melancholy, as if he were about to die on the spot. A precondition of his neurosis was his innate bisexual disposition, and Freud associates his epilepsy with the guilt that ensued on 'defending himself with special intensity against dependence on a specially strong father'. Dostoevsky 'told his friend Strakhov that his irritability and depression after an epileptic attack were due to the fact that he seemed to himself a criminal, and could not get rid of the feeling that he had a burden of unknown guilt upon him, that he had committed some great misdeed, which oppressed him.'[2] This throws some light on what the novels of Dostoevsky, Sade and Genet have in common. With all three, ability to empathize with the criminal mentality is inseparable from the compulsion to project the self into fantasies of criminality.

In October 1785, Sade was at the end of the thirtieth day of his narrative, and he had made detailed notes for the remaining ninety, but instead of developing them he decided to make a fair copy which could be hidden more easily. By sticking together

[1] 'Dostoevsky and Parricide', *Complete Psychological Works*, Vol XXI.
[2] Ibid.

small sheets of thin paper about five inches in width, he made a forty-foot roll. Working intensively from 22 October until 28 November, he filled both sides of it in minute handwriting. His intention was to treat the last ninety days of his story in as much detail as the first thirty. There are many interpolations in the draft about points he meant to check and defects he wanted to remedy. Addressing himself consistently in the second person plural, he wrote notes like: 'Curval buggers her for the last time and then they kill her with fearful torments which you will describe in detail.' He even wrote a memorandum about the width of the margin he intended to leave.

That he opted against finishing *120 journées* means that he arrived at the point of not feeling any strong compulsion to bring the crimes of the final ninety days to the same degree of realization as the perversions of the first thirty. Not that this was, in any case, a very high degree. Even in the most detailed passages of narrative, a great deal is left unrealized. There are flashes of vividness, but the novel proceeds rather like a film in which the camera settles only momentarily on subordinate characters, even if we are meant to assume that they are there all the time. The presence of Fanchon, for instance, is not effectively felt throughout most of the action. We are told that she is sixty-nine, short, fat, dirty with only two teeth left in her stinking mouth, vaginal cancer, haemorrhoids as big as a fist, and a habit of farting without being aware of it. But once he has described her, Sade seems to forget all about her, and when Curval licks her feet we are not forced to picture what happens in any more detail than we would an incident in an anecdote. Like the stories told by Mme Duclos, the main narrative proceeds very rapidly, summarizing, chronicling, cataloguing, never lingering to dramatize or solidify. Sade had been influenced by *Candide*, in which the comedy depends partly on Voltaire's technique of reducing an earthquake to a laconic sentence or dismissing a massacre with six words.

In the roll of paper thirteen yards long on which Sade had written all that survives of his work on *Les 120 journées de Sodome*,[1]

---

[1] Found by Arnoux de Saint-Maximin in Sade's cell, the roll remained in the possession of the Villeneuve-Trans family for three generations. At the beginning of this century it was sold to a collector. The first published version appeared in 1904, edited by Iwan Bloch, who used the pseudonym Eugen Dühren.

about four-fifths of the draft are devoted to the first thirty days, and most of the notes which fill the remainder of the long roll are summaries of the 450 episodes to be described by the last three story-tellers. These notes constitute a hundred of the most horrific pages currently in print. By the beginning of December a libertine in one of the stories is deflowering not only children of five and seven but babies in the cradle. A mass is celebrated for naked whores and, by the end of the month, crucifixes are being used for flagellation. *Love* is a word that Sade uses very seldom, but before the year has ended, the Duke is in love with the fifteen-year-old Augustine. After taking her frontal virginity, he has seven orgasms inside her before morning.

The third story-teller talks about a libertine in the habit of having sex with a turkey, whose neck is held between the thighs of a girl lying on her stomach, so that it looks as if he is buggering her. He is being simultaneously buggered, and as he comes, she cuts the bird's throat. Sade goes on to stories about a nobleman who buggers a dead girl, a libertine who has a prostitute hanged while her daughter masturbates him, and another who sticks pins all over a girl's body. Meanwhile the Duke, increasingly aroused by the stories, whips Augustine viciously, and refuses to eat except out of her mouth. After wounding her in the arm, he brings himself to orgasm by sucking her blood. The next step towards human sacrifice is taken when they break the finger of Adelaide, Durcet's wife. By the end of the month, the victims in the stories are being blinded and having nipples, buttocks, and ears cut off. Pieces of flesh are roasted and eaten. Tortures are inflicted with hot irons and molten lead. The stories excite the libertines to the point of burning Adelaide with a hot iron inside the vagina, under the armpits and on the nipples.

The last of the story-tellers begins February with several variations on the theme of watching paupers starve to death. She says that one of the most refined pleasures available is that of buggering a girl with a black silk cord around her neck, and strangling her at the moment of orgasm. There are stories about burning bodies with a candle, and stuffing gunpowder or fuses into orifices. Some of the stories about gratuitous evil-doing have no connection with sexuality. One anecdote is about poison planted in the earth to kill anyone who walks above it; this is reminiscent of Marlowe's Jew of Malta:

> As for myself, I walk abroad o' nights,
> And kill sick people groaning under walls,
> Sometimes I go about and poison wells.

Both the torturers and their victims were Sade's victims in one of
his most extreme attempts to push beyond the limits of reason.
As in polluting crucifixes with Jeanne Testard or in desecrating
the holiest day of the Christian year with Rose Keller, part of his
object was to find out how far he could go; but this time he was
also testing Durcet's dictum about 'things which are not here'.
The Duke is making essentially the same point when he says: 'The
idea of evil is more exciting than the fact of libertinage.' How
excited could Sade himself become about sadistic pleasures that
were not available to him or about crimes he was not committing?
The death instinct, as Freud would later define it, is never apparent in its pure state, but the structure of Sade's novel was carrying
him unusually close to a verbal adumbration of it, and to a direct
confrontation with the schizoid elements in himself. In schizo-
phrenia, the libido withdraws narcissistically from the external
world into an overvaluation of words, but this, according to
Freud, represents 'the first of the attempts at recovery or cure'.
Complete cure would involve a return to the external world and
a rediscovery of objects corresponding to the lost objects of childhood. Sade's imprisonment resulted in a withdrawal which was at
once more complete and more artificial than the withdrawal of the
schizophrenic, but can we compare the writing of *120 journées* with
an effort at self-cure? If his notes for the final ninety days con-
stituted an attempt to horrify himself, the fact that he abandoned
the book may mean that they succeeded. Adelaide, he noted,
would be slaughtered 'in fearful torments which you will describe
in detail'. He never did. The writing of the draft may have
brought him to terms neither with the actions of his persecutors
nor with the destructive pressures operating inside him, but it
made him turn to a very different kind of literary project. The
novel for which he gave up *120 journées* is a philosophical
novel with little violence and no description of the sexual act.
There was now obviously much less interdependence between
the act of writing and the act of masturbation. It may also
be significant that he abandoned an action which was leading
towards wholesale slaughter in favour of an action in which

one of the heroines, feigning death, uses a coffin as a means of escape.

In so far as the abandonment of *120 journées* represented a failure, it was a failure to solve a problem which was partly moral, partly one of language. During the first thirty days, the physical assaults on the victims' bodies had been, in effect, secondary to the indoctrination that assaulted their innocence, so it had been possible to sustain the paradoxical equation of good with evil, which works well enough when perversion is being represented as natural. But Sade seems to have been partly aware that he would run into difficulties, and his notes suggest a semi-conscious pressure to manœuvre himself into a position where his argument would become untenable. Writing to Renée-Pélagie about his plays, he had once said there was no need for viciousness to be denounced: it was enough that the reader should come to dislike it. No reader of *120 journées* can fail to dislike the four libertines before February is over.

Embedded in the language Sade was using were the values of the culture in which it had evolved. The word *good* confused the ethical with the desirable. Not unaware of the difficulty, Sade was focusing on the problem of truth in his notes for the second week of the final month. Severe punishments are being meted out to the boys and girls who cannot provide excrement for the libertines who want to eat it. They are guilty of breaking the rules if they have conformed with the normal rules of hygiene and flushed it down the lavatory; they are innocent if the reason they cannot provide any is that they have given all they had to another libertine. But what if he deliberately gets them into trouble by denying it? This happens twice. There is also an episode in one of the stories about a man in the habit of hiding objects in his servants' trunks, and then calling in the police to denounce them as thieves. If they are hanged, he watches; if they are not, he strangles them, exciting himself to the point of orgasm. Meanwhile, in the main story, Augustine has been plotting to escape with one of the four 'fuckers' with large penises, but when one of the old women discovers the plot, she denounces them. The man is tortured to death; Augustine is made to assist in the tortures; the old woman has one of her breasts cut off. When she objects that there is no justice in this, the Duke explains: 'Had it been just, it would not have given us an erection.'

A great deal of blood flows in the final weeks. Breasts, buttocks, arms and legs are cut off, fingernails and teeth are torn out, burns are inflicted, and in one of the stories, a little girl is boiled. None of the victims on either level of narrative ever seems to offer any resistance. The notes seldom go into detail about the tortures, but they give a full account of one gruesome episode which starts when the Duke makes love to Augustine for the last time, and which ends with her vivisection. However much Sade was horrifying himself with what he wrote, he did not sever the umbilical cord of empathy with the Duke, for whom, as for himself, orgasm is associated with anger. 'He discharged, but he was angrier when he withdrew.' As the girl finally gives up the ghost, Sade's note ends: 'So perished at the age of fifteen years and eight months one of the most heavenly creatures nature had ever formed. Etc. Eulogy of her.' The use of 'heavenly' as a compliment is one indication of the way Sade's vocabulary was at odds with his cynicism, and had he tried to finish the book, he would have found it increasingly difficult to maintain a balance of sympathy.

It is possible that he felt he could not complete *120 journées* until he had written *Aline et Valcour*: it may be that he wanted to investigate the same moral problems from a different angle. The new novel explores the opposite hemisphere of human experience, and the hero's name inverts Curval's. Writing, fifteen years later, about *Aline et Valcour*, Sade said: 'I do not want to win sympathy for vice. It is not my object . . . to make women love the men who deceive them . . . Those of my heroes who follow the path of vice I made so frightful that they will surely inspire neither pity nor love.' As a retrospective statement of intention this is not altogether specious, but it is one-sided. It filters out all the negative elements, rather as Sade had in his apologetic letters to his father, and to police and government officials. Neither the positive nor the negative elements in his writing are intrinsically as interesting as the tension between them.

To shift from one novel to another may seem like an act of impatience. Possibly Sade may have felt—as when he ignored Canon Vidal's attempts to make him stay away from Lacoste in 1778—that he was in the grip of an irresistible hand. But the actual work on *Aline et Valcour* called for much more patience than anything he had yet written. Even in the completed part of *120 jour-*

nées, the action shifts rapidly from one incident to the next and from one level of narrative to the other. In *Aline et Valcour*, an epistolary novel in the manner of Richardson, the action is extremely slow. Treated less summarily, some of the incidents are actualized much more vividly. As a writer, Sade may have become impatient with his own impatience, sensing that he needed to master a more leisurely narrative style.

To some extent the technical problems and the moral problems were interdependent. Most of the letter-writers in *Aline et Valcour* are men and women who abide by the moral conventions and express strong disapproval of libertine behaviour. Sade gives them a great deal of free rein, contenting himself with a footnote to correct Léonore's assertion that libertinage suffocates the natural impulses: 'It does not suffocate natural impulses but it leads to egoism. The libertine's desires are in conflict with social duties ... and it undermines them.' It is partly because the question of social duties is central to the novel that the attitude to libertinism is so much more critical. The novel dramatizes a genuine ambivalence: this time, instead of being used to reinforce the same principles, argument and action begin to pull in different directions.

Cannibalism on the African island of Butua symbolizes the sadistic exploitation of the weak by the strong, and there is an intricate argument in favour of the system. Sarmiento, the Portuguese favourite of the King, admits that violence and injustice are always basic to monarchical government, but he maintains that: 'The necessity of slavery was established by nature when she buried gold in the entrails of the earth. Human arms would be needed to dig it out.' He also argues that pleasure does not need to be shared. Fontenelle is quoted in a footnote: 'The desire to give other people happiness is only the result of self-love and conceit. Is not the sultan in his seraglio a thousand times more modest?' According to Sarmiento, Nature creates only to destroy, and human vices are her instrument. The crimes of the tyrannous Roman emperors were her means of contriving the Empire's disintegration. But the action bites back at the argument when Sarmiento, having plotted to destroy his cannibal King, is himself destroyed.

In many ways, life on the cannibal island is reminiscent of the château in *120 journées*. Women, according to the Butuans, are made to be used, not adored. It offends the gods if the adoration due only to them is lavished on a simple creature. When Sainville arrives on the island, he is inspected as a bull is by a butcher. Sarmiento pronounces him too lean to be eaten and too old to be enjoyed, although the prince is bored with women. There are too many of them. They are divided according to age. As sexual fodder they are best between childhood and the age of sixteen. Human sacrifices are made from the age-group sixteen to twenty, but these girls are not eaten because boy-flesh tastes better. Female slaves are between twenty and thirty. A father has absolute rights, including those of life and death, over his women, children and slaves. Nor does he discriminate between them. His wife must kneel to address him. If she produces an heir, disgust will be her reward.

Just as the project of diversifying the sexual 'passions' was built into the structure of *120 journées*, the narrative of *Aline et Valcour* is designed to proliferate contrasting attitudes to the problem of social duties. Butua generates its antithesis: on the utopian island of Tamoë, the King, Zamé, is a vegetarian. He argues that all men are equal 'in the hands of Nature . . . and wherever they are equal, they can be happy'. It is only opinion which creates the differences that make one part of a nation live at the expense of the rest. The legislator should work for the common happiness, and there should be no punishment for incest or sodomy, which do no harm to society. Like Gustavus III of Sweden, Zamé boasts of being 'the state's first citizen'. He is more concerned to be liked than to be respected, maintaining that government exists only to guarantee liberty.

Through Zamé's mouth Sade comments on the disparity between current reality and the ideal. 'Everywhere I can divide men into two classes, both equally pitiable. In one are the rich slaves of their own pleasure; in the other, the unfortunate victims of their fate.' Zamé is also Sade's spokesman for a direct attack on the Parlements, which are 'useless because they cannot alleviate monarchical despotism, and they prevent equality from being established'. In his indignation at the magistrates, Sade forgets that the King is not a Frenchman. His heart bleeds, he tells us, 'it breaks in pieces when I recall how this infamous class has spread evil all over my country'. Nor would anyone but a French nobleman have been quite so outraged at the way the French nobility 'consents to give authority over itself to a magistracy which is no longer drawn from its own ranks'. This, says Zamé, is what puzzled him when he was passing through France. Though Sade pulls him badly out of character in using him as a mouthpiece, he is not presented uncritically, and again the criticism is introduced quite subtly through the situation. Zamé would not be willing to introduce parliamentary government of the English sort. 'Less dangerous for the people, no doubt, but much more restricting for me. The more I divide my power, the more I reduce it, and since my only desire is to do good, I do not want anything to stand in my way.' This exposes the egotism of the benevolent despot, and it points to the central flaw in the French system of government. The country, as Turgot realized, had no constitution.

For Louis XIV this had been an advantage. He used the old nobility and the new bureaucracy like stilts, keeping one foot on each and never losing his balance. For Louis XVI, who had a weaker personality and a greater sense of social responsibility, it was a disadvantage. Even if he had been less easily confused by conflicting advice, he would not have been able to eliminate more than a small minority of the crucial abuses, though he could hardly have had a better adjutant than Turgot. When he was appointed Minister of Finances in 1774, Turgot had been Intendant of the *généralité* of Limoges for twelve years, so he was familiar with the difficulties of bridging between central government and local needs. Constitutionally, all the executive power was in the hands of the King, who had six councils to advise him. None of the councillors was likely to be well informed about local variations in the price of bread or possible improvements in methods of tilling the fields or of milling the grain or about cattle epidemics or conditions affecting the crops. In September 1775, Turgot instructed Du Pont de Nemours to draw up a *Mémoire sur les municipalités*, which would have been presented to Louis XVI if Turgot had not been removed from office too soon. It characterized the French nation as

a realm composed of different social orders which have no real unity and of people who have very few social ties. It is a country where, in consequence, each man is concerned with his private interest only, where hardly anyone takes the trouble to fulfil his duties or to recognize his relationships with his fellows,

with the result that there is a perpetual conflict of competing
and particularist interests which reason and common enlightenment have never regulated.

Ideally, the remedy was to introduce a constitution, which is what
Turgot would eventually have done if he had been given the
power. But even if Louis had wholeheartedly wanted to support
Turgot, they would not have been able to carry the programme
through unless they could have created either a dictatorship based
on military strength or an alliance with the masses.[1] The revolution
was inevitable because reform could not have been carried very
far without more inroads into privilege than the privileged classes
would have tolerated. During his twenty months in office Turgot
did a great deal towards eliminating waste, but while he understood that the health of the economy depended on the free flow
of capital through the national bloodstream, he could do little to
relieve either the sclerosis caused by the restrictions on trade or
the taxation that fell crushingly on farmers, traders and labourers.
Those who enjoyed fiscal privileges would have fought hard
against innovations that threatened to deprive them of both
money and prestige.

The vested interests supported each other. Zamé's puzzlement
at the nobility's acceptance of the magistrates' authority could be
taken as a comment on what had happened when Turgot wanted
to abolish the guilds, which were keeping the price of food on an
unnecessarily high level. The *gens du palais*, nervous of losing the
litigation that the guilds initiated, argued that without them the
markets would be flooded with inferior produce, while the Prince
de Conti led the magistrates in their resistance to Turgot's re-
forms. Sade may have had strong private reasons for hating the
magistracy, but his satire bears pertinently on the social situation.
In one episode Léonore and her friend Clémentine find themselves at the mercy of four lecherous Portuguese magistrates, who
want to enjoy the girls before restoring the luggage which has
been stolen from them.

'Should you make conditions when it is a matter of returning
what belongs to us?'

[1] Cp David Dakin, *Turgot and the Ancien Régime in France*, Methuen,
1939.

'This logic is not ours,' said one of the distinguished rogues.
'The strongest are always the master of the law.'

This corresponds with the premiss from which Hue de Miro-
mesnil, the Keeper of the Seals, argued against Turgot's proposals for reform. The abolition of privilege, he maintained,
would jeopardize the whole social fabric and the military great-
ness of the French nation. Countering the attack, Turgot went
straight to the central issue. If taxation is nothing but a burden
imposed on the weak by force, the King, who 'is raised above all
for the good of all', has become, in effect, an enemy of his own
people.

As a barometric reading of the pressure towards revolution,
Aline et Valcour is remarkably accurate. Sainville forecasts: 'The
energy of your citizens will soon break the sceptre of despotism
and tyranny, trampling underfoot the sinners who serve them.'
Claiming to be a prophet, the bandit Brigandos announces that:
'France will undergo terrible revolution. She will shake off the
yoke of despotism.' The Curé de Berseuil evokes Sodom in his
reading of the future: 'Your modern Babylon will be annihilated
like that of Semiramis . . . and the state, enervated in beautifying
this new Sodom, will be engulfed in the same way under your
gilded ruins.' And Zamé predicts: 'You Frenchmen will finish up
by throwing off the yoke of despotism and by becoming republicans in your turn.' Admittedly, since the novel was not published
until 1793, there was nothing to prevent Sade from prophesying
the event after it had occurred, but in a careful consideration of
this question, Jean-Marie Goulemot[1] concludes that at least the
first three of these forecasts were written before 1789.

Turgot, who had contributed five articles to Diderot's *Encyclopédie*, shared the Physiocrats' belief in the importance of freeing
the grain trade; Sade makes the Curé de Berseuil propose the
same solution: 'diminish taxation; honour, encourage agriculture.' But Sade would not have wanted to concern himself in any
detail with social and economic problems, even if he had known
more about them. He goes to the opposite extreme, working in a
social vacuum with random political and geographical details
introduced perfunctorily to surround the argument with a semblance

[1] 'Lecture Politique d'*Aline et Valcour*', in *Le Marquis de Sade*, Centre
Aixois.

of situation. Whereas the best writing in Rousseau's novel *La Nouvelle Héloise* is the description of landscape, nothing in *Aline et Valcour* is worse than Sade's attempts at descriptive writing. He had not looked at a landscape or at furniture in a home for eight years. A forest in his fiction is an indeterminate place of danger; a castle symbolizes either safety or imprisonment. Nor could his characterization or his study of motivation be anything but schematic. He had not observed the expressions changing on human faces; he had not been involved in complicated relationships.

During the last four years before the outbreak of revolution in 1789 he was writing rapidly and prolifically, but all his information was second-hand. In describing sand-storms and tropical animals he drew on the travellers' books that Renée-Pélagie had been providing, and his Africa is fabricated haphazardly out of details from miscellaneous sources: the rivers are 'edged with lilies, jonquils and tulips'. For information about Portugal and Spain, countries he had never visited, he was dependent on his correspondence with her, and in the middle of December 1786 he was still waiting for her answers to questions he had formulated on 25 November. Topographically the book might have been less inaccurate if she had been visiting him more frequently during the three years he was working on it—November 1785–October 1788. But in the summer of 1786 Le Noir had been replaced as Lieutenant-General of Police by de Crosne, and when Renée-Pélagie appealed to him for permission to resume regular visits to Sade, he consulted de Launay. The Commandant's reply is dated 7 July: 'The prisoner, who is extremely difficult and violent, constantly made scenes with her, especially on the day when he did not want to obey the rule about speaking out loud.' This enabled the prison officer to monitor conversations.

Police records contain many letters from him full of horrors about his wife, his family and us. When he took exercise, he insulted the sentries for no reason at all . . . Since he has not been seeing anyone, his behaviour has improved. The goodness and decency of Mme la marquise de Sade makes her ask to see him, but almost invariably she receives nothing but torrents of insults and imbecilities. The truth is that she is afraid for her life, if the time should come when his liberty is restored.

It was not until February 1787 that she was again able to pay regular visits.

Perhaps there would have been an equally striking resemblance between the villains of the novel and the Montreuils even if he had been seeing more of her. In *120 journées* two of the libertines had been noble, two bourgeois. In *Aline et Valcour*, all the sympathetic characters are noble, while the two villains are members of the same professions as Durcet and Curval—a financier and a president of a Parlement. Dolbourg and the Président de Blamont are remarkably similar in outlook and strategy to the four 'champions' of *120 journées*. Sade again chews over his experience as the victim of an arranged marriage, showing parents in the process of sacrificing their children to their own convenience. But unlike the libertines of *120 journées*, Dolbourg and de Blamont are unequivocally characterized as villains. The experience of writing the earlier novel had forced Sade to reconsider his evaluation of those who discard all moral restraints. He had discovered that fiction could help him towards a crystallization of his attitudes, and to some extent he was even moving towards a new synthesis between aristocratic and bourgeois values. Birth, breeding and honour are still rated very highly, but while Valcour considers it *infra dig* to work for a living, Léonore does not. Like Richardson's bourgeois heroines, she has only one weapon—her brain—for defending her virtue against the persistent attacks of ruthless predators, while loss of virtue would be a greater degradation than loss of status.

All through the novel, the epistolary method swings Sade between male and female viewpoints. The long letter from Léonore (No 38), anticipates his later narrative in the first person about a beautiful girl who has to shift for herself in a series of dangerous adventures tirelessly resisting the superior strength of the male. The theme will become central in several of the stories in *Les Crimes de l'amour* and in the three successive versions of the same story: *Les Infortunes de la vertu, Justine* and *La Nouvelle Justine*.

It took Sade only a fortnight (23 June–8 July 1787) to write *Les Infortunes de la vertu*—138 pages—although, as he noted in the margin of the final page, 'I have had trouble with my eyes while doing it.' But the discomfort did not prevent him from giving his sense of humour more play than it could have had if he had been writing up the notes for the final sections of *120 journées*. In *Aline et Valcour* too there is some welcome comedy. When Léonore is forced into a convent by parental opposition to her marriage with Sainville, he rescues her after persuading a sculptor to co-operate in a plot. She has to pose as a statue which will later be removed from the chapel. During the night an old nun comes in to pray. She wants finally to kiss the statue's face but it is dark, and after an hour of motionlessness Léonore is tickled on a part of her body that no hand has ever touched. Taking the movement for a miracle, the nun prays with redoubled fervour.

'What use are novels?' Sade asked later in *Idée sur les romans*, which he published in 1801. 'As a picture of secular manners, the novel is as necessary as history to the philosopher who wants to understand humanity. History is an etching of the actions in which man lets himself be seen, but at those moments he is not seen as himself—his face is masked with ambition and pride. But the novelist catches him when the mask is off, and the painting, which is much more interesting, is also more true.' His own novels are lacking in domestic details, but it is almost as if he were anticipating this criticism when he wrote in *Aline et Valcour*: 'Instead of the fancy furniture that does not produce a single idea, I wish people had in their houses a kind of tree in relief, with the name of a vice written on each branch, beginning with the slightest of deviations, and working up by degrees to the crime engendered by oblivion of fundamental obligations. Would such a moral picture not have its use?'

With sufficient expertise at turning things upside down, even the immoralist multiplication table of *120 journées* can be given a moral application.

He praised Richardson and Fielding for their success in 'sketching male characters who, playthings and victims of that cardiac effervescence known as love, show at the same time its dangers and its miseries. Only through this kind of observation is it possible to achieve those developments and passions which are so well realized in the English novel . . . Only the deepest study of the human heart—that veritable maze of nature—can inspire the novelist, whose function is to make us see not only what man is . . . but what he can be, what vice and the shocks of passion can make him become. It is therefore essential to know all of them and to use all of them if one wishes to work in this genre.'

Sade was sufficiently a man of his century to believe in the possibility of providing a clear and comprehensive map of the maze. His ambition was encyclopaedic: the listing of 600 passions in *120 journées* was intended not as representative but as complete. Alongside *Aline et Valcour* he was working on a project for four volumes of stories under the title *Contes et Fabliaux du XVIIIe Siècle par un Troubadour Provençal.* In his opinion, Boccaccio, Dante and even Petrarch had been influenced by the Troubadours' ideal of chivalry. Sade's attitude was anti-chivalric, though his sympathy is divided when Sarmiento tells Sainville: 'You still love in the style of the tenth century. You remind me of the gallant heroes of antiquity, and I find this virtue charming, though I am far from being inclined to adopt it.' Sade's ambivalence expresses itself through his irony, his parody and his inversion of the mode he used for his stories, adapting the moral tale to the purposes of immoralism.

The plan for *Contes et Fabliaux* formed the base from which he made all his subsequent excursions into fiction. The unpublished story *Les Infortunes de la vertu* was intended for inclusion in the collection. The notes he made for it show that his planning was no less schematic and no less mathematical than it had been for *120 journées.* He made a numbered list of seven 'harassed virtues' which were to serve as the basis for ten incidents:

1. Shame, 2. Shame, 3. Horror of Evil, 4. Shame, 5. Pity, 6. Charity, 7. Piety, 8. Prudence, 9. Love of Goodness and Truth, 10. Charity.

Though he was to abandon the two episodes he sketched out to illustrate Pity and Prudence, and to add an unplanned sequence about lecherous monks, the blueprint served him well. He had realized (as he later formulated it in *Idée sur les romans*) that 'it is not necessary to make virtue triumph . . . If, after the toughest of trials, we see virtue finally floored by vice, our souls are inevitably rended and, having moved us exceedingly, having, as Diderot says, "bloodied our hearts inside out", the work should undoubtedly arouse the interest that alone wins laurels.' The comment, like the story, may have been based partly on the Abbé Prévost's *Manon Lescaut.* Sade went on to say: 'What tears one sheds in reading this delicious novel. What description of Nature! How the interest is held! How it increases by degrees! What difficulties are surmounted! What philosophy emerges from this interest in a lost girl! ... It was from her that Rousseau learned how, despite imprudence and stupidity, a heroine can still claim to soften our hearts.'

Sade's heroine was lost for different reasons, while her imprudence and stupidity are of a different order. The intention of the book, as declared on the first page, is to teach the 'unhappy individual biped', who is 'perpetually buffeted about by the caprices of the being who, it is said, controls him so despotically', that the virtues 'have never encountered anything but thorns, while the wicked gathered only roses'.

But is this despotism malevolent or merely chaotic? If there is no justice either in our dealings with each other or in providential interventions, is it because there is never any connection between an action and the apparent sequel or because our ideas of justice are misconceived? The pattern of *Les Infortunes de la vertu* is that Justine's actions are consistently virtuous and the sequel invariably unpleasant. She rebuffs the advances of a financier, refuses to steal for a miser, to join a band of robbers or to help the man she loves in a plot to poison his mother. She rescues a twelve-year-old girl who would have been vivisected by two surgeons. After preserving her virginity throughout these adventures, she takes refuge in a remote monastery, where she is helpless in the hands of four libertine monks. When she finally escapes, she has her purse stolen as she takes it out to give charity. When she helps a man who seems to be dying, she is raped, kidnapped and forced to work for a gang of coiners. Warning a man that he is about to be robbed, she is robbed herself and accused of a murder. Trying to save a baby from a fire, and killing it accidentally, she is accused of arson. The framing irony is that the lovely woman listening to Justine's account of her misadventures turns out to be her sister, Juliette, who by ruthlessness has risen to the top. Her career, which will later be given a long novel to itself, parallels that of Beauvoisin and other actresses Sade had known. Many of them had worked their way up through 'cruel apprenticeships'. As he said, some of the bodies now lying in the beds of princes might still carry humiliating marks left by depraved libertines. Juliette's current lover is powerful enough to save Justine, but she is on her way to the scaffold when she is killed by lightning, which strikes her breast and contorts her beautiful features.

The narrative presents a succession of events with no apparent causal connections. If Sade's prose had been as advanced as his thinking, it could have been said of *Les Infortunes de la vertu*, as Jean-Paul Sartre later said of Camus's novel *L'Etranger*, that the discontinuity of the sentences models itself on a temporal discontinuity. Fictional narrative, said Sartre, 'demands continuous duration, a process of becoming, the manifest presence of the irreversibility of time. But in *L'Etranger* each sentence is clean, unsmudged, self-enclosed . . . Between each sentence and the next, the world is annihilated and reborn. . . In *L'Etranger* a sentence is an island. And we cascade from sentence to sentence, from nothing to nothing.'[1] Sartre thought Camus was borrowing from Hemingway, and certainly the stylistic similarity is striking, but the deeper debt is to Sade.

Sade's negativism is at the root of Camus's notion of the Absurd. In Sartre's summing-up, absurdity manifests 'the divorce between human aspirations to unity and the insurmountable dualism of mind and nature, between man's impulse towards the eternal and the finite character of his existence, between the "concern" which is his very essence and the vanity of his efforts. Death, the irreducible pluralism of truth and creation, the incomprehensibility of reality, accident—those are the keypoints of absurdity.' Justine, the martyr of merciless accidents, is the female forerunner of Absurd Man.

She is isolated like no previous character in Sade's fiction. He had to separate Léonore and Sainville for them to have their adventures, but each of them strives constantly for reunion with the other. Aline finds that in the end she can be faithful to Valcour only by killing herself, so she is a martyr to the idea of love, whereas Justine's experience erodes her belief in the possibility of mutual goodwill. Each time she offers her love, her help or her services, she lays herself open to vicious exploitation, whether it is fate that is being vindictive, or a man. The only glimpse of social justice occurs in the episode of the coiners, which, as Philippe Roger points out,[1] suggests a feudal utopia. The cut-throat Dalville is replaced as leader of the gang by the fair-minded Roland, who treats his serfs more equitably than any normal seigneur, accommodating them comfortably in a castle and feeding them

[1] 'Explication de *L'Etranger*', reprinted in *Situations I*, Gallimard, 1947.
[2] *Sade: La Philosophie dans le pressoir*.

well. Justine no longer wants to escape, but the happy interlude is illegal. As Roger says, 'the reality of an evil society irrupts into the feudal dream, and the utopian forgers are put in chains by the disorderly forces of law and order: "in a totally corrupt world", Juliette will not be able to "recommend anything but vice".' Between evildoers, alliances are possible. Juliette has her lover; the lecherous monks, like the libertines in *120 journées*, form a quartet. But altruism will not be reciprocated. 'One of our greatest prejudices,' wrote Sade, 'arises out of our gratuitous supposition that we can form a bond with someone else. The bond is chimerical . . . absurd.'

Aline et Valcour had represented a tentative and abortive attempt to compromise with the optimistic humanism of the Enlightenment and the stress it laid on the social virtues. D. H. Lawrence said:[1]

> the 'good man' of today was produced in the chemical retorts of the brain and emotional centres of people like Rousseau and Diderot . . . You must be honest in your material dealings, you must be kind to the poor, and you must have 'feelings' for your fellow-man and for nature . . . In order to get nice 'feelings' out of things, you must of course be quite 'free', you mustn't be interfered with. And to be 'free', you must incur the enmity of no man, you must be 'good'. And when everybody is 'good' and 'free', then we shall all have nice feelings about everything.

In *Aline et Valcour*, Sade's characters talk about social duties and social relationships, but, in spite of himself, Sade revealed his lack of respect for the *honnête homme* by making all his bourgeois characters unsympathetic. In *Les Infortunes de la vertu* the only male characters who behave decently are bourgeois, but Sade is less concerned with social or personal relationships than relationships between the individual and Nature. The law that features most prominently is the natural law of destruction. Of the men Justine encounters, the one who most resembles Sade is the Marquis de Bressac, whom she sees committing alfresco sodomy with his eighteen-year-old valet. His excuse for planning to kill his mother is that her corpse will be food for worms, whose life is of no less value than hers.

[1] 'The Good Man' in *Phoenix*, Heinemann, 1936.

When Sade turns to social problems in other stories, it is to make the point that institutions and laws are counterproductive. In 'Faxelange', for instance, he again uses bandits to represent an alternative justice, and he uses the leader of the gang to advance the argument that punishment causes crime:

> Do not be surprised that men turn criminal when, albeit innocent, they are degraded. Do not be surprised that they prefer crime to shackles, when one situation is as shameful as the other. Legislators, if you want less crimes to be committed, do not be so eager to stigmatize. A nation that learns to worship honour can dispense with scaffolds.

This is once again to reassert the values of the aristocracy, while deriding the activities of the magistracy.

The abrasiveness of Sade's fiction contrasts oddly with his effusive reaction when Renée-Pélagie gave him a miniature portrait of herself in August 1787: it was a 'precious, divine present' which gave him feelings that, 'constantly multiplied until the day of his death, will cause a thousand fresh flowers to blossom above the thorns of his life'. In October she brought a new oculist to attend him, and in June 1788 he was allowed to consult a doctor about his eyes, though de Losme suspected that Sade was hoping Dr Lassaigne would recommend exercise. When his right to take walks had again been suspended, he tried to ignore the order confining him to his cell, only to find that an armed warder had been stationed outside. Sade was forced back at gunpoint.

But in September, after agitating for a change of cell, he was moved up to the sixth storey of the same tower. The cell overlooked the rue Saint-Antoine, and it is possible that Sade had been asking for the change because, knowing the streets were full of disorderly crowds, he wanted a better vantage point.

France was on the verge of the revolution he had predicted. The King had been forced by the Paris Parlement to summon the Estates-General. The French Revolution was to be dominated by the bourgeoisie, but at this stage the conflict was still between the monarchy and the Parlement, and the convocation of the Estates-General was not even a gesture in the direction of democracy. In 1614 nobility, clergy and 'third estate' had each had an equal number of representatives. Even when it was agreed that the third estate should now have twice as many as the others, the bourgeoisie would still have been powerless if each order had voted separately, as in 1614. As Abbé Sieyès argued in his pamphlet, *Qu'est-ce que le Tiers-état?*, the French people consisted of the third estate, which had constantly been deprived of its political rights. The clergy was really less an estate of the realm than a profession, while the aristocracy was elevated by unfair privileges. It was high time France had a constitution. The people must be represented in the Estates-General, and the Estates-General must have legislative power.

The influence of the pamphleteers was evident in the slogans shouted by the revolutionary crowds. But despite the high proportion of peasant voters, it was the well established middle-class citizens—mostly lawyers—who were elected as deputies. When they had their first meeting on 5 May 1789, it still looked as though double representation was not going to save the third estate, but by 16 June it was being proposed that it should constitute itself into a national assembly, and on 17 June the proposal, reformulated by Sieyès (who had been elected as a deputy) was carried. Without royal sanction the assembly was implicitly claiming legislative power. On 19 June the clergy voted in favour of joining it, but on 20 June the third estate was locked out of the hall in which it was due to meet. Writing to Gaufridy two days later, Renée-Pélagie described the rumours she had heard about the meeting it had held on a tennis-court, about angry mobs and anti-clerical sentiment.

In 1789 the average unskilled labourer in Paris was earning about 25 sous a day, and by the beginning of February a 4 lb loaf of bread, which normally cost 8 or 9 sous, was costing 14½. But it was not until August that the first of the bread riots occurred. At the end of the month soldiers fired on a mob of 600 demonstrators, killing seven or eight. In September shots were fired on a crowd attacking the house of the Chevalier Dubois, the unpopular commander of the Garde de Paris, and at the end of the month he resigned.

The winter of 1788–9 had been extremely severe. After the bad harvest, hungry, unemployed countryfolk converged on the capital where they mingled in the street with jobless workmen. Dissidence was fomented by mob orators, who played on the suspicion that grain was being hoarded by the rich. By the end of April dangerous riots were breaking out. Several hundred workmen congregated near the Bastille, and, armed with sticks, marched behind a drummer, picking up recruits until there were 3,000 of them. Employers were burned in effigy, two houses were destroyed, food shops were raided. During a siege on the house of a wallpaper manufacturer, troops were ordered to fire on the crowd bottle-necked into a narrow street, and several hundred people were killed. Thousands of dissidents took to rallying every night at the Palais Royal. Orators and pamphleteers mooted new ideas for action. At the end of June, a crowd was sent to liberate eleven guardsmen who had been imprisoned in the Abbaye for refusing to fire on demonstrators at Versailles. The rioting became more organized. Internal customs barriers were burned and the customs officers' documents destroyed, but looting was checked. Grain and weapons were collected in a series of organized raids. Defectors from the army were joining the revolutionaries, and a civilian militia had been formed to counter the dual dangers of internal anarchy and military intervention from outside.

At the Bastille, de Launay had given orders for the cannon to be kept loaded and for prisoners to be barred from the towers. In Sade's cell there was a long tin pipe with a funnel at one end; it had been given to him for disposing of urine and dirty water through the window. At midday on 2 July he used it as a megaphone. Yelling to the people in the street, he gathered a crowd, and then appealed for help. Prisoners in the Bastille were being slaughtered, he shouted. Unless the citizens came to his aid, his own throat would be cut.

Alarmed, de Launay wrote to M. de Villedeuil, Minister of State: 'At a time like the present, it is very dangerous to have this man here . . . It would be desirable to transfer this Prisoner to Charenton or some establishment of that kind, where he would be unable to disrupt discipline, as he constantly does here. This would be the right moment to be rid of this person whom nothing can daunt, no superior officer can break.'

M. de Villedeuil acted swiftly. At 1 o'clock in the morning Sade was pulled out of bed by six men armed with pistols. They forced him to dress very quickly, and, as before, he could take nothing with him. He was pushed into a cab and driven to the asylum of Charenton, five miles outside Paris, leaving behind not only his furniture, his clothes and 600 books, but fifteen volumes of his own work in manuscript.

Ten days later the Bastille was besieged by about 900 people. They had not come to liberate Sade or the seven remaining prisoners but to commandeer the gunpowder that had been sent from the arsenal. At 10 o'clock in the morning a deputation arrived to negotiate with de Launay. The emissaries were invited inside for luncheon. The crowd outside became restive, suspecting a trap. Shouts went out demanding the surrender of the fortress. A second deputation went inside. The cannons were withdrawn from the battlements, and de Launay promised not to fire unless attacked. One of the drawbridges had been left raised but undefended. When two men from the crowd climbed the wall and cut the chain to lower it, de Launay thought an attack was beginning. He gave the order to fire. Ninety-eight people in the crowd were killed, and seventy-eight wounded. Reinforcements were called. Taking their orders from a former non-commissioned officer, two detachments of the National Guard marched to the Bastille with five cannons that had been removed from the Invalides. De Launay offered to surrender on condition that his men's lives were spared, but the crowd was in no mood for conditions. His next idea was to blow up the fortress, but he allowed himself to be dissuaded, and the main drawbridge was lowered to the invading soldiers and civilians. Of the 110 men inside the fortress, six or seven were slaughtered. De Launay was promised a safe conduct to the Hôtel de Ville, but on the way a cook cut off his head with a butcher's knife.

Chapter 10

Revolution

Unlike the Bastille and Vincennes, Charenton was not a state prison but a lunatic asylum run by friars. In the file they opened for Sade on 4 July 1789, it was noted that he had been imprisoned since 1777 at the request of his family and was to be detained indefinitely. He had been found innocent of sodomy and poisoning, but had indulged outrageously in libertinage, and was prone to periods of madness.

Anxious to recover his manuscripts and his other possessions from the Bastille, Sade appointed Renée-Pélagie as his trustee, signing an authorization for the seals on the cell door to be broken in her presence; but she did nothing until after the siege, when she wrote to Chenon, the commissioner who had put the seals on the door, asking him to remove her husband's property in her absence and to have it all delivered to the asylum.

The mob had broken into Sade's cell and taken everything in sight. 'I had been extremely busy in prison,' he told Gaufridy. 'Just imagine, my dear lawyer, I had fifteen volumes ready for the printer ... With an unconcern that is unforgivable, Mme de Sade has let some be lost and others taken, which means thirteen years simply wasted! ... Everything has been torn up, burnt, carried off, pillaged. There is nothing I can do to recover a scrap of it. And all because of Mme de Sade's pure negligence. She had ten days to recover my things. She must have known that the Bastille, which was being stuffed all this time with weapons, gunpowder, soldiers, was being prepared either for attack or defence. Why then did she not hurry to remove my things? ... My manuscripts? ... For the loss of my manuscripts I have shed tears of blood! ... Beds, tables, chests of drawers can be replaced, but not ideas ... No, my friend, no, I will never be able to describe for you my despair at this loss. It is irreparable for me.' In the fiction he wrote from now on, he compulsively recreated parts of the lost *120 journées*, knowing that his memories would be inaccurate, and that the fragments he could reproduce would be different in a different context.

In August, after denying responsibility for the loss, Renée-Pélagie sent a message: she was doing what she could to extricate him from the lunatic asylum, but he should not expect his liberty to be restored. Since the fall of the Bastille, many aristocrats had emigrated. Unemployment was rising while food supplies dwindled. The high prices were being blamed on corn-speculators and counter-revolutionaries. As the Paris mob grew more belligerent, the moderates petitioned the King to move the National Assembly outside the city, but it still seemed that the country was drifting towards constitutional monarchy. On 4 August, the Duc d'Aiguillon and the Vicomte de Noailles took the lead in proposing to the Assembly that feudal privileges and tax exemptions should be abolished, while all citizens should become eligible for public office. In the euphoric close to the session, the King was praised as if the initiative had been his. But when legislation was drafted, he refused to sanction it. Nor would he consent to the Declaration of Rights, in which the moderates defined the natural rights of the individual as 'liberty, property, security and the right to resist oppression'—a phrase which implicitly legalized the storming of the Bastille. No one must be arrested or imprisoned except through legal processes. Torture was condemned, freedom of speech and of religious opinion asserted. But on 15 September, when Louis XVI was again petitioned to sanction the decrees about feudal rights, his response was to bring the Flanders regiment from Douai to Versailles.

In a letter to Gaufridy dated 17 September, Renée-Pélagie wrote: 'It is the confusion of the Tower of Babel. Everyone wants to be master . . . Everyone here carries arms and many have left for England . . . It is a great strain constantly to be on guard against compromising oneself, to distrust everybody one meets, not to know the people one is living with, to listen to threats of force. It would be much better to be a galley-slave: at least one would know what one was expected to do.' A few days later, hearing that the peasant revolts had spread to Provence, she wrote to him again, asking him to take possession of the family papers.

The price of a four-pound loaf had been reduced to 12 sous but, despite the good harvest, there was a severe shortage of flour and the crowds were ready to believe the popular orators who said that the King could help them against the profiteers. On 5 October hundreds of angry women marched fifteen miles from Paris to Versailles, where they petitioned for cheaper bread and for the troops to be dismissed. In the afternoon they forced all the women they met—'even women in hats' said an English observer—to join the demonstration. Renée-Pélagie escaped from Paris with her daughter and a maid 'in a hired carriage, following the general flood. I did not want to be dragged off by the women of the people, who were forcing all the ladies from the houses to march with them through the rain, the dirt etc. to Versailles to capture the King . . . He has been taken to Paris. The heads of two of his bodyguards were carried in front of him on pikes.'

The next day crowds of women dumped 150 barrels of rotten flour in the Seine. On 21 October the Assembly made a desperate bid to hold the mob in check: martial law was introduced, together with press censorship, and the death penalty for 'rebellion'. Paris settled into an uneasy calm. On 26 November, Renée-Pélagie, who had come back, wrote to Gaufridy: 'We are threatened with slaughter every day. It is useless for the nobility and the clergy to go on giving in to all the demands that are made. They can always ask for more. At the moment, since the scene at Versailles nothing has happened, but in going to sleep at night one never feels safe about the morning. The day before yesterday, at the Palais Royal and la Halle, they were confiscating shoe-buckles and ear-rings, and forcing people to empty their pockets on pretext of taking everything to the Treasury.'

Although the women had compelled the King to give his assent to the Declaration of Rights, Sade was still a prisoner. His restiveness was increasing; by causing trouble he was improving his chances of being released. On 12 January 1790, the Prior at the asylum did exactly what had been done by all the commandants who had been responsible for him—asked for him to be sent elsewhere. Unless he could be kept in solitary confinement, the President of the National Assembly was informed, he was liable to cause trouble.

All this time the behaviour of the revolutionary mobs had been confirming his theory about the naturalness of 'criminal' aggressiveness. The tradition of exploitation had been turned upside-down: noblemen, priests and civic officials were at the mercy of the men they had oppressed. Writing to Gaufridy about the 'fearful slaughter' in Meaux, where the mayor had been hanged, Renée-Pélagie said: 'The password for violence is "There's an aristocrat! He wants to rescue the King!" They hang people immediately, without a trial!'

On 13 March the Assembly took action to liberate prisoners held under *lettres de cachet*: if no new charge had been made against them, they must all be released within six weeks, unless they were either mad or under sentence of death. Alarmed though she was by the prospect, Mme de Montreuil was nervous of drawing attention to herself by intervening. When her two grandsons, now twenty-two and twenty, wanted to visit their father and tell him about the decree, her reaction was: 'I hope he will be happy but I very much doubt whether he knows how to be.'

They went to the asylum on 18 March. Neither of them had seen him for nearly fifteen years. The friars let him take them out for an unsupervised walk and entertain them to dinner. A fortnight later, on Good Friday, he was released. He was now within three months of his fiftieth birthday; he had been twenty-seven on the Good Friday he spent with Rose Keller and thirty-six when Marais took him to Vincennes. He left the asylum wearing a black ratteen waistcoat and trousers instead of breeches. (Breeches were a hallmark of nobility—which was how the *sans-culottes* got their name.) Having no money, he went straight to the office of his Paris lawyer, de Milly, who gave him a meal, 15 livres, and a bed for the night. In the morning he went to visit Renée-Pélagie at the convent, but she refused to see him.

Writing to Gaufridy the following day, she did not explain herself. 'I have only enough time to tell you, Monsieur l'avocat, that M. de Sade has been free since Good Friday, which was yesterday. He wishes to see me but my reply was that my firm intention is to separate, that it cannot be otherwise. Send my effects and papers to my mother's address.'

That she had decided to sue for separation was not altogether surprising. Since her visits had been resumed during his last two years in the Bastille, he had noticed a worrying change, which he attributed to the influence of her confessor. She had been ill after nursing La Jeunesse through his final sickness. She had been constantly short of money, and her family had done nothing to help her. She no doubt felt guilty about her procrastination over recovering Sade's manuscripts and possessions from his cell, although she would not have admitted it. In the austere but peaceful convent she could feel safe, and it would be dangerous to expose herself all over again to his savage temper. How could she know whether a future with him would repeat the past? Her talent was for self-denial in the cause of dutiful devotion. First as a daughter and a believer, later as a wife, she had been happy to sacrifice her own happiness. Letting herself be beaten, disguising herself as a man to rescue him from Miolans, litigating against her mother, appealing to have her husband freed, walking across Paris to visit him, she had subordinated her own needs to his, dedicating herself piously to his service. Latterly, though, there had been nothing she could do for him, and, surrounded by nuns, she turned back to serving God. She knew from experience that it would now be easier to keep the door shut tight against his emotional needs than to open it half an inch. She even refused to give back the manuscripts he had entrusted to her or the fair copies she had made for him. She had given some of them to people who had burnt them, she said. Perhaps she meant the nuns.

Desperate for a friend to confide in, he wrote forgivingly to the treacherous Gaufridy:

It was not your fault if I was arrested at Lacoste. I thought I was safe, not knowing what an abominable family I was saddled with . . . You can have no idea of the hellish, cannibalistic treatment they had in store for me . . . My eyesight and my lungs have been ruined. For want of exercise I have become so enormously corpulent I can scarcely move.

The letter grows more intimate:

All my sensations have been snuffed out. I no longer have any taste for anything; there is nothing I like. It was foolish to feel so much longing for the world. It now seems dismal and boring. Sometimes I feel inclined to become a Trappist monk, and it is possible that one fine day I will disappear without anyone's knowing what has become of me. I had never felt so misanthropic as I have since being amongst people again, and if to them I seem like a foreigner, they can be sure that they produce the same effect on me.

He complains particularly about Renée-Pélagie:

> Anyone else would have said 'He is unhappy, I must dry his tears'. But she has no interest in any such logic of sentiment. I have not lost enough. She wants to destroy me.

After fifteen years of isolation Sade was frantic for human contact, but he had no friends, no one to talk to, no one to write to even, except legal advisers. Later on in May, Reinaud, the lawyer in Aix, received an almost equally intimate letter:

> Important business to settle and the fear of being hanged in Provence on a democratic gibbet will keep me here until next spring . . . if God and the nobility's enemies allow me to live . . . But do not take me for a fanatic. I protest that I am no more than impartial, angry at having lost much, still angrier to see my sovereign in irons . . . but otherwise feeling very little regret for the *ancien régime*. Indeed, it caused me so much misery I cannot weep for it . . . You ask for news? The Assembly has refused to let the King have anything to do with making war or peace. For the rest it is the provinces that concern us most. Valence, Montauban, Marseilles are theatres of horror, where cannibals daily enact tragedies in the English manner. One's hair stands on end. But I have long been saying that, straddling cruelty and enthusiasm, this lovely gentle nation, which had eaten the buttocks of the maréchal d'Ancre on the grill, was only waiting for the chance to erupt, to show that, given the opportunity, it would revert to its natural tone. But that is enough. One needs to be prudent in one's letters. Despotism never unsealed so many of them as liberty does.

Corpulence had reduced but not ruined Sade's attractiveness to women, and by the end of May he was living with a lady of forty who, like his mother-in-law, bore the title *Présidente*. She had been married to M. de Fleurieu, a President of the Grenoble Parlement. They had separated. 'She has been unhappy herself,' Sade reported to Gaufridy:

> and knows how to sympathize with others who have. She is intelligent and talented . . . In her company I always forget my

unhappiness ... All my strength is used up in coping with my overwhelming maladies—the coughing, the trouble with my eyes and my stomach, my headaches, my rheumatism ... I am lodging with this lady in a small apartment for 300 livres a year. There is scarcely room to turn round, but it is pleasant, with a good view, good air, good company. I shall wait here patiently for the spring, when I will certainly come to see you, bringing my two boys. You will find them extremely agreeable, decent, intelligent, but cold ... They have something of the Montreuil haughtiness, and I should prefer them to have the Sade energy.

His reaction to Madeleine-Laure, who was now nineteen, was even less favourable: 'My daughter is just as ugly as I described her to you. I have seen her three or four times since then and have looked at her carefully. Intellectually and physically she is a good, fat farm-girl.'

Most of the Sade energy was now going into efforts to arrange for productions of the plays he had written in 1781–3. He met François-René Molé, who had played the Count in Beaumarchais's *Le Mariage de Figaro*. He may have been instrumental in arranging the reading Sade gave in August of his one-act blank verse drama *Le Boudoir ou le mari crédule* to a committee of Comédie-Française actors. They rejected it, but another one-act play in verse, *Le Suborneur*, was accepted by the Comédie-Italienne where, twenty-six years earlier, he had met Mlle Colet.

It is astonishing that after more than twenty years of promiscuity, followed by thirteen years of imprisonment, a man should be capable of settling down into a relationship that would last twenty-four years. When Sade met the actress Marie-Constance Renelle, she was not quite thirty. She had a child, but her husband had abandoned her. So while Renée-Pélagie was suing for a separation order, Sade was already extricating himself from one relationship to start another.

In September, his five-act verse comedy *Sophie et Desfrancs* was unanimously accepted by the committee of the Comédie-Française. It was never produced, but it went on earning money for him until 1795. He was, as always, in financial difficulties. Renée-Pélagie was demanding the repayment of her dowry, and in June 1790, when the Châtelet Court issued the separation order, he was commanded to pay her 160,842 livres. Legal wrangling continued until September, when he accepted the separation order and acknowledged the debt in return for her agreement not to ask for settlement during his lifetime. His only liability to her was to pay interest at the rate of 4,000 livres a year. A week earlier, 1,500 livres had been stolen from him by a servant who had been recommended by his former valet Langlois. But Audibert, a Catholic farmer from Bonnieux who was now collecting all the rent from him at Lacoste, advanced him 15,000 livres, and in November Sade set up house near the Opera. He told Gaufridy that he felt like 'a good fat country priest in his parsonage'. He employed a housekeeper, a cook and a valet. 'Is this too much?' He was trying to arrange for furniture to be sent from Lacoste, and in December, convinced that he had not received what was due to him from his mother's legacy and that the Montreuils had misrepresented the revenues from his estates, he informed them that, since he could not live on less than 10,000 livres a year, any interest he paid to Renée-Pélagie would have to come from income in excess of that. In January 1791, Marie-Constance moved into the house with him.

Justine is dedicated to her. 'Yes, Constance, I address this work to you—at once the model and the honour of your sex, combining the soundest, most enlightened mind with the most sensitive of spirits.' His nickname for her was Sensitivity, and, uneducated though she was, he found her criticism of his work much more useful than Renée-Pélagie's had been. He would read out chapters to her and make detailed notes of her comments. He had probably started expanding *Les Infortunes de la vertu* into *Justine* when he was still in the Bastille, and though the new version was not published until 1791, it cannot be said that her influence is visible in the treatment of relationships. Nor is there evidence in the description that he was now a free man. From internal evidence, the novel might as well have been finished in the Bastille.

In his *Idée sur les romans* Sade put forward his view of what a writer ought to do when redrafting:

Take advantage of your right to interfere with the line of the story . . . You are not required to be truthful—only to be convincing. Once you have your outline, work intensively to expand it without feeling obliged to stay within the limits it originally seemed to dictate . . . What we want from you is panache, not discipline. Go beyond your own plans. Change them. Add to them. It is only while working that ideas come. Should the ones that press in on you while you are writing be any less valid than those incorporated in your rough sketch? ... In essence I am asking only one thing of you: to hold the interest until the last page ... You owe compensation to the reader when you force him away from what interests him. He will forgive you for interrupting but not for boring him.

Justine is over twice as long as *Les Infortunes*, and the heroine is less cramped than she was by the exigencies of the argument, though she is still exceedingly slow to learn that God does not intervene to protect the innocent, that virtuous behaviour is not rewarded, that other people cannot be trusted to respond gratefully when they are helped, that priests and judges abuse their positions of power. She never becomes suspicious of a man's motives until she is in a situation where he will be able to use his superior strength. Describing her frequent experiences of rape, her language is always euphemistic, though Sade pulls her rather out of character in making her use the imagery of pagan worship. When Rodin rapes her, the incident is described in half a sentence: 'and to Rombeau's homage the cruel man added his, which consisted of those harsh and savage caresses that degrade rather than honour the idol.' Throughout her first-person narrative, the words 'altar', 'sanctuary', 'incense', and 'sacrifice' recur as circumlocutions: 'facing him, raised upon my flanks, the fifteen-year-old girl, her legs spread open, offers his mouth the altar at which he sacrifices to me.' 'Sévérino uses only his hands to molest what is offered him and hastens to engulf himself in the sanctuary of his whole delight.' Surrounded by naked girls, 'Sévérino is able to see nothing but a multitude of those obscene altars in which he delights.' Justine is more in character when she is piously periphrastic about an erection or an outsize penis: 'exhibiting himself to me in a state over which reason is seldom triumphant, and in which the opposition of the object that causes reason's downfall serves only to foment delirium.' 'This monster was outfitted with faculties so gigantic that even the broadest thoroughfares would have been too narrow.'

But at least she is now capable of wondering seriously whether vice is not, after all, preferable to virtue. When her money has been stolen by the beggar-woman she was about to help, she considers whether to join the gang of robbers or to accept the offer of a 30,000-livre salary to work as procuress for St Florent, a libertine who likes to take two virginities every day. Though she goes back to the path of virtue, she is less ingenuous than the Justine of *Les Infortunes*. Determined to rescue the beautiful young wife of the Comte de Gernande, who has a passion for bleeding her, Justine pretends to be hostile towards the girl. She will have a better chance of helping her to escape if the Count is unaware of any sympathy.

Gernande is typical of Sade's libertines in seeing nothing regrettable about the miseries of the oppressed: they are fulfilling their duties towards their social superiors. Another of Justine's tormentors says there would be no need to complain about the number of beggars in France if seven or eight thousand of them were hanged. The body politic should be handled like the body, and who would feel sympathy for the vermin that try to feed on his flesh?

Generally there is little correspondence between the violence of the fiction and the violence of the revolution. At one point, while planning to kill his daughter, Rodin makes light of the bloodshed by comparing it with that of a King who feels entitled to sacrifice twenty or thirty thousand soldiers in a single day. But when Roland amuses himself by putting a noose around Justine's neck, and when he lowers her into a dungeon full of corpses, there is no allusion to current events. Sade does not seem to have been considering the violence of the mob in relation to what he had written about natural aggressiveness.

Obviously, the social system which had victimized him was disintegrating. If his imagination went on working in the same groove as it had in Vincennes and the Bastille, it was more because of the impetus that had been generated than out of any continuing desire for vengeance. The central drive was still towards self-justification. Ever since his education in a Jesuit boarding-school —and possibly since being brought up as the playmate of a prince —he had been subjected to an elaborately vicious system of punishments. Irrigating his novel like an underground river is the compulsion to prove that victimization does not destroy innocence, and that no one is responsible for his own sexual needs. Far from being whitewashed, the libertine is always represented as a bloodthirsty villain, but Sade can divide his empathy between him and his incorruptible victim because both represent their author.

In *Justine* the thirst for blood is depicted most directly in an episode which did not occur in *Les Infortunes*. Until Sade's letters from Vincennes were published between 1949 and 1953, no one would have guessed at the closeness of his identification with the Comte de Gernande. The Count is fifty, monstrously fat, with wicked black eyes, a long nose, a large, ill-furnished mouth, a raucous voice and enormous hands. When blood is spurting out of the Countess's arms, which have both been lanced, he screams and staggers about like a man having an epileptic fit. He lashes out at everyone and everything within reach, recovering his senses only when, with great difficulty, Justine, kneeling between his legs, has sucked him to orgasm. The liquid is abundant and extremely thick.

If Justine ever comes near to being corrupted, it is at this moment. Knowing she will not be allowed to staunch the Countess's bleeding until her husband has climaxed, Justine, overcoming her revulsion, does her utmost to speed him. As she says, 'Kindness forces me into prostitution, virtue into libertinism.' The image crystallizes the duality of the identification. Like the fragile Countess whose health has been destroyed by voracious blood-letting, Sade has been victimized by a punitive system that has drained away the prime of his life and ruined his health. From his own point of view he is as innocent as Justine, but he is also tormented with guilt at the literary revenge he is taking. He could have been thinking only of himself when he made Armande, one of the girls victimized by the monks, compare the vicious abbot with 'those perverse writers' who go on instigating crime after their death by having their appalling doctrines printed.

The Comte de Gernande is also used to re-angle the argument about reciprocity in love-making. Though his appetite is large, his penis is extremely small. How could he possibly consider himself obliged to satisfy his wife? Unless the obligation is mutual, there can be no need to share pleasure, but two people can be equally well equipped to do each other harm. Here is another rationale for the alliances that recur in Sade's fiction between two or four libertines. Being equally formidable, they can share and exchange pleasures as they never could with their feeble victims. According to St Florent, benevolence has nothing to do with Nature. The wolf will do anything to draw the lamb into its clutches. Charity is a human concept and occurs only when people are weak or believe they will become weak. Slaves use it to propitiate their master.

Justine is not a self-indulgent book. Any novel depends to some extent on the writer's sexual fantasies but in spite of having catalogued so many in *120 journées*, Sade allows himself only a few of the old ideas, adapting them carefully to the different tempo and different requirements of the new novel. Justine's adventures with the coiners are given a much fuller treatment than in *Les Infortunes*, and their leader, Roland, is now addicted to the refined pleasure—so highly praised by the fourth story-teller in *120 journées*—of looping a black silk cord around the girl's neck and pulling it at the moment of orgasm. His 'formidable member' (as the polite Justine calls it) is so huge that he has great difficulty in gaining the anal intromission he wants. It 'slides to the brink of the neighbouring canal and, battering vigorously, penetrates nearly half-way.' When she cries out, he withdraws peevishly and 'hammers at the other gate with so much force that the moistened dart goes in, sundering me'. He becomes even more violent, and he tightens the noose as he penetrates more deeply, amused by her screams, but he relaxes the pressure as she begins to lose consciousness, and before she faints she is aware of his shouts and of being flooded. This time, instead of merely summarizing, Sade is fully dramatizing a sexual incident, creating suspense about whether the well-meaning heroine will survive.

Another new feature in *Justine* is the libertine's insistence on reversing every situation he contrives. After sparing her life, Roland insists on putting his in her hands, as they play a dangerous game with a stool and a halter. If the pressure of the rope around his neck produces an orgasm, she is ordered not to cut him down until it has taken its course; if it produces only death-throes, she is to cut him down at once. This time there is not much tension for the reader: it is predictable that Justine, subjugated by Sade's schematic structure, will not be given any freedom of choice. But the pattern of reversal was not merely satisfying—it was topical. The King, who had put his signature to so many *lettres de cachet*, was virtually a prisoner, with his head in the mouth of the underdog.

Sade was deriving considerable enjoyment from quiet domesticity. What he wrote about Mme de Staël must, as Gilbert Lely suggests, have been inspired by Marie-Constance: 'In a woman the cares of domestic life have a singular grace. The most ravishing of all, the wittiest and most beautiful, do not feel in the least superior to those good and simple tasks which so sweeten domestic life.' He was also making arrangements for the publication of *Aline et Valcour*. By March 1791, two of his plays had been accepted for production at the Théâtre Italien, and three at other theatres, though only one of the five would actually be performed.

Some of the furniture now arrived, finally, from Provence, badly damaged; Gaufridy had been equally negligent in arranging for books and papers to be sent to Paris in three chests. A jar of jam was upset over a blue tapestry, and something gluey had leaked over the books, gumming up the pages.

The financial squabbling with Renée-Pélagie was likely to be protracted. She was trying to hold Sade to the promise of 4,000 livres a year, while he was trying to prove that she had defrauded him of the 9,000 livres due from his mother's estate. His immediate problem was to find enough cash to buy food. In June, paper money was losing its value so rapidly that shopkeepers were refusing to accept it. Nor would they give credit. Sade and Marie-Constance were sometimes going to bed hungry, though he had high hopes for *Justine*, which was being printed by Girouard. As Sade wrote to Reinaud, 'My printer asked for it to be well *peppered*, and I made it fiery enough to smoke out the devil . . . Burn it and do not read any of it if by chance it comes your way. I am denying authorship of it.'

Paris had been divided into forty-eight sections. As an 'active citizen' of the Place Vendôme Section, Sade was issued with papers that entitled him to vote, and in June 1791 he was summoned to the general assembly. In May, when one of his elderly aunts had been imprisoned, he had professed outrage at the 'abominable horror' perpetrated by the revolutionary 'brigands', but after the King had escaped to Varennes and the National Assembly had issued a warrant for his arrest, Sade understood that he would have to be more cautious. The exodus of aristocrats had been continuing: soon about one family in four would be affected.[1]

[1] Robert Forster, 'The Nobility in the French Revolution' in *French Society and the Revolution*.

Sade wrote *Adresse d'un citoyen de Paris au roi des Français* and had it printed by Girouard as an eight-page octavo booklet:

> What have you just done, Sire? . . . You, the strongest, you, who commanded us . . . have resorted to the odious ruses of feebleness . . . You complain about your situation. You groan, you say, in irons . . . Deign to think for an instant of those wretched people, the former victims of your despotism. You had only to be coaxed or misled into signing your name, and they were wrenched in tears from the bosom of their family to be thrown for ever into the dungeons of those fearful Bastilles your Kingdom bristled with.

Later he would claim that he threw a copy of the pamphlet into the carriage of the King when he was on his way back from Varennes on 24 June. The obligation to work as a writer, Sade complained to Gaufridy, now for one party, now another, produced a volatility which affected his deepest mental habits. He felt nothing but hatred, he said, for the Jacobins, the radical Society of Friends of the Constitution. (The Club had its headquarters in a former Dominican monastery, and Dominicans had been known as Jacobins because of St Jacques.) 'I adore the King but detest the old abuses. I like innumerable articles in the new constitution; others revolt me. I want the nobility to have its lustre restored: to have taken it away helps no one. I want a monarchy and no national assembly but two chambers, as in England, which limits the King's authority, balancing against it the consensus of a nation necessarily divided into two orders. The third is useless.'

On 22 October 1791 his three-act prose drama, *Le Comte Oxtiern ou les effets du libertinage,* was produced at the newly built Théâtre National Molière, which had opened in June. The director of productions was a member of the National Assembly, and most of the plays were tendentiously anti-royalist or anti-aristocratic. *Oxtiern* is about a girl brave enough to challenge her seducer to a duel, but the old rogue takes advantage of the darkness to trick her into fighting against her father. The audience at the first performance was so disorderly that the second was postponed for nearly a week. It was interrupted when someone in the audience shouted for the curtain to be lowered. It came down half-way, but other people shouted for it to be raised again. There was some hissing at the end, but the majority of the audiences was enthusiastic, calling Sade on stage to take a bow.

But in March 1792, when his one-act play, *Le Suborneur*, had its première at the Théâtre Italien, a group of Jacobin hecklers in the stalls made the dialogue inaudible. The disturbance grew worse in the second scene and worse still in the third. In the fourth, the actors had to admit defeat. One of the interruptors shouted that from now on the red bonnet would be a rallying signal for patriots in all public places, especially theatres, where the aristocracy would be fought remorselessly by the friends of liberty.

In April Sade was asked to send the municipal officers of Lacoste a statement of loyalty to the revolution and the constitution. The day after he complied, he heard that the local commune had voted in favour of removing the battlements from his château. In a long letter of protest he described himself as the man with more reasons than anyone else for detesting the old regime. 'Am I not an active citizen in my section? Do I ever claim any other title than *man of letters*?' He signed the letter Louis Sade. Read out at the next meeting of the constitutional club at Lacoste, it was greeted rapturously. His battlements were safe, he was informed. A week later he received another letter signed by all twenty local Friends of the Constitution, assuring him of the 'fraternal and inviolable attachment and friendship of all the citizens'.

Monarchy in France died very slowly from a blow delivered by Robespierre in September 1791, before the Constituent Assembly was dissolved. When he proposed that members should be disqualified from sitting in the new Legislative Assembly, the extreme royalists joined forces with the extreme revolutionaries to carry a motion that would have the effect of eliminating all the moderates. In revolutionary situations, democratically elected bodies are liable to act self-destructively: fearing defeat, they precipitate it. In the Legislative Assembly there was only a minority of republicans, but they divided their opponents by pressing for measures to be taken against the aristocratic *émigrés*. In April 1792 the outbreak of the war with Austria exacerbated both the economic crisis and the general panic. All over the country, mobs were on the rampage. On 20 June, the third anniversary of the Tennis Court Oath, a procession of National Guards, citizens with pikes and red bonnets, women and children marched through the streets to the National Assembly, where they paraded in front of the deputies singing a revolutionary song. One of them was brandishing a calf's heart at the end of a stick: it was labelled 'Heart of Aristocrat'. The crowd went on to the Tuileries. Finding a side-entrance to the palace unlocked, demonstrators pushed into the royal apartments. Someone put a red bonnet on the King's head; someone else poured him a glass of wine, and they shouted slogans at him. He managed to disguise his fear and preserve his dignity, but, without knowing what they were doing, they had plucked away the veil of sanctity that had inspired superstitious respect. They went away without doing him any harm, but there was nothing to stop them from coming back.

After Robespierre's speech of 29 July attacking the constitution, agitation grew rapidly for the King either to abdicate or to be deposed. An ultimatum was delivered to the Assembly: if he was still on the throne after 9 August there would be an armed rising. On the night of the 9th, three representatives from each Section were called to the Hôtel de Ville, and a revolutionary commune was set up. In the morning an armed mob marched to the Tuileries. After some of the crowd had broken into the palace, the guards started shooting. Infuriated, the invaders set fire to the palace and slaughtered 600 guards. Sade was later to claim that in the square outside the palace he had fought side by side with a friend who received a wound. 'I was boiling with impatience for the tyrant and his ignoble spouse to pay the penalty for their crimes.' In a similar attempt to prove that he was reliably anti-monarchist, he wrote to M. de Montreuil, Renée-Pélagie and his two sons, who had both emigrated, condemning their disloyalty to the republic. Sade made copies of all three letters, securing two witnesses to vouch for the accuracy of each copy. At the beginning of September he was appointed as Secretary of his Section, which had been renamed the Section des Piques.

The prisons were full of priests, suspected counter-revolutionaries and people found with faked identity papers. On 17 August, under pressure from the Commune, the Assembly established a revolutionary tribunal to judge cases of crime against the state. On the 26th the news arrived that one of the frontier fortresses had been surrendered to the advancing Prussians by anti-revolutionary French troops. The panic that spread over Paris was inflamed by rumours: a counter-revolutionary coup was imminent; the prisoners were plotting a break-out; all the National Guards in

Paris were liable to be called to the front. The Assembly, which had already decreed that a National Convention should be elected, was clashing with the Commune. At Danton's instigation, house-to-house searches were organized to disarm everyone whose loyalty was suspect. On 1 September, after Danton had made another inflammatory speech in the Assembly, a group of prisoners on its way to the Abbaye prison was massacred by the waiting crowd, and within a week over a thousand prisoners had been slaughtered—prostitutes and thieves alongside priests and aristocrats. 'There is nothing to equal the horror of the massacres,' Sade wrote in a letter of the 6th. Cautiously he afterwards interpolated, 'but they were just'.

The September massacres produced tremors of reaction all over the country. At Lacoste about eighty villagers attacked the château, smashing all the glass, throwing the smaller pieces of furniture out of the windows and breaking the bigger pieces, all without any interference from the National Guard. This was not an isolated incident, but the culmination of a hostility that had been latent for a very long time. The villagers fuelled their passion with wine stolen from the cellars. Doors and shutters, ripped off their hinges, were shattered against the surrounding rocks. A smaller crowd came back to complete the devastation on the same day that, in Paris, the Assembly was replaced by the National Convention which immediately voted for the abolition of the monarchy. Its next major decision was that the King should be brought to trial. As a nobleman, monarchist and secretary of his Section, Sade was already under considerable strain before hearing about the vandalism. 'With actions like that those swine will soon win hatred for their regime, whatever reasons one has for supporting it . . . There is death in my heart.'

That his fellow citizens in the Section des Picques were willing to forgive him for his noble birth was confirmed when he was made responsible for organizing cavalry, and then appointed as commissary to advise on hospital administration. In a speech he made on the 28th, he read out five recommendations on the role of commissaries in hospital administration. It was agreed that his speech should be printed and circulated to the forty-seven other Sections. His November speech on how to support legislation by sanctions was also printed for distribution.

It was even more gratifying when his fellow-citizens made him responsible for investigating the houses which had been put under seal when found abandoned. One of these belonged to the Montreuils. What if he found evidence that they were enemies of the revolution? After so much suffering and so many years of day-dreaming impotently about revenge, he was actually going to have them in his power. 'If I find anything aristocratic,' he told Gaufridy, 'as I certainly shall, I will not spare them. Did you laugh, lawyer?'

At the trial of the King, the verdict of guilty was unanimous, though the death sentence was carried only by a majority of 53— 387 votes to 334. Twenty-six of the fifty-three had previously voted in favour of suspending the death sentence. The inconsistency was so embarrassing that a fresh vote was taken on whether the execution should be deferred. A majority of seventy was now in favour of killing the King. On the morning of 21 January 1793 the watching crowd was silent as he was carried to the guillotine in the Place de la Révolution, which used to be called Place Louis XV. At 10.22 his head was cut off.

Chapter 11

Degrees of Terror

'When all men are free,' said Saint-Just, 'they will be equal, and, when equal, just.' This was the philosophy of the Terror, in which 30,000 people were killed. External reality was taking the shape of Sade's dream. After years of arguing that humanity should emulate the cruelty of nature, Sade found himself suddenly in a position from which he could shed as much blood as he liked. Given the opportunity, he did not want it.

Early in 1793 food prices again rose steeply. By February sugar was costing twice as much as it had in 1790. The first victims of the mob were city wholesalers and big merchants suspected of hoarding, but the violence spread outwards. Condemning the riots, Jacobin orators blamed them on counter-revolutionaries and disguised aristocrats.

The other European nations were throwing more weight into the war against revolutionary France, and in March, after crossing the Meuse, the Austrian army occupied Liège. The endemic anxiety was exacerbated by a peasant rising in the west to resist the military levy, and on 10 March a Revolutionary Tribunal was given powers for the summary trial of anyone accused of crimes against the State. Nine days later the Convention decreed that military commissions of five members could execute rebels captured under arms. Revolutionary committees were set up in every commune to round up foreigners and suspects. On 5 April the French general Dumouriez, who had just sustained two major defeats, went over to the enemy. Panic made it inevitable that governmental power should pass into the hands of a small group, and on 6 April the Committee of General Defence became the Committee of Public Safety.

In the afternoon of the same day M. de Montreuil appeared at the Section Assembly. He had not spoken to Sade for nearly fifteen years. They chatted amicably for about an hour and within a week Montreuil had visited his ex-son-in-law's house. The attempt at reconciliation was prompted by a healthy instinct for survival.

Sade was now an assessor on one of the revolutionary committees that were trying *assignats*—cases of forged promissory notes issued by the state. 'I am a judge,' he wrote to Gaufridy, 'yes, a judge! Assessor for the prosecution! Who would have expected that, lawyer, fifteen years ago? You see, my brain has ripened and I am beginning to grow wise . . . So congratulate me! And above all do not forget to send some money to His Honour the Judge, or, devil take me, I will condemn you to death!' With his income drastically depleted by the uncompensated abolition of feudal rights, according to the decrees of June and August 1792, and by the difficulty of collecting rent, Sade had been pawning his silver and borrowing money at an interest rate of 7 per cent. The letter he wrote to Gaufridy three weeks later was less jocular: for four days he had been without servants; his furniture might be taken away any day; he had been thinking seriously of blowing out his brains. 'Well, do something! In the name of God do whatever you like with Saumane, with Arles, with Lacoste! Levy taxes, make cuts, mortgage them, sell them, do what the hell you like, but send me some money. I need it immediately or I shall be driven to desperate remedies.'

But the main dangers were external. His life was saved twice during 1793 by coincidences, and the first of these occurred a few weeks before the murder of Marat, who had been on the Commune's vigilance committee since September. He had read a most unflattering account of Sade's libertine career, but thanks to a confusion, it was the Marquis de la Salle who was denounced on 2 June in his paper, *L'Ami du Peuple*, and subsequently executed. If Michelet's *La Révolution française* is to be believed, Marat discovered his mistake, and (by an irony which Peter Weiss does not seem to have discovered) Charlotte Corday unwittingly saved Sade's life when she killed Marat on 13 July.

The moderates in the Convention could not survive long after the speech of Robespierre's younger brother at the Jacobin Club, inciting the Sections to demand the arrest of the 'disloyal deputies'. By the middle of April thirty-five of the Sections had declared themselves in favour of removing the twenty-two deputies whose names had been listed, and on 19 May the Commune invited the Sections to send representatives to discuss how to go about it.

Out of this assembly the Central Revolutionary Committee emerged. On 29 May, it went into permanent session, and within less than a week an ex-customs clerk, François Hanriot, had been appointed to command the National Guard and a revolutionary militia of 20,000 *sans-culottes* had been created. On 2 June, several battalions of National Guard, reinforced with *sans-culottes*, surrounded the Tuileries where the Convention was now meeting. The arrest of two ministers and twenty-nine other deputies not only gave the Jacobins a majority but showed the Convention that its power was limited.

In June Sade was one of four delegates from the Sections chosen to address it with a call for the revocation of the decree that a paid militia should be enlisted in Paris. Sixteen of the forty-eight Sections had already committed themselves to opposing the idea. But he exerted more personal influence in his hospital work. The overcrowding in the wards was atrocious. According to the naturalist Cuvier, patients were crammed two or three to a bed, 'choking, feverish, unable either to move or to breathe, sometimes feeling a dead body or two next to them for hours at a stretch'. With two other delegates appointed by the Hospitals Commission, Sade inspected five hospitals. Their report, which consisted of eighty-eight foolscap sheets, seems to have been genuinely influential: soon patients could be sure of having a bed to themselves. And in July he was in the chair at the meeting which decided that each Section should send a list of hospitalized citizens to the Commission of Welfare and Health, so that individual checks could be made on their situation.

The documents Sade now drafted are full of revolutionary clichés: 'liberticidal manifestations', 'counter-revolutionary projects', 'the great republican family we have just organized', 'delights of the new regime'. But he was successful, temporarily, at proving his loyalty to the republicans. In July he became President of his Section. 'There I am,' he wrote to Gaufridy, 'higher still up the ladder.' The Montreuils were totally in his power. Madame did not dare to confront him, but 'Papa Montreuil', as Sade called him in the letter, had put in another appearance at a sectional assembly. One of Sade's duties as President was to instruct citizens of his Section about how they must contribute on 10 August to the celebrations for a new constitution, which had been hastily prepared by a Jacobin committee, declaring that the purpose of society was the happiness of the people. Landlords and innkeepers must paint their façades with the words: 'UNITY, INDIVISIBILITY OF THE REPUBLIC, LIBERTY, EQUALITY, FRATERNITY OR DEATH.' And they must put a tricolor pennant in front of their houses, crowned with a red liberty bonnet.

The Committee of Public Safety had been re-elected monthly until a series of military defeats undermined confidence in its leadership, and on 10 July 1793, it was replaced by a committee with nine members instead of fourteen. Dominated by Robespierre, the new committee made concessions to the extremists, imposing the death penalty for food-hoarding. The meetings of the Sectional Assembly became 'stormy'; Sade felt 'overwhelmed, shattered'. At the beginning of August he was spitting blood. On the 2nd, too ill to continue in the chair, he resigned from the Presidency. He was under pressure to put to the vote a proposal he found 'horrible, inhumane'. He told Gaufridy: 'I never wanted to. Thank God I have finished with it.' Before exchanging positions with his Vice-President, he made sure that the names of the Montreuils were entered on a list that would guarantee their survival. 'That is the revenge I take!'

On 29 September, ignorant of Marat's attempt to have him guillotined, Sade paid tribute to the martyr of the revolution in a speech delivered from the plinth of the monument in the Place Vendôme, which was then known as the Place des Piques: 'Though slaves called you bloodthirsty, you wanted only to sacrifice those who overburdened the earth. You great man! It was only their blood you wanted to shed, and you were lavish with it only to spare that of the people. With so many enemies how could you survive? You pointed out traitors; treachery struck you down.' The woman who had saved Sade's life by killing Marat was reviled as a 'savage assassin . . . like those hybrid creatures who cannot be assigned to either sex, vomited up by hell for the despair of both'. Applauding Sade's speech for 'its principles and its forcefulness', the Sectional Assembly voted to have it printed and circulated.

In November, as Vice-President, he was invited to make proposals to the Sectional Assembly for re-naming streets in his district. Rue des Capucines was to become rue des Citoyennes Françaises, rue Saint-Nicolas rue de l'Homme Libre, and the rue Neuve-Sainte-Croix the rue du Peuple Souverain. He also played a prominent part in the revolutionary campaign to replace Christianity with a religious cult of reason. The Bishop of Paris was frightened into resigning, and on 10 November a festival of Reason was held in Notre-Dame. In the dechristianization of the calendar, which made Year I start from 22 September 1792 when the monarchy was abolished, the months were given new names based mainly on the weather, while the saints disappeared from the calendar to be replaced by plants, fruits and flowers. Notices were posted outside the churches to proclaim: 'Death is an eternal sleep', and on 15 November 1793 Sade addressed the Convention proposing that the Virtues should be worshipped with hymns and incense at the altars where the Catholic Mass had been celebrated. 'For a long time Philosophy laughed quietly at the ape-like antics of the Catholics; but if it ever dared to raise its voice, it was in the dungeons of the Bastille, where ministerial despotism could soon silence it. It was in the interest of Tyranny to prop up superstition.' The speech was received favourably and the proposals were referred to the Committee for Public Education.

But on 8 December, abruptly and incomprehensibly, Sade was once again arrested. He had had less than four years of freedom. After asking the commissary to convey some sheets of corrected proofs for *Aline et Valcour* to Girouard, the printer, he was taken to the Madelonnettes, a converted convent which had been used as a reformatory for prostitutes. He was again in danger of being guillotined: he had been denounced for volunteering in 1791 to serve, together with his two sons, in the King's *garde constitutionelle*. He immediately wrote to his colleagues at the Section, but instead of vouching for him the Vigilance Committee not only confirmed the allegation but added several new accusations.

For six weeks he was made to sleep in the latrines of the Madelonnettes. As so often before, he channelled all his energy into desperate bids at self-justification. He wrote to the Committee of Public Safety, insisting that he was a loyal citizen imprisoned by some mistake: 'The miseries of a true patriot bring joy to enemies of the Revolution.' On 8 January 1794 Girouard was guillotined. A few days later Sade was transferred to a converted Carmelite convent in the rue Vaugirard, where he had to share a cell with six victims of a malignant fever. During the eight days he was there, two of them died. On 22 January he was moved to the maison Saint-Lazare, which had been built as a lepers' hostel. The report from the Vigilance Committee was dated 8 March: he had pretended to be a patriot and made much of having been a prisoner in the Bastille, but if he had not been of noble blood, his punishment would no doubt have been more severe. The citizens in the Section had not been deceived by his zealous display of sympathy for the revolution. He had revealed himself in his true colours when he opposed the formation of a paid militia. He had consistently been hostile to the republican clubs, and habitually made references to Ancient Greece and Rome in his attempts to argue that it would be impossible to establish a democratic republic in France.

He defended himself vigorously. 'Yes, I wrote to Brissac in 1791, as a former officer in his regiment. Like many others, I was mistaken about him, believing him to be a friend of the revolution . . . Brissac knew me better than I knew him . . . He said to one of my friends *publicly* that he did not want me because he did not want to recruit men who had as much reason as Sade to complain of the King.' Since 1789 his behaviour had always been motivated by sincere commitment to the revolution. He could cite his harangue to the crowd from the window of the Bastille, his involvement in the fighting on 10 August 1792, the letter he had written to the King, his pleasure at the death of the 'most cowardly, most villainous, basest of tyrants' and the speeches he had made on behalf of his Section. He had never been noble, he insisted. His ancestors were farmers and merchants.

At the end of the month, he was moved to another converted convent which had been made into a prison hospital at Picpus, near the Place de la Nation. Choderlos de Laclos was one of the other prisoners there. Sade later described Picpus as an 'earthly paradise—beautiful house, superb garden, choice company, pleasant women. But suddenly there was the place of execution positively under our windows and the middle of our beautiful garden became a cemetery for the victims of the guillotine.' It had been in the Place de la Concorde until residents objected to the smell of blood. 'We have buried 1800 bodies, my dear friend, in thirty-five days, a third of those coming from our own unhappy house.'

Under the *ancien régime* no one had been able to live in ignorance of the torture that so often preceded execution. The fastidious would never join the crowds that gathered to watch a criminal being broken on the wheel, but they could not fail to hear the dying moans of criminals on gibbets. As Henry Fielding had pointed out after a visit to France, these were fixed

> at some little distance of about ten or twenty Poles from those Roads where now are the usual places of Execution, that their Cries may not much disturb the common Passengers, and yet not so far off out of hearing, but that they may a little reach the Ears of their offending Brethren at their passing by, in Order to remind them of the dismal end they are likely to come unto.

Death by guillotine was quick, not for humanitarian but for practical reasons. There were too many death sentences to carry them out slowly. To Sade, who wrote so much about cruelty and killing, the reactions of the crowd, yelling, jeering, enjoying itself, must have been as horrific as the bloodshed. No book could possibly afford so much excitement to its public as the guillotine did, and the experience was an unforgettable object lesson in the theatricality of cruelty. Behind the spectacle lay the viciousness of the Public Prosecutor, the tribunals and the executioner, but their power was rooted in the will of the people which was itself rooted, like the public reaction, in eroticism. From now on Sade will write with more understanding about something he had already apprehended intuitively: in his relationship with his victim, the libertine is like an executioner or a murderer.

On 24 July, the sixth day of Thermidor, there were twenty-eight names on the list drawn up by Fouquier-Tinville, the Public Prosecutor, and the eleventh was 'Aldonze Sade'. The indictment said 'Sade, ex-count, captain of Capet's Guards[1] has been in communication with the enemies of the Republic. He has not ceased to fight against the republican government, maintaining in his Section that such government was impracticable ... It appears that the proofs of patriotism he was at pains to give were no more, so far as he was concerned, than means of evading investigation of his complicity in the conspiracy of the tyrant whose vile satellite he was.'

The second coincidence to save Sade's life during 1793 was that the bailiff failed to find him. He had been moved four times since

[1] Louis XVI was now known as Louis Capet.

his arrest in December. There were so many executions, the turn-over in the overcrowded prisons was so rapid and the administration so inefficient that only twenty-three of the twenty-eight accused were delivered to the tribunal through the bailiff. He must have called at Picpus on his way to the tribunal because one of the twenty-three had been imprisoned there. The trial was brief and perfunctory. The only two to escape the death sentence were a farmer and a woman who threw a fit when she was led into the courtroom. The twenty-one condemned prisoners were pushed into the tumbrils that were to take them to the guillotine. Twice their lives were almost saved. This was the day that the conflict between the Convention and the Commune came to a head. Early in the afternoon Robespierre was prevented from addressing the Convention and a warrant was issued for his arrest. Paris was in turmoil as the armed forces received conflicting orders from the two centres of government. Fouquier-Tinville was asked whether the executions should be postponed, but he insisted that nothing should delay the course of justice.

The second incident that could have saved the twenty-one victims occurred in the rue du Faubourg Saint-Antoine at about 3 o'clock in the afternoon. Usually the people in the street jeered at the aristocratic victims in the passing tumbrils, but now, after hearing rumours of Robespierre's arrest, they crowded around the carts, asking for the condemned prisoners to be reprieved and even trying to unharness the horses. At the crucial moment, Hanriot arrived on horseback with three of his officers, trying to rally support for Robespierre. They used sabres to disperse the crowd, and the tumbrils proceeded to the place of execution where the twenty-one heads were quickly sliced off. 'Imprisonment by the nation,' Sade wrote later, 'with the guillotine under my eyes, did me a hundred times more harm than all the Bastilles you could imagine.'

At 7.30 in the evening of the following day, 28 July, Robespierre, Saint-Just and Hanriot were guillotined.

When Sade, four weeks later, again petitioned the Committee of Public Safety for his release, the citizens of his Section were again invited to report on their former President. This time their verdict was quite different: Citizen Sade had worked 'with zeal and intelligence' in the local hospitals, and they knew nothing about him 'which might be contrary to the principles of a good patriot or might cast doubt on his civic spirit'. Eight weeks were to go by before he was released. He then had to make arrangements with Girouard's widow about *Aline et Valcour*, half of which had been printed when he was guillotined.

Gaufridy and his son Elzéar were in hiding. Wanting to help them, Sade sent a message through Audibert, who had not been forwarding any rent from Lacoste. As soon as Gaufridy replied, Sade repeated the offer: 'My detention has won some friends for me in the Convention and I will always be pleased to make use of them for you.' With debts totalling 6,000 livres, Sade was soon writing to Gaufridy again, complaining about his slowness over the sale of the house at Saumane. It was still unsold when Sade succeeded in obtaining an official pardon for the notary.

It would have been a hard winter even if Sade had been less impoverished. Everything was in short supply, and it was so cold that, working on *La Philosophie dans le boudoir*, he had to keep his inkpot in a bowl of warm water to stop it from freezing. 'What is more, there is no wood. One lot every two months for 40 livres. Everything is the same: on 25 livres a day you die of hunger!' By the end of February 1794, he was desperately trying to find a job either on a newspaper or as a librarian or curator of a museum. It was not until the end of March that Gaufridy was able to announce his success in selling the house—to one of his relatives.

The acid internal logic of *La Philosophie dans le boudoir* is partly distilled from the harshness of the surrounding circumstances, and the book is quite unlike *Justine* in its references to current events. Though written in dialogue, it is less like a play than a novel or a moral tale, but the tension is always entertainingly theatrical and despite inconsistencies, contradictions and absurdities, Sade comes surprisingly close to synthesizing the libertine philosophy of his earlier fiction with the ideas he had championed in his political speeches. A radical pamphlet, which may have been written separately, is interpolated into the dialogue, and the characters find it easy to reconcile the substance of it with their orgiastic behaviour.

At the Collège Louis-le-Grand, as in Jesuit schools all over France, the teachers had used their power to inculcate moral vetoes at the same time as introducing the adolescent mind to the pleasures of learning and literature. Sexual freedom diminished as articulacy increased. Already the French language had effectively been made into an accomplice of the Catholic restrictiveness which outlawed all sexuality that was not harnessed to the reproduction of the species. In launching a thoroughgoing attack on this moral tradition, Sade invented a different kind of educational programme. A fifteen-year-old girl, well endowed both physically and mentally, is instructed by two libertines, Dolmancé, a man of thirty-six, and the ironically named Mme de Saint-Ange, who is twenty-six. The teaching has to be both sexual and moral. Techniques of love-making will be of no practical value to Eugénie unless she can be liberated from the moral indoctrination that has been inhibiting her from exploring the pleasures her body offers her. At the same time her vocabulary must be widened. She cannot understand male and female anatomy while deprived—as she has been—of the words to describe the parts of the body, and the processes that occur when people enjoy each other sexually. Mme de Saint-Ange's brother is also involved in the story, partly to make the sexual permutations and combinations more complex, partly to mediate between the action and the reader's violation of the boudoir's privacy. Secrecy is conducive to shame, and shame must be exorcized.

In *La Philosophie* the immoralist and the comedian work happily together. Having succeeded better than most of his contemporaries in curing himself of religious indoctrination, Sade is able to parody Jesuit teaching methods. Eugénie is threatened with punishment if she does not learn her lessons, but in this situation, no one will conceal the pleasure derived from whipping a well-shaped bottom. The scientific pretensions of Enlightenment writing are mocked by the pretension to experimental objectivity, while schoolroom didacticism is mimicked: ' "Listen, my child, that is called a cock, and this movement," he continued, guiding my wrist with rapid jerks, "this movement is called masturbation. So, at the present moment, you are masturbating my cock." ' Later on in the lesson the girl is asked to describe exactly what she feels when two tongues press into her two orifices. Among the topical allusions is a casual comment on the pleasure that the guillotine gives to executioners: 'While guiding the law's blade, the criminal satisfies his own passions.'

The arguments against the existence of God are in line with

those of *Dialogue entre un prêtre et un moribond* but the statement is more forceful. God is 'an inconsistent and barbarous being, creating today a world he disapproves of tomorrow ... a feeble being who can never make men do what he wants ... If he had made them good enough, they would have been incapable of doing evil, and only then would the work be worthy of a God.' Eugénie's conversion is as unrealistically rapid as the Priest's in the *Dialogue*. She immediately renounces this feeble God. Though still handicapped by the impossibility of breaking free from the categories of good and evil, virtue and vice, Sade makes the point, as in *Aline et Valcour*, that norms have varied from one century to another and one country to another. What is new is his anti-authoritarian insistence that citizens of a republic should have no need of the religious dogma which has been a tool of monarchical autocracy.

> Yes, citizens, religion is incompatible with liberty. You have sensed that. Never will the free man bow to the gods of Christianity, never will its dogmas, rites, mysteries and morals suit a republican. One more effort. Since you are labouring to destroy all prejudices, do not let a single one survive, or the rest will all be restored ... No, we want no more of a god who goes against Nature.

Sade never understood how exceptional he was in not feeling frightened of freedom. As Dostoevsky's Grand Inquisitor tells Christ in *The Brothers Karamazov*: 'Man is tormented by no greater anxiety than to find someone quickly to whom he can hand over that gift of freedom with which the ill-fated creature is born. But only one who can appease his conscience can take over his freedom.'

Though not alone in wanting to set up Nature as a god and to dispense with priestly appeasers of conscience, Sade was almost alone in refusing to pretend that Nature was moralistic. Still relying on La Mettrie's premiss that Nature must want us to indulge the impulses she has implanted, he goes on to make suggestions for reforming the legal system. He was right to insist that the death of monarchy must lead to changes in manners: in a society based on liberty and equality there should be fewer legal prohibitions, fewer actions which are branded as crimes. Capital punishment should be abolished. Even murderers, he suggests, should be treated as Louis XV treated Charolais: 'I grant you pardon,' said the King, 'but I will also pardon whoever kills you.'

Nor should stealing be regarded as a crime, according to *La Philosophie*. It breeds courage, skill and tact—virtues useful to a republican society, and it tends towards a more even distribution of wealth. Is it not unjust that the man who has nothing should be forced by the law to respect the man who has everything? A social contract to respect property is a weapon of the strong against the weak.

Rape does less harm than theft, because nothing is taken away. Nature's intention is that women should belong to all men. Exclusive ownership is as bad as slavery, and no woman should have the right to reject any man who makes advances. If men were not entitled to compel submission, why would Nature have given them superior strength? Love is anti-social, serving only the happiness of two people. Women, like roadside fountains, are there for everybody.

The separation of sensation from emotion was essential to the underlying equation of liberty with libertinism. Love had to be discredited. 'What is the base of this sentiment? Desire. What are its consequences? Madness ... The aim is to possess the object. Well, let us try to succeed, but prudently. Let us enjoy it when we have it, and console ourselves when we fail. All men and all women are alike ... nothing is more deceptive than this intoxication which so upsets our senses as to make us think that we do not see, do not exist, except through this madly adored object.' The libertine is concerned only with his physical sensations. Eugénie has no interest in raising a family. Childbirth is not only bad for the figure, it reduces sensitivity. Eugénie is taught that: 'Whether daughter, wife or widow, a woman should have no other object, occupation or desire than to be fucked from morning till night.'

Much of Sade's argument is sound, much is silly. The most unpleasant sequence is the climax in which the liberated girl collaborates with her libertine teachers to torture her thirty-two-year-old mother, who is a beautiful prude. As in *120 journées*, the plot's movement towards bloodshed reflects a fundamental ambivalence towards the immoralists. It cannot be evil to strip away superstitions, prejudices and inhibitions when they stand in the way of harmless physical pleasures, but Sade compulsively develops his narrative to culminate in evil-doing that cannot fail to alienate his readers. Personally he had no reason to think highly of mothers, and it is dramatically effective that Mme de Mistival should suddenly be confronted with a daughter who has been totally transformed, emancipated to the point of murderous hostility. But though she is tiresome, the mother does not make us dislike her enough to be glad when she is first tortured and then raped by Dolancé's valet, who has been ordered to infect her with his venereal disease.

Chapter 12

The New Justine *and* Juliette

Inflation followed in the wake of revolution, and in 1795 it was rumoured that a military government would be formed. Sade was afraid, as he wrote on 5 August, that it would

> revive all the horrors of the revolutionary regime. We have a constitution and we have peace, but we still do not seem to be at the threshold of happiness . . . Everything that used to cost 6 livres is costing 60, while some commodities are infinitely more than ten times as much as they used to be. In consequence of hoarding, jam, oil and candles, for example, are 30 times as much . . . The most austere life—in short the life I am leading, with stew and bread from the Section, vegetables five days a week, never a visit to the theatre, never any frills, my lady, our cook and myself—well, 60 livres a week disappear.

In August, Gaufridy had not sent the 60,000 livres from the sale of the house at Saumane. Interest rates were abnormally high but instead of bringing Sade a good monthly income, the money, which had been outstanding since March, was bringing it to Gaufridy. Nevertheless, as soon as *Aline et Valcour* was printed, Sade, forgiving as always, sent him two copies. In March 1796 Sade and Marie-Constance, who was now divorced, took a year's lease on a house outside Paris. His elder son came to visit him there—'a very pleasant boy . . . very active, passionate about the arts, devoted to painting and music.' In June, Sade was still grumbling about Gaufridy's procrastination, but still ineffectually:

> Money, money, money! I would rather die than be unable to change this pernicious management of my affairs. My doctor says that the only cause of all my troubles is the dreadful anxiety you keep me in. Everybody grumbles at me for being dependent on your vagaries, and certainly that will have to

change. It will change, I swear ... The insecurity and the
anxiety you have given me since 3 April 1790 have done more
damage to my health than my 12 years in the Bastille.

The threat had no effect. At the end of July 1796, Sade had to
serve a writ on the notary. And in October he had to sell everything he owned at Lacoste—château, contents, mill, farm, buildings, land. He was paid nearly 75,000 livres, but he spent most of
it on two properties, one near Chartres and the other at Malmaison, even closer to Paris. Renée-Pélagie immediately started
litigation to secure herself a share of the income from the new
properties. 'My mother is well,' she wrote to Gaufridy. 'During
the Terror, she was arrested with my poor father, who passed
away six months after his release ... My daughter and I have been
in exile, and the exiles were destined to refill the prisons when
they were empty.'

In April 1797 Sade moved into Marie-Constance's house at
Saint-Ouen, a suburb of Paris, and in May he took her with him
on the first lap of an extended visit to Provence, trying to recover
arrears of rent from the past six years. Imprudently he accused a
tax-collector of stealing some of it. The repercussions were
humiliating and expensive, involving a public apology and legal
costs. Nor did Sade succeed in selling the property at Arles. Sym-
pathizing with Renée-Pélagie, who had received none of the
interest Sade had promised to pay, Gaufridy was secretly working
to prevent the sale. Her letter of gratitude is reminiscent of her
mother's correspondence with Gaufridy, though the manner is
slightly adapted to revolutionary democracy: 'You can be confident that I will not compromise you in anything and that my
gratitude for your devotion to the interests of my children always
has pride of place among the sentiments of esteem and consideration with which I am your fellow-citizen.'

La Nouvelle Justine ou les malheurs de la vertu, Sade's third and
longest version of the story, was published in 1797, together with
L'Histoire de Juliette sa soeur ou les prospérités du vice. The only one
of the three versions to be drafted outside a prison cell, this is the
one in which the fiction interpenetrates most intricately with the
world he was again allowed to live in. The narrative is written
in the third person, which tends to increase objectivity, making it
easier for Sade to comment critically on Justine's naïvety. The

language is no longer chained to the circumlocutions a pious girl would use in describing what impious men have done to her. At the same time, the perspective is widened. Human crimes are viewed against a background of cosmic criminality. This affects the imagery. The monk Jérome identifies with Mount Etna: in fantasy his orgasms are volcanic eruptions. The destructiveness of Nature is concentrated in his sperm as neighbouring cities are inundated with lethal lava.

In *Juliette* Sade reverts to the first person, but with this narrator there is no need for circumlocution. The novel is nearly as long as *War and Peace*, though the main strain on the reader is the progressive brutality. Like Eugénie in *La Philosophie*, we must be liberated not only from shame and inhibition but from the scruples that make us condemn violence. Action and argument work like battering rams to break down three ancient doors—Christianity, truthfulness and chastity. Dismissing the idea of love, one of Sade's libertines quotes Voltaire's definition of it as imagination's embroidery on nature's homespun.

In fictional defences of conventional morality, virtue is either rewarded—in this world or the next—or presented as its own reward. A clear conscience and the prospect of heaven are offered as enticements for rationing the body to a small fraction of the pleasures for which it is equipped. But even the fiercest enemies of promiscuity, like Richardson, are prone to ambivalence. Lovelace, who rapes Clarissa, dreams of her, garbed in white, ascending with angelic choirs while a chasm opens at her guilty feet; but Richardson (like Choderlos de Laclos) felt more sympathy than he could reveal for the villains. Virtuous heroines are entertaining only in proportion to the lechery they stimulate, but, to preserve appearances, the seducers who provide the fun must afterwards be punished. The punishments in *Les Liaisons dangereuses* are the only unconvincing part of the book.

While owing a great deal to Richardson—and probably to Laclos—Sade felt no inclination to pass sentence on his libertines. If punishment in actuality could be as grossly disproportionate to crime as his imprisonment had been, the whole system must be rotten, and the revolution had failed to overturn it because France was ignoring the warning of *La Philosophie*: Frenchmen were not making the 'one more effort' it would have taken to abolish God. If the old hierarchy was merely being replaced by another one, with God still at the apex, justice would still be dispensed in public according to an unacceptable scale of values. The only trustworthy judges were the most sensitive parts of the body.

But why did Sade need so much brutality? Why not simply write hymns of praise to the orgasm, indulging his preference for anal intercourse by implanting similar tastes in his heroes? He was still using literature as a means of unpicking the past, inverting reality. In reality, he did not want the blood of the Montreuils; in fantasy, his thirst for vengeance was unquenchable. In theory he could prove that any action, however base, was natural and therefore did not need to be justified; in practice he could not shake off the compulsion to infiltrate self-justification into everything he wrote. Addiction to the habit had merely made him more skilful in designing elaborate superstructures.

Unlike Baudelaire, he seldom used the word evil, not because he disbelieved in evil but because he believed it to be all-pervasive. So what effect could his writing have? If it did harm, it would only be helping Nature to achieve her purposes, though, in his ambivalence, he could not help trying to persuade himself that it would do good by demystifying, disabusing the credulous victims of hypocrisy—the majority that was so willingly deceived. The public must be taught, for instance, that churchmen are not motivated by altruism. Of all the priests and monks in his fiction, there is scarcely one who does not use religion as a cloak for lechery. In one comic sequence, Juliette's confession gives the priest an erection, and in the ensuing orgy with the Carmelites, the Mass is profaned: the circumlocutory image Sade had so often put into Justine's mouth to describe the sexual act is developed into action as the Mass is celebrated with a naked woman as altar.

Of all Sade's corrupt priests the most cynical is the most powerful—the Pope. In a sequence between him and Juliette, which prefigures the confrontation between Dostoevsky's Grand Inquisitor and Christ, she attacks the Church's accumulation of wealth and power. Has it not betrayed the central purpose of a religion based on poverty, equality and hatred of the rich? The Pope cannot deny that intolerance has become the fundamental principle. Without implacable rigour, the authority of both Church and State would be overthrown. In the end he confesses his own lack of faith. He ought to enlighten those who still believe, but if he told them the truth, he would starve to death. Is it so urgent, Juliette asks, that for the sake of his digestion fifty million people are still benighted by error? Yes, he says. Self-preservation has priority over all other natural laws. ⸱⸱

It makes more sense to condemn the book as propaganda than as pornography. Sade is less interested in arousing us sexually than he was in *120 journées*, and more interested in convincing us. He knows that, unlike Eugénie, we are not going to be converted by a single discourse, but if he can make us read on he is making us his accomplices, at least to the extent of acquiescing in a flow of events which we will be unable to stop. Like Juliette, we are receiving lessons in apathy. Her first comes from the Mother Superior, who advises her to hold back from interfering in other people's sufferings. A quick-witted pupil, she immediately points out that apathy will lead to criminality.

To survive the assault course of horror Sade presents, we may —without becoming criminals—cultivate a certain apathy that will remain with us. This danger is increased by his usual strategy of dividing the narrative into two levels: as in *120 journées*, the interruptions illustrate the aphrodisiac effect the chronicle of crime is having on the listeners. 'We soon lit the fire of the passions from the torch of philosophy.' Once again, words are leading to actions within the narrative, and this makes it more difficult to treat the whole fictional world of crime as if it were merely verbal. In the same way that the Jesuits encouraged children to emulate the saints, Sade structures his stories on the way student libertines emulate virtuoso sinners. The pattern of *La Philosophie* is developed. When Juliette sees how evil Lady Clairwil is, she decides 'to become identical' if she possibly can. She is soon receiving lessons in how to suppress compassionate impulses, and, in a later footnote, Sade recommends warm-blooded ladies to take advantage of the instruction Juliette is receiving from her other principal mentor, the Comte de Saint-Fond. He is an advocate of habituation as a means of overcoming shame and remorse. This is the teaching method Sade adopts in his narrative, habituating us to the attitudes, and the violence they admit, by means of action and argument which are both repetitious.

Saint-Fond stands in for all the Ministers and highly placed officials who have helped Mme de Montreuil to her vengeance. He gives Juliette six blank *lettres de cachet* as playthings: she can amuse herself by selecting six names to fill in. Normally Saint-Fond sells the letters. Among the 30,000 people wasting their lives in dungeons is a libertine who used to enjoy prostituting his wife to strangers. 'The respective families became involved in the affair.' There is also a retaliatory reference to the King of Sardinia, and Sade indulges in some unsubtle satire against law-courts. In one sequence Juliette and Saint-Fond try to revive their flagging appetites for sex by planning a frightening fancy-dress for him. 'Costume and accessories are essential: in our law-courts those incomparable jesters, the judges, resemble characters from a comedy, or else charlatans.' Later there is a mock trial that culminates in sadistic tortures and executions.

As Saint-Fond's mistress and accomplice, Juliette is paid out of public funds. Diamonds, carriages, enormous sums of money are lavished on her. Mme de Montreuil's treatment of Nanon is echoed when Saint-Fond arranges life-imprisonment for a pregnant girl on a charge of stealing. The revelation that the girl is innocent gives Juliette an orgasm. She goes on to derive progressive pleasure from theft and from the power unscrupulousness is giving her over the innocent. As in *120 journées* and *Justine*, the basic irony follows the pattern of the dialogue between Mme de Montreuil and de Losme in Sade's letter of 4 September 1784: 'Punish him for his virtues . . . What else are you being hired for?'

In *Juliette*, more obviously than in any novel since *120 journées*, Sade enjoyed his absolute power over characters who themselves had absolute power over an unlimited supply of victims. Instead of identifying with the victim, as in so many of the intervening fictions, he was writing from the libertine's blinkered viewpoint. When Clairwil and Juliette torture Olympia, there is one lifeless sentence to describe the tears from her beautiful eyes that splash down in pearly drops on her beautiful bosom. The energy of the writing goes into matter-of-fact reporting of what they do—stroking and poking at every part of her body, sticking hatpins into her bottom and pulling out pubic hairs. Finally Juliette bites her clitoris almost in two. The reader is to wear the same blinkers as the libertine. ' "In orgies like these," said Clairwil, "we have to be able to enjoy the delicious idea of believing ourselves to be alone on the earth." ' The victim becomes a depersonalized representative of a submissive Nature. The action is fulfilling the promise of the Mother Superior, Mère Delbène, who told Juliette that after a few years of breaking laws that seemed to be natural, she would have Nature fawning at her feet, grateful to have been violated and pleading for further degradations. Writing *Juliette*, Sade was living out Jérome's dream. Nature is represented as masochistic, and the fiction is a gigantic literary orgasm to ejaculate lava all over the globe.

When, in the second half of the novel, Sade sends his characters out on their travels, his object is to fortify private experience with a semblance of cosmic validity, but he fails to make the world seem real. The narrative technique is the accomplice of action and argument in their campaign to devalue external reality: nothing is given any solidity in its own right. He does even less than in *Aline et Valcour* to make landscape or objects into felt presences. The word *Nature* keeps recurring, but if natural scenery is described, it is only in terms of its effects on the imagination. The Lombard plains produce torpor, while the volcanoes of a 'constantly criminal Nature' encourage a spiritual turbulence which may provoke great actions. Mount Vesuvius inspires Juliette and Clairwil to the gratuitous murder of the beautiful Olympia, which is recounted with a laconic indifference to realism. After torturing the girl for two hours, they carry her to the brink of the volcano, drop her inside, and listen for several minutes to the sound of her body crashing from ledge to ledge, torn by the sharp outcropping rocks.

Sade is aware that he is arrogating the right to remodel Nature according to the momentary needs of his narrative. His aesthetic assumptions are as solipsistic as his imaginative premiss. Durcet's negativistic inclination to abolish reality in favour of an imaginary alternative is developed when Belmor tells Juliette that the main pleasure in love-making is mental:

How delicious they are—the pleasures of the imagination . . . The whole earth is ours in those exquisite moments. Not a single creature resists us. Everything presents to our excited senses the sort of pleasure our seething imagination believes it wants. We lay waste to the world and repopulate it with new objects, which we go on immolating . . . Truly, Juliette, I do not know whether reality is worth as much as fantasies are, or whether the pleasures of what one lacks are not worth a hundred times as much as what one possesses. There are your thighs, Juliette—I can see them and I find them lovely—but my imagination, always more brilliant than nature and more skilful, I dare say, creates still lovelier thighs. And the pleasure this illusion gives me, is it not preferable to the one truth is going to make me enjoy?

Implicitly the novel is giving divine status to the imagination, while relegating Nature to an inferior position, but at the same time the libertines are challenging Nature to revenge herself for the outrages they perpetrate against her. She gives no sign of wanting to, but in all the philosophizing the possibility that she may be unconcerned about human behaviour comes to the surface only twice: Noirceuil, who has defined crime as something that conflicts with natural laws, recognizes that nothing can conceivably 'outrage a Nature which is ceaselessly in flux'. But within a page he is talking of 'Nature's learned hand', which generates order out of chaos, and reasserts the equilibrium by implanting the same destructive instincts in men as she has in the animals. We get the other glimpse of the possibility when Sade makes the Pope declare: 'Mankind has no relationship to Nature; nor has Nature to man.' This was an extraordinarily advanced position to adopt, even momentarily, in the eighteenth century, and it should not surprise us that Sade's pontiff immediately retreats into talking as if creatures 'do well by Nature' if they destroy each other. Nature abhors propagation, he maintains, and delights in destruction. The cruelty that leads to murder is a disposition received from Nature. The irreligious Pope is merely secularizing the idea that Saint-Fond formulated in religious terms: 'What I designate as evil seems to be a great good from the viewpoint of the Being who created me . . . the evil I do to others makes me happy just as God is made happy by the evil he has done to me.'

Objects and actions are devalued in relation to sensations and fantasies. Even works of art—products of the imagination—are assessed according to their effects on the imagination of the characters. In the Uffizi Gallery the paintings and sculptures are exciting only if they are provocative. Titian's Venus prompts Sbrigani to remark that Raimonde, a girl who is with them, resembles her. This prompts Juliette to give the girl 'a fiery kiss'. Juliette's reaction to the Venus de Medici is not analysed: she merely claims 'no one else will ever appreciate her quite as I did'. Sbrigani admires the bottom of 'The Hermaphrodite', which reminds him of a bottom he once enjoyed. Paolo Veronese and Guido are mentioned by name, but nothing else is described except a waxwork of an overflowing sepulchre with corpses representing various phases of the body's decomposition. This makes Juliette reflect on the innumerable bodies that have gone through those phases as result of her actions. In writing the Uffizi sequence Sade did not have to depend on memories of his visit to the gallery in 1775. He had a copy of Abbé Richard's *Description historique et critique de l'Italie* in his library, and he was also drawing on Montaigne's *Voyages*. Montaigne devoted thirty pages to the Uffizi Gallery. He visited it in December and January 1728–9, enthusing particularly about the bottom of the Venus de Medici.

Sade made more use of his own experience in the Neapolitan episode. The Frenchman who mistook him for an embezzling cashier reappears as the Frenchman who announces that Juliette and Clairwil are two whores. The orgy scenes—in France, in the King of Naples's palace and in the castle of the Muscovite giant Minski—are derived from Sade's memories of sadistic adventures when he was in his twenties and early thirties, on his prison fantasies and on his previous elaborations of memory and fantasy into literature. His descriptions of living human bodies are as perfunctory as his descriptions of landscapes, objects and works of art. This bosom, he tells us, or this bottom, is the most beautiful in the world. Faces are 'the most heavenly one could hope to find', eyes are 'glorious', skins are 'faultless', breasts 'make one's mouth water', thighs are 'appetizing beyond words'. But he never troubles to find the words that will put readers in a position to form pictures of their own. He prefers statement to dramatization or objectification or suggestion. Even with moments of action, there is less dramatic realization than in *La Philosophie*, though each incident is given very much more narrative space than in *120 journées*.

The body which is realized most vividly is that of a woman who resembles the well-preserved story-tellers in *120 journées*. Mme Durand is still good-looking in her fiftieth year, with a clitoris as long as a finger. Sade is able to make her vivid because he identifies with her, going so far as to use the word 'epileptic' when describing her shouts and convulsions during orgasm. He also gives her sophisticated libertine tastes: the greatest pleasures, she says, are 'born from revulsions which have been overcome'. Her sexual expertise delights Juliette, as does her ambitiousness. Together they will become mistresses of the universe.

The immensity of Sade's destructive fantasies stands in the same ratio to the modesty of his living conditions, as fiction did to fact when he was a prisoner. Sometimes he had barely enough money to pay for food, while the sophisticated cynicism of the writing is oddly discordant with his naïve, absurd and almost masochistic stubbornness in continuing to trust Gaufridy. Having saved the notary's life, Sade expected gratitude—a mistake Juliette would have outgrown at a very early stage of her education. Sade was clever enough to forge an injunction against himself in order to antedate an injunction taken out by a creditor who was hoping to dispossess him of his new properties. But it was unrealistic to count on Gaufridy to help him. When the creditor succeeded in impounding Sade's furniture, he made yet another appeal for sympathy:

> I am hastening to a hiding place where I shall stay for several days. You see how badly I need your help!—Miserable journey! . . . Cruel and cursed wife! . . . My condition and my despair are infinitely worse than those of the damned. I embrace you. —Some money, in the name of God, some money!—To crown my misfortunes I am on the verge of losing an eye. I can no longer read what I am writing to you.

When a sequester was put on his properties, Sade would have no rental income until his name was removed from the *émigré* list. He could prove that he had not been outside France since 1776, but the confusion over his Christian names and the inconsistency in his signatures made it impossible to prove that he was the Sade whose name had been crossed off the list in 1793. In September 1798, he and Marie-Constance were so short of money they could not go on living at Saint-Ouen and they were forced to separate. She stayed with friends while he took refuge with a farmer on his land at Beauce, but within a few weeks he had outstayed his welcome and had to move on.

At the beginning of 1799 he was living in Versailles. 'There,' he wrote to Gaufridy, 'at the back of a barn, my lady-friend's son, a servant-girl and I are living on carrots and beans. We warm ourselves (not every day but when we can) with some faggots, which we can buy on credit half the time. Our desolation has reached the point at which Mme Quesnet, when she visits us, brings food in her pocket from her friends.' *La Nouvelle Justine* and *Juliette* were selling extremely well, but in clandestine editions which yielded no share of the book-sellers' profits to the author.[1]

By February 1799, when the sequester was finally lifted, Sade was working at the Versailles theatre, earning 40 sols a day and still appealing to Gaufridy for help. Even in October, when Gaufridy sent a post-dated letter of credit which lost a quarter of its value if it was cashed earlier, Sade went on hoping for a change of heart: 'In the name of God, you must alter your behaviour and start doing everything you can to raise funds, because I am dying, literally, of hunger, am quite naked and am obliged to keep alive by having recourse to dirty work. Yes, dirty work . . . I have been reduced to *stealing* furniture from my son's room because I needed the money to buy bread.'

Sade's humiliation coincided with the end of parliamentary government. After Napoleon had defeated the Austrians in 1797, his Egyptian campaign was a failure, but, returning to France, he used his army to intimidate the two chambers of the Directory into appointing three provisional consuls. The deputies were then dismissed. Within two years, his own appointment as First Consul was made permanent, and in 1804 he was crowned as Emperor of the French.

In December 1799 *Oxtiern* was produced at Versailles with Sade as Fabrice, the inn-keeper, but his earnings were negligible and Marie-Constance, who had been pawning her clothes, finally took a job. On the third day of the new century he was taken into the hospital at Versailles. When he wrote to tell Gaufridy that he would otherwise have 'died in the street', he received a reply from one of the lawyer's sons, Charles: 'I have money for you, but I am taking it upon myself to delay sending it.' Sade did not want,

---

[1] The Italian poet Ugo Foscolo reported: 'I happened to see this book in the year 1804 in a small town between France and Flanders in the house of a poor printer who was preparing its twentieth or maybe thirtieth clandestine edition for a Paris bookseller.'

even now, to take legal action. Two weeks later he was informed that Charles Gaufridy had been in Arles, where he could have collected some rent, but it had been too cold.

'Everyone here who sees my situation is revolted by your behaviour,' Sade wrote to Gaufridy *père*. 'It makes them all shudder, and when I show them Charles's letters, they sympathize with me for being in the hands of such a fool. In a word I can wait no longer. Send my money or I will go to any lengths to extricate it from your crooked and barbarous hands.' In February, threatened with imprisonment by the owner of a local restaurant where he had not been able to pay his bills, Sade warned Gaufridy: 'The people who will come to find you will know how to make you disgorge. You can be sure that they will have a dose of emetic strong enough to clean out your gullet.' But the threat was not carried out until June 1800, when Marie-Constance travelled to Provence with a lawyer empowered to inspect both Sade's properties and Gaufridy's accounts. If only Sade had taken action five or ten years earlier, he, Marie-Constance and her son could have been living very much more comfortably. As it was, he had no sooner used the law as a weapon than it was used, far more viciously, against him.

On 6 March 1801 he was arrested again. His new publisher, Nicolas Massé, had denounced him, and he was at Massé's office, discussing *Les Crimes de l'amour*, when police officers arrived to arrest both men, and to search the premises for obscene manuscripts. They found several, including *Juliette*. Sade was then escorted to Saint-Ouen. After ransacking the house, the police impounded three pictures and a tapestry illustrating sequences from *Justine*. Before he was taken away, the distraught Marie-Constance made a promise not to abandon him. He was secretly detained for two days and two nights in a small room at the prefecture. Meanwhile Massé obtained his own release by surrendering the stock of *Juliette*: a thousand copies were taken from their hiding-place and destroyed. Sade, who was submitted to three two-hour bouts of interrogation within three days, consistently denied authorship. He was only the copyist, he said. Marie-Constance made several attempts to see him, but in vain. After a fortnight, he was moved into a cell and kept there for over three months before he was told that he was going to prison. It had been agreed between the Prefect and the Minister of Police that public proceedings would cause too much scandal: an 'administrative punishment' was preferable. As the author of the 'infamous novel' *Justine* and of 'the still more frightful work' *Juliette*, he was transferred to Sainte-Pélagie on April 5.

Chapter 13

Prison and Asylum

'The entr'actes of my life have been too long', is a phrase Sade noted down to use in the memoirs he was planning. At the age of sixty-two he had not had as much as six consecutive years of freedom since his early thirties. Only a few hundred yards from the Collège Louis-le-Grande, Sainte-Pélagie was another converted convent which had been used as a prison during the revolution. Marie-Constance had obtained permission to visit him three times every ten days and on her first visit 'she seemed to be harbouring suspicions of family intrigues against me ... I noticed a lot of inconsistencies in what she said, and from that moment I was aware that the system of numbers would be working against me, as at the Bastille.'

In most ways his situation was worse. He was not allowed the books he wanted to read. Though he had writing materials at his disposal, everything was subject to censorship and there was little prospect of being allowed to publish. Knowing that if he admitted his authorship of *Justine* and *Juliette*, he would lose all chance of being released, he denounced them in his notebooks, hoping to convince the censors of his innocence. How absurd that *Justine* should be reprinted while publication of *his* work was delayed—perhaps even prevented. Men of letters, as Diderot had said, were always the victims of stupidity. 'Bravo, my friends! You would be inconsistent if you did not resist the good and champion the bad. Our revolution was in vain. It was written up above that the worst abuses would persist in our country as long as there is a sun in the sky.'

After fifteen months of imprisonment without a trial, he wrote to the Minister of Justice to demand one. 'I am the author—or not —of the book imputed to me. If I can be convicted I will submit to judgement; if not, I want my freedom.'

The appeal was ignored, and Sade went on denouncing *Justine* as infamous, disgusting, full of filth. But once he starts to condemn his own work, for whatever reason, a writer is only too liable to find himself partially in agreement with the criticisms he voices. 'What would you say,' Sade wrote, 'of the man who purposely dragged his favourite coat through the mud?' The apparent point is that he would not have jeopardized the reputation of *Aline et Valcour* by writing *Justine*; but he may also have meant that he was betraying his favourite novels. He was saying that *Justine* could be used as ammunition by those who wanted to defend conventional morality. Was it not obvious that all the characters who philosophized were evil?

As before, he had no notion of how long he would be living in a cell. According to another prisoner at Sainte-Pélagie, the novelist Charles Nodier, Sade was mostly in a deep depression:

> At first I noticed only the enormous obesity which so hampered his movements as to deprive them of the traces of grace and elegance that were still visible in his manners and his speech. However, his weary eyes still had something indescribable, something brilliant and fine which came to life from time to time, like a dying spark on a dead coal . . . He was courteous to the point of obsequiousness, affable to the point of unction and he spoke respectfully of everything that is respectable.

There is no evidence of any violence. He seems never to have slapped a warder's face. But after two years of sexual solitude, he used, according to police records, 'all the means suggested by his depraved imagination to . . . seduce and corrupt the young people who were confined in Sainte-Pélagie because of unhappy circumstances and whom chance had situated in the same corridor.' The youngsters complained about him, with the result that Sade was transferred to Bicêtre, the notorious prison which had been known as 'the rabble's Bastille'. It was now full of lunatics.

Ensuing on the Declaration of Human Rights, the decree of 13 March 1790 had grouped lunatics with criminals in exempting both from the ruling that prisoners held under *lettres de cachet* must be set free. That madmen needed help, not punishment, was implicit in the decree: after being interrogated by magistrates and interviewed by physicians they should be either released or treated 'in hospitals indicated for that purpose'. The problem was that these hospitals did not yet exist. The law of August 1790 bracketed madmen with 'vicious and dangerous animals', entrusting both to the vigilance of the municipal bodies. Madmen from all over Paris were sent to Bicêtre, which had been a prison, a hospital and, in effect, a poorhouse. As the administrator complained in 1794, nine years before Sade arrived, the poor and the old 'have before their eyes nothing but chains, bars and bolts. Add to this the groans of the prisoners . . .' But at least madmen were no longer being kept in chains: the turning-point had come earlier in the year, after a visit by Philippe Pinel, the philanthropist, who was to produce the authoritative *Traité médico-philosophique sur l'aliénation mentale* (1801).

Sade was at Bicêtre for only forty-four days, but he was to spend the rest of his life among the insane. Thanks to an appeal made by his sons to the Prefect of Police, he was transferred to Charenton, where special precautions were taken to prevent him from escaping. The family agreed to pay 3,000 livres a year for his accommodation and food.

The prominence of water in the therapy provided at Charenton was due partly to superstition. Immersion was associated with purification, baptism, rebirth; water was naturally beneficent, and extravagant ideas could be washed away. As in the Middle Ages, it was believed that a maniac should be pushed under water repeatedly until he had 'lost his strength and forgotten his fury'. At Charenton there were two forms of hydrotherapy: the shower and the surprise bath. For the shower the patient was tied into an armchair. About eight foot above his head was a vertical pipe leading down from a huge reservoir. When the tap was turned, the water poured down with great force. A jet of cold water on the head, said Pinel, would put the lunatic out of countenance and dislodge a fixed idea by giving him a violent surprise, but the harshness of the remedy should be counterbalanced by kind words and even jokes.

Pinel disapproved of the 'surprise bath', but it was used a great deal at Charenton, according to Hippolyte de Colins, an ex-cavalry officer who in 1812 wrote a confidential report on the asylum for the Minister of the Interior. 'Imagine a pool of water 10–12 feet long, 7–8 feet wide and 5–6 feet deep . . . Two of the male nurses seize hold of him, undress him, blindfold him and lead him backwards down the vaulted corridor. After these frightening preparations, he is seated on the edge of the pool, taken by the hair and pulled suddenly into the cold water, where he is held for some time, totally submerged.'

In 1803 Charenton was no longer in the hands of the friars, as it had been when Sade was there fourteen years earlier. It had been closed in 1795 and reopened in 1797 under the control of the Minister of the Interior, but in practice all the administrative power was in the hands of the director, de Coulmier, a short, ugly man of the same age as Sade. He had been an abbot and a member of the Constituent Assembly. Establishing an excellent international reputation for the asylum, he was able to spend 150,000 livres on new buildings and on improving the gardens between 1806 and 1812.

There were about 350 patients, mostly male, and a staff of about fifty, mostly male nurses, who had unlimited opportunities for taking sadistic pleasure. Administering the cold showers, they would abuse the patients instead of giving them kind words and jokes. Of the punishments they could impose, the most dangerous was solitary confinement in the damp rooms below ground level where a great deal of rheumatism was induced. Standards of hygiene were extremely low, if Colins is to be believed. Sade was put in a small room on the first floor of a four-storey building where only the top floor was kept clean, thanks to the male nurse in charge of it. Coulmier, who hardly ever made tours of inspection, left his staff very much to themselves, and few of them troubled to sweep floors, clean walls or even to keep inmates provided with drinking-water. Ventilation was poor, and smells spread along each corridor from the lavatory in the corner. There were not enough sheets; blankets were filthy and badly torn; chamber-pots, glasses and crockery were not properly washed. There was no segregation of inmates according to their ailments: melancholics who wanted to be left alone were importuned by maniacs. Those who became violent were beaten and locked up.

Sade went on objecting obstreperously to being interned without a trial, but within a few months he was reading and writing steadily. Mme de Staël had published her novel *Delphine* in 1802, and the following year, when Sade was reading it, he was sufficiently impressed to copy out forty-two passages, mostly concerned with adversity and the process of ageing: 'It is horrible to see the circle of years closing in on one without one's ever having enjoyed happiness.'

The violence of the Revolutionary mob had left vivid images in his mind. His notebooks compare the women from the court of Catherine de Medici, who came out of the Louvre to look at the naked bodies of the massacred Huguenots, with the women of Paris on 10 August 1792 staring at the corpses of the Swiss Guards in the Tuileries. He began writing notes for a new epistolary novel which would have had affinities with both *La Philosophie* and *Les Liaisons dangereuses*. He started the preliminary notes for a massive new novel, *Les Journées de Florbelle ou la Nature devoilée suivie des Mémoires de l' Abbé de Modose et Les Aventures d'Emilie de Volnange servant de preuves aux assertions*. He completed this in April 1807, reconstituting some of the lost material from *120 journées*. And he was working on two collections of stories.

As before, his output seems to have been unaffected by the danger that at any moment the police could seize all his papers. The first time this happened was in May 1804, when he received an ultimatum from the Prefect of Police that he would be sent back to Bicêtre if his behaviour did not improve. He was still protesting, uselessly, against the violation of human rights by which he was deprived of his liberty. In September the Prefect of Police and the Minister of Police issued a joint report which characterized him as 'an incorrigible man . . . in a permanent state of libertine dementia . . . There are grounds for leaving him at Charenton, where his family pays for his board and where, for the sake of its honour, it wishes him to remain.' The official attitude was exactly the same as before the revolution.

Marie-Constance had been living in the asylum with him since July. The other inmates were told that she was his illegitimate daughter, and even in his diaries he keeps up the pretence, though sometimes *amie* is crossed out for *fille* to be substituted. She was free to go to Paris whenever she wanted; sometimes she spent several nights there. In allowing her to move in, Coulmier had accorded Sade a very rare privilege: the relationship between the two men had improved as Sade's hopes of liberation dwindled, and, unlike most of the inmates, he was given complete freedom of movement inside the house and the park.

To catch the attention of the fashionable public Coulmier mounted theatrical entertainments at the asylum every month.

With his professional experience, Sade was useful, not only as a writer but as a director and sometimes as an actor. The performance was usually a double-bill consisting of a comedy, a drama or an opera combined with a ballet. Occasionally there was a firework display. Invitations, worded to arouse curiosity, were distributed in Paris and the suburbs. It was generally assumed that the performers were all lunatics and that spectators would see for themselves how theatre dispelled illusion from the diseased mind. In fact the chief performers were a former male nurse, who had been made Coulmier's secretary, a wine merchant from the village, the chief clerk of a local bailiff, dancers from the Opera and men recruited from the Café Touchard, a rendezvous for unemployed actors. Money was spent lavishly on costumes, decor and music. In the auditorium about forty seats were reserved for patients—convalescents and melancholics, with the men segregated from the women. The maniacs and the violent could not be admitted, and the others squabbled over the tickets.

Sade coached the actors, selected the plays and directed the performances, besides writing a good deal of material, including verse for interpolation into plays by other writers. He wrote a rhymed eulogy of the imperial family, several eulogies of M. Coulmier and, once, a play in his honour. Sometimes he sang, and one of his most effective characterizations was of a villain. According to the disapproving de Colins, 'he played with a veracity that came straight from the criminality in his heart. I saw the whole audience tremble with horror at this spectacle, while M. Coulmier went red with anger at not hearing any applause in the auditorium.'

There were also concerts at the asylum and every Thursday there was a ball. According to de Colins, the therapeutic value of the music might have been greater if fewer strangers had been invited, but M. Coulmier loved to have contact with the *beau monde*. 'In an asylum where the passions that cause the disease should be damped down, there is no scruple about inflaming them by bringing the sexes together . . . by dancing, physical contact, postures etc! And these are nervously excitable women. It is hysterics and nymphomaniacs who are being made to dance.'

In January 1806, at the age of sixty-five, Sade made his will. To thank Marie-Constance for the sincere friendship she had shown since 25 August 1790, he wanted her to have 80,000 livres in cash together with all his furniture, linen, clothes, books and papers, except the papers that had belonged to his father. These were to go to his children. His body must not be dissected and must be kept in the room where he died for forty-eight hours before being placed in a wooden coffin, which was to be fetched by M. Le Normand of Versailles, the timber merchant, who was to carry it on his cart to the wood on Sade's property at Malmaison, and to supervise while the farmer dug a grave in the copse. The coffin was to be buried without any ceremony, in the presence of any relations and friends who wished to attend, and acorns were to be planted on the grave so that 'when the copse becomes as thickly wooded as it was before, the traces of my tomb disappear from the face of the earth, as I expect to disappear from human memory, save in the minds of those few who wanted to love me until the last minute and of whom I carry a fond memory to the grave.'

Soon after this, he wrote his last letter to Gaufridy, again treating him as an old friend: 'And you, my dear lawyer, you, my life's contemporary, my childhood companion, how are you?' He went on to enquire about the people he knew at Lacoste. 'And what state is it in, the château? And my poor park? Is there still anything of me there that people can see? . . . Perhaps you would now like a word about me. Well, *I am not happy*, but I am in good health. This is all I can answer to the questions I hope friendship still asks.' He signed the letter 'Yours for life' and concealed the fact of being in an asylum: 'Our address is—care of M. de Coulmier, President of the Canton and Member of the Legion of Honour, Charenton-Saint-Maurice.'

Though he was now enjoying more freedom of movement and more deference than he had received in prison, he could not manage without his mad numerology. It was not merely a means of calculating how much time he still had to serve, it had become a source of semi-mystical satisfaction. On 5 June 1807, when the police once again seized all his papers, he calculated that it was three years, one month and five days since they had last been taken away. Among the manuscripts confiscated this time were the drafts of the long novel *Les Journées de Florbelle*. He was assured that anything 'useful to him' would be returned: the novel was never returned. On 2 August he noted that the number 2 was being signalled to him: 'I was sent 2 newspapers, 2 people from Mazan came to see me, etc.' On 12 September, the figure 1 was being signalled all day. Louis-Marie had written on the 10th to say that he would come to Charenton on the 12th. He returned Volume I of *Les Crimes de l'amour*, which he had borrowed, and borrowed Volume I of *L'Histoire de France*. At dinner one extra course was served, and his son talked about the first volume—the only one he was to complete—in his own *Histoire de la nation Française*.

On the forty-first anniversary of his father's death, in January 1808, Sade wrote: 'I think about him all day, and do not go to bed without shedding tears for him. Ah! If he were still alive, would he have tolerated all the idiocies I have had to suffer!!!'

Coulmier frequently came under pressure—both from doctors at the asylum and from the Prefect of Police—to give Sade less freedom, and in May 1808 the family was plotting to have him imprisoned in a fortress where he would have been shut more securely away from the public eye. On 31 May 1808 he received a surprise visit from Donatien-Claude who wanted his consent to marry. Sade, who raised no objection, was asked to sign the contract at a notary's office. Coulmier at first refused permission for him to leave Charenton but eventually agreed, on condition that it was in the evening. An express letter then arrived from Louis-Marie, who appeared the next day to warn his father that it was a trap. He would have been taken from the notary's office to the Tower of Ham or the Mont-Saint-Michel. After that, though Sade refused to have anything to do with either the notary or the contract, the danger was not over.

In August 1808, the Chief Medical Officer at Charenton, Royer-Collard, wrote to tell the Minister of Police that the author of the infamous novel *Justine* was not mad. 'His delirium is that of vice ... He preaches his horrible doctrine to some of the inmates, lends his books to others ... For the public performances he has a certain number of tickets at his disposal and he helps to do the honours in the hall ... I must suggest to Your Excellency that a prison or a fortress would be more suitable for him than an establishment dedicated to the treatment of the sick, who need the most assiduous supervision and the most delicate moral precautions.' On 2 September, the Prefect made a report to the Minister recommending that Sade should be transferred to a state prison, and on the same day the Minister decided on the Tower of Ham. It was only by calling on him that Coulmier could persuade him to postpone the move. In November the date was fixed for 15 April 1809, and in April it was postponed indefinitely. Six weeks later Louis-Marie was on his way to rejoin his regiment in Italy when he was ambushed and killed by Neapolitan rebels.

His mother outlived him by just over a year. Blind and fat, she was living with Madeleine-Laure in the château at Echauffour, which she had inherited. She died on 7 July 1810. Sade does not seem to have been much affected by the news of her death.

He was allowed to have dinner-parties in his room, where he entertained some of the most celebrated actors and actresses. Together with the power he wielded as producer and Master of Ceremonies, his privileges caused a good deal of jealousy. This gave rise to complaints, and some of them filtered through to the Minister of the Interior, the Comte de Montalivet. In October 1810 Coulmier was ordered to keep Sade in solitary confinement. He retorted that he was not a gaoler, and in the circumstances he could only ask for M. de Sade to be transferred elsewhere. But when one of Sade's nieces called on the Count, he allowed himself to be persuaded that things could continue as they were. There were more complaints, of course, especially after the police discovered that copies of *La Nouvelle Justine* were being sold by two booksellers. One of them had 100 copper plates from which he was printing and selling illustrations to *Juliette*. When Sade's imprisonment came under discussion at the Privy Council in July 1811, Napoleon finally ruled that he should stay on at Charenton. Even then the subject was not closed; it came up again in April 1812 and yet again in May, but Napoleon did not change his mind.

In November 1812, a girl of fifteen whose mother worked at the asylum paid her first visit to Sade's room; they slept together for the first time in the middle of May 1813, when he was not quite seventy-three. He had first noticed Madeleine Leclerc when she was twelve; she seems to have been apprenticed either to a dressmaker or a laundress, and she was earning only 3 livres a week, so she was glad to be given some extra money, some pairs of stockings and some tuition in reading and writing. Sade compulsively noted down the number of times she came to his room and the number of times they made love. He was upset when she seemed cold and passive; often she was responsive and eager to please him. She took her cues from her mother, who was keen for the relationship to continue. Madeleine was tolerant when he could not go on for long enough to satisfy her, and she would appease his jealousy with promises—which she did not always keep—not to go to the asylum balls. 'She made me great promises of submission and fidelity,' he noted on 25 September 1814, 'promised never to go with anyone who would displease me, or cause me anxiety.'

A student doctor, J.-J. Ramon, who joined the staff at Charenton on 11 November 1814, later described him rather in the way his father might have been described in old age:

> In the corridor outside his room I would often meet him, dressed very carelessly, walking alone, with a heavy, dragging gait. I never saw him in conversation with anybody. I would acknowledge him as I passed, and he responded to my salutation with that cold politeness which shuts out any possibility of entering into conversation ... I would never have suspected that he was the author of *Justine* and *Juliette*: the only impression he made was of a haughty, morose old gentleman.

On 1 December Sade found that he could no longer move his legs. He was moved into a different room, with a servant to look after him. In the afternoon Donatien-Claude, now a man of forty-five, came to see him. Marie-Constance, who had been quarrelling with him about Madeleine, may have been in Paris. Donatien-Claude asked Dr Ramon to spend the night in his father's room. 'I had nothing more to do than give him some mouthfuls of herbal tea and a medicine which had been prescribed. His breathing, which was noisy and laborious, became more painful. Towards the middle of the night, shortly after giving him a drink, I was surprised at hearing no sound from him. I went over to his bed and I can confirm that he was dead.'

He was buried in the cemetery at Charenton near the border dividing it from the Bois de Vincennes. The gravestone was engraved with a simple cross, no name, no inscription. At his death, as during his life, his own wishes were ignored. Donatien-Claude, who asked the police to destroy *Les Journées de Florbelle*, went along to watch the burning of the manuscript.

A few years later, when several of the tombs at Charenton were exhumed, Dr Ramon obtained possession of Sade's skull. He lent it to a phrenologist, Spurzheim, who promised to return it together with several plaster casts, but apparently lost it somewhere in America. In the opinion of Ramon, who had studied phrenology, its dome was beautifully developed, indicating benevolence, and there were no signs of ferocity, pugnacity or excessive carnality. 'His skull was in all points similar to that of a father of the Church.'

cA Negative Strain

If we were not still afraid of de Sade, why would we still be keeping his books on the poison shelf? Nearly twenty years have passed since the trial that vindicated the Penguin publication of *Lady Chatterley's Lover*, but in England it is still impossible to buy a translation of *Justine* or *Juliette*. That they are boring is a rumour propagated by people who have never read them: in the United States the hardback editions of 1965 and 1968 were rapidly followed by paperback editions which have since gone through several reprints.

It is not hard to explain why Sade's work has been considered dangerous. 'Our civilization,' wrote Freud, 'is, generally speaking, founded on the suppression of instincts . . . Each individual is potentially an enemy of civilization, though civilization is supposed to be an object of universal human interest . . . So one gets the impression that civilization was imposed on a resisting majority . . . built up on the coercion and renunciation of instinct.'[1] No one has ever argued more uncompromisingly than Sade that we should give free rein to our destructive impulses, overcoming all inclination to altruism and remorse. Many of his contemporaries were sceptical about the doctrine that the interests of the individual coincided with the interests of the majority; none came so close as he did to anticipating Freud both in his explanation of conscience as the product of guilt feelings and in his insistence that aggression is fundamental to all sexuality, as eroticism is to all human energy. It was Nature's intention, suggested Sade, to merge love with cruelty. 'Why would the paroxysm of pleasure be a kind of madness unless the mother of the human race had wanted anger and sexuality to express themselves in the same way?'

In the seventeenth century Pascal's view of human nature was no less derogatory. Without the Christian religion, he said, humanity, nature and history would become monstrous and chaotic. In the eighteenth century, Diderot was similarly con-

[1] *Civilization and Its Discontents.*

vinced that civilization could not have been achieved without producing an unresolvable tension between instinct and restraint, or, as he put it in *Le Supplément au voyage de Bougainville* (1772), an interminable war between natural man and artificial man. Pascal had his stabilizing faith in God, and Diderot did not believe that sexual liberation would necessarily produce an anarchy of aggression, but Sade had nothing to hold him back from taking a totally negative view of human existence.

He even had the advantage of writing from prison, which gave him greater freedom of expression than any of the other free-thinking *philosophes*. Until recently historians of philosophy and literature consistently excluded him from this category, but some are now acknowledging that he belongs to the same movement of intellectual liberation as Voltaire, Rousseau and the other Encyclopaedists.[1] They had to work against powerful resistance from Church, state and reactionary *littérateurs*. Many of their books were burned by order of the courts and publication of the *Encyclopédie*, which had started in 1751, was banned by royal decree in 1759. At different stages of their careers, Diderot, Voltaire and his friend Marmontel, who contributed many of the articles on literature, were disciplined with periods of imprisonment; Rousseau escaped only after orders had been issued for his arrest. This helps to explain why the tenor of Diderot's unpublished dialogues is so different from that of his articles in the *Encyclopédie* and of his other published work. The disparity seems to date from his imprisonment in Vincennes after the *Lettres sur les aveugles* had been printed in 1749. Even by circulating his dialogues among friends he was running the risk that he would be betrayed, so he was careful—in *Le Neveu de Rameau* for instance—not to take an unequivocal position between the viewpoints of his personae. Most of the talking is done by the nephew, who reads *L'Avare* and *Tartuffe* with a view to picking up hints from Molière on how to be avaricious and hypocritical without seeming to be. It is not evil that upsets people but the indications of it. Erect a façade of virtue, and behind it you can be true to nature—your own nature. Genuine virtue, he says, can lead only to unhappiness; 'I achieve happiness through natural defects which I have acquired with no

[1] See for instance Lester G. Crocker, *Nature and Culture*, Baltimore, 1963, and Pascal Pia, 'Sade à notre horizon', *Magazine littéraire*, No 114, June 1976.

trouble, preserve without effort and which tally with the *mores* of my country.' There is no hint of Diderot's sympathy for 'Lui' in anything said by 'Moi', who finds him entertaining but disapproves and disagrees. It is 'Lui', though, who is brought warmly, vividly and amusingly to life, while 'Moi' remains little more than a foil. Lui's viewpoint has much in common with Sade's, but while Sade was writing from prison he had almost nothing to lose. When he was released after the Revolution, his freedom depended on denying that he was the author of *Justine*.

Not that either Voltaire or Rousseau had been looking optimistically forward to liberty and equality: the view they took of human nature made it impossible for them to entertain the idea of popular democracy. Rousseau's *Emile* begins:

> Everything is good as it leaves the hand of the Author of all things, everything degenerates in the hands of man.

Natural man must be transformed into 'l'homme civil':

> Good social institutions are those which are best able to denaturalize (*dénaturer*) man, take away his absolute existence in favour of a relative existence, transporting the self into the common unity, so that each individual no longer believes himself to be a whole, but part of a whole, and is sensitive only in relation to it.

While condemning the chains that a corrupt civilization had put on humanity, he had to believe that 'natural impulses' would lead only to good behaviour, that conscience was a 'divine instinct which would speak only with the voice of Reason'. The seeds of despair are strongly evident; without his faith in God he could not have stopped them from germinating.

According to Walter Benjamin, Baudelaire was the first poet to express modern alienation, but his negativity is Sadean. The influence is unmistakable in such declarations as: 'Nature can advocate nothing but crime . . . Everything that is beautiful and noble results from reason and calculation. Crime originates naturally: the human animal acquires the taste for it inside its mother's stomach.'[1]

The phrases *Les Fleurs du mal* and 'Spleen et Idéal' (the title of

[1] 'Le Peintre de la vie moderne', reprinted in *L'Art romantique*.

the first section) are indicative of Baudelaire's awareness that he was growing something beautiful out of filthy soil—'*l'horreur et l'extase de la vie*'. He was the first Romantic to be totally free from the romantic fallacy of continuing reciprocity in the love relationship. It was Sade who taught him that it can be cruel to inflict enjoyment on another human body, and, in making the point that one lover was almost invariably more eager than the other, he used the Sadean image of executioner and victim; sometimes he compared the sexual act with a fight between two warriors. But when he wrote 'the unique and supreme pleasure of love lies in the certainty of doing evil', he was not merely saying that self-consciousness about giving sensations is partly sadistic: he was echoing Sade's statement that 'horror, nastiness and the frightful are what give pleasure during fornication'. If the instinct is animal, the sense of evil and nastiness can only have been imposed by civilization.

In the alienation that is so prominent in modern literature, revulsion against human nature interpenetrates with revulsion against our environment. It was characteristic of nineteenth-century Romantics to concentrate on individual moments of intense experience; eighteenth-century Classicism thrived on the assumption that nature was something that could be *copied* in both senses of the word. Moral lessons could be derived from her example, while the function of art was to reproduce the harmony God had created between man and his surroundings. The French word *aliénation* means both alienation and madness: as Michel Foucault has pointed out, it was no accident that Sadism appeared during the Age of Reason. He calls it 'a massive cultural fact . . . which constitutes one of the greatest conversions of Western imagination: unreason transformed into delirium of the heart, madness of desire, the insane dialogue of love and death in the limitless presumption of appetite.'[1] Classicism had denied the animality of human nature, transforming passion into sentiment, restraining the imagination on the leash of refinement. The poet could no longer group himself with the lunatic and the lover; an eighteenth-century equivalent of Shakespeare or Rabelais is unthinkable. Language became a system of signs that corresponded as uncreatively as labels with what they represented. Everything that could be discussed could be categorized; nothing could be

[1] *Madness and Civilization.*

admitted to exist unless it could be discussed. Sexual fantasies were rigidly repressed by a decorum that rendered them inarticulate.

The French language was even more restrictive than English. There had been no Shakespeare to bring the rhythms and idiom of verse closer to those of everyday speech, and while education was dominated by the Jesuits the taboo on vulgarity was even stronger than in Dr Johnson's London. The lower parts of the body, like the lower classes of society, were almost unmentionable. Crudity must be avoided at whatever cost of circumlocution. For Racine, to tame a wild horse is 'to bridle an untamed charger into gentleness'; a commonplace animal like a dog must be dignified with some such otiose epithet as 'devouring'.

By 1740, when Sade was born, literary convention, like morality, was already beginning to crack under the tension. 'Pleasures always gain from being ennobled,' said Crébillon *fils*, who wrote *Le Sopha* in 1742, while his father was the dramatic censor. Neither the erotic fiction of the son nor the spell of imprisonment it had earned him in 1734 prevented him from succeeding to the position of dramatic censor in 1759—the year in which the *Encyclopédie* was banned. Choderlos de Laclos, the most important of Sade's predecessors in the tradition of the libertine novel, was even more cynical than Crébillon in submitting passion and pleasure to ruthless analysis, but there is no deviation from politeness in his fiction, and no direct description of sexual encounters (though the illustrations in the original of *Les Liaisons dangereuses* left little to the imagination). When Louis XIV's long reign ended in 1715, the French aristocracy had been largely dispossessed of its political importance and its social responsibilities. Its values still derived from its traditional function of service to God and King, but the secular morality of the Enlightenment was becoming influential. Deprived of its power, the nobility was not losing its appetite for power, which was partly diverted into the game of seduction. The sophisticated letters that constitute *Les Liaisons dangereuses* centre on two pleasures which are sadistic but not physical: one is outmanœuvring a skilful opponent; the other is corrupting someone beautiful, young and virtuous. The second theme appealed equally to Sade, and in Huysmans's *A Rebours* (1884) and Oscar Wilde's *The Picture of Dorian Gray* (1891) we find a direct continuation of the same line.

Seduction was a form of self-assertion, and the more expensive eighteenth-century coquettes learned how to make the moment of capitulation seem more meaningful by delaying it. Actresses used their professional skills in private dramas. Sade was no less concerned than Laclos with domination, but much less concerned with tactics. By choosing isolated locales for his action, he gives his libertines more power over their victims, who seldom even take advantage of the little opportunity they have for resistance. While the pleasure-seekers in *Les Liaisons dangereuses* are more interested in their victims' emotions than their own, Sade's seem to experience no emotion except anger and no pleasure except in sensation. Direct description of the sexual act is indispensable, so he cannot avoid euphemisms and circumlocutions which are almost reminiscent of Racine's, even when a certain irony is present. As Roland Barthes has said, Sade used a fastidious combination of rawness and rhetoric to scorch away the patina left by centuries of literary politeness.

Sade is given a prominent place in Camus's book *L'Homme révolté*. It defines 'metaphysical rebellion' as 'the movement by which a man ranges himself against his condition and the whole of creation'. Camus maintains that there was no 'coherent' example of it until the end of the eighteenth century, when 'the modern age began with a loud noise of collapsing walls . . . Historically the first coherent attack is that of Sade, who collects in a single, enormous war-machine all the arguments of libertine thought up to Meslier and Voltaire. It goes without saying that his negation is also the most extreme.' The word 'libertine' had been in the French language since the fifteenth century (as it had in English since the fourteenth) as a translation of the Latin *libertinus* (freed from slavery). By the sixteenth century it had acquired a double meaning in both French and English: free-thinking and profligate. Criticism of orthodox dogma was associated with indifference to morality. (Language often operates in this reactionary way, vilifying heterodox phenomena and sensuous pleasure with pejorative connotations. Even today it is hard to feel innocent when talking about sexuality: so many of the relevant words are either intrinsically ugly or loaded with obscene associations.) In the sixteenth century, *Libertins* was the name of a religious sect, and the libertine thinkers of the seventeenth century, whom Molière attacked in his *Dom Juan*, were the intellectual ancestors of the Enlightenment *philosophes*, but by the eighteenth century the connotation of licentiousness was so strong that 'pious libertine' would have seemed like a contradiction, though it was still possible to talk about a pious atheist. After the death of Louis XIV, the word *libertinage* became more fashionable. In his old age the King had turned to religion, prompting a display of holy zeal among his courtiers. It is usually assumed that immorality increased under the Regency, but the change may have been mainly superficial. According to one witness, 'Some were as bogus in their libertinism as they had been in their piety, believing they could win favour by affecting the pursuit of pleasure.'[1]

There was nothing unusual about Sade's pride in calling himself a libertine. What was exceptional was his obstinacy in refusing to dichotomize theory and practice, ideas and sensations. As Edgell Rickword has said: 'The most astonishing thing about Sade is the integrity with which he suggests a cosmology and devises a sociology and an ethic based on an unrelenting fidelity to the experience of his own organism, wherever it might lead him.'[2] In other words he was a pre-Romantic individualist, though he was also typical of his period in so far as he believed in the possibility of using his experience to evolve categorizations which would have a general validity. No pervert has ever been a more avid cataloguer. His *120 journées de Sodome* was intended as a comprehensive listing of the destructive sexual passions. He also had an extraordinary talent for self-analysis and it is only prejudice and historical myopia that has denied him his importance as an originator of the alienated art in which case-history is inseparable from *œuvre*: Sade, Baudelaire, de Nerval, Lautréamont, Rimbaud, Artaud, Genet. As in the work of Kafka and Kierkegaard, the letters and journals take their place alongside the 'creative' work —the best of Sade's letters from Vincennes are better written than his fiction—and deprivation of love in childhood survives into the adult malaise. As an artist, of course, Sade cannot be placed on the same level as Baudelaire, de Nerval or Rimbaud, but in all these French *poètes maudits* the rebellion against the conventional language was inextricable from a rebellion against conventional

---

[1] 'Les Confessions du Comte de * * * écrits par lui-même à un ami', *Oeuvres*, 1821.

[2] 'Notes for a Study of Sade' in *Essays and Opinions 1921–31*, Carcanet, 1974.

morality and the idea of God, while the thirst for beauty and intensity of experience was imbued with a death-wish. What matters is to penetrate, at whatever cost, to the unknown.

Baudelaire ends his *Fleurs du mal* with a triumphantly joyful hymn to death:

Plusieurs réligions semblables à la notre,
Toutes escaladant le ciel; la Sainteté,
Comme en un lit de plume un delicat se vautre,
Dans les clous et le crin cherchant la volupté;

L'Humanité bavarde, ivre de son génie,
Et, folle maintenant comme elle était jadis,
Criant à Dieu, dans sa furibonde agonie:
'O mon semblable, o mon maître, je te maudis!'

Robert Lowell adapts these two stanzas as:

and everywhere religions like our own
all storming heaven, propped by saints who reign
like sybarites on beds of nails and frown—
all searching for some orgiastic pain!

Many, self-drunk, are lying in the mud—
mad now, as they have always been, they roll
in torment screaming to the throne of God:
'My image and my lord, I hate your soul!'[1]

As Artaud said, de Nerval's verse effectively accuses God of original sin, while Lautréamont's Maldoror lives virtuously until he

noticed that he had been born evil: extraordinary fate. For many years he hid his character as best he could; eventually this concentration, which was unnatural to him, made the blood rise to his head every day; until, unable to go on with such a life, he threw himself resolutely into a career of evil . . . pleasant atmosphere! When he kissed a small pink-faced child, he would have liked to cut its cheeks off with a razor . . .

[1] *Imitations*, Farrar Straus, 1961; Faber, 1962.

Rimbaud was sixteen and under the influence of Baudelaire when he mapped out his future career.

> Now I am debauching myself as much as possible. Why? I want to be a poet and I'm working at making myself into a Visionary (*Voyant*) ... It's a matter of penetrating to the unknown by means of a disordering of *all the senses*.[1]

Artaud's project for a Theatre of Cruelty was based on a Sadean idea. 'Cruelty is above all lucid, a sort of rigorous discipline, submission to necessity.' There could be no cruelty without consciousness. Consciousness was what 'gives its blood-red tinge to every act of living, its hue of cruelty, because it is understood that life is always the death of someone else.'[2]

Like Sade, Artaud spent a major part of his adult life behind bars; like Sade he was a violent extremist and genuinely dangerous. Roland Barthes is right to argue that 'the invention of a paradoxical discourse is more revolutionary than provocation'. The violence of the theatre that Artaud proposed is a Dionysian violence in which the floodgates of delirium and desire could be thrown wide open and the restraints of church and state, morality and hierarchy, swept aside in the onrush of libido.

By the time Genet started writing, his Weltanschauung was no less negative than Sade's. In social origin their lives could hardly have been more different; the affinity is most evident in their worshipful attitude towards crime and violence. Developed by their prison experiences, this can be seen to have originated from constant frustration of the hunger for love. Abandoned by his mother, Genet simultaneously blamed himself for being unlovable and entertained childhood fantasies of revenging himself by destroying her. Developing as a homosexual, he was asserting independence of the female sex, while in choosing the female role he was perpetuating the emotional frustration. Though he felt love towards the men who used him, he could neither share in their physical pleasure nor sense any reciprocal warmth. In his novels, as Sartre has pointed out,[3] the loved one is always described in negative terms—unyielding, immobile, inflexible, im-

---

[1] Letter to Georges Izambard, 13 May 1871.
[2] Letter of 13 September 1932 to Jean Paulhan.
[3] *Saint Genet, comédien et martyre*, Gallimard, 1952.

penetrable. As a male prostitute, Genet became involved with pimps who treated him brutally. Taking masochistic pleasure in this, he also took sadistic pleasure in treacherously outwitting them. As thief, prostitute, convict, betrayer, he became alienated from himself, actively embracing the rejection imposed by other people. At the same time, like Sade, he was able to detach himself from his own abjection, using it to construct a system of thought. 'Abjection is a methodical conversion,' said Sartre. 'It establishes the world as a closed system which consciousness regards from outside, in the manner of divine understanding.'

Whether the prisoner is alone in his cell, as Sade was, or sharing it, confinement induces new, quasi-meditative habits of thinking. After six and a half years at Vincennes, Sade had nothing he valued more than what was going on in his mind:

> My way of thinking is the fruit of my reflections; it is a part of my existence, my constitution ... [It] is my only comfort; it alleviates all my sufferings in prison, provides all the pleasures I have in the world and I value it more highly than life.[1]

It was a way of thinking that depended on a rejection—partly involuntary, partly voluntary—of external reality. He had no means of knowing how much distortion there was in the accounts that reached him of what was going on in the world outside the cell; as he wrote retrospectively in 1803, 'Wanting peace of mind, I preferred to believe nothing, scoff at everything.'[2] This affected the formative period of his development as a novelist. His fiction has little purchase on the objective world of people and things. If you try to read it as realistic narrative, it is boring. As Roland Barthes says: 'The spectacle consists entirely of discourse.'[3] Unlike D. H. Lawrence in *Lady Chatterley's Lover*, Sade was not trying to dramatize erotic action as vividly as the medium would permit. John Fraser has noticed[4] that the victims of the violence are abstracted from contact with workaday routines, which makes it more difficult for the reader to empathize with them. As with Genet, we are seldom shocked.

[1] Letter written at the beginning of November 1783.
[2] *Cahiers personnels* (*1803–4*).
[3] *Sade, Fourier, Loyola*, Seuil, 1971.
[4] *Violence in the Arts*, Cambridge, 1974.

Both Sade and Genet dissolve crime and sexuality in rhetoric. The action is subordinated to the imaginative and verbal embroidery. It is almost certain that neither man would have become a writer if he had not spent so much time in prison, and the experience which engendered the writing also engendered a habit of masturbation. Fantasies of revenge against society and against women began to revolve around vivid visualizations of other men's penises, punitively large. Sade also pictured women as victims of aggression. Genet's rhetoric is more poetic than Sade's, but in neither corpus of fiction are the characters endowed with independent vitality. Solitary fantasies of sexual activity are being verbalized, while crime is being sexualized. As Simone de Beauvoir has pointed out,[1] theft features in Sade's work as a sexual act, the mention of it sometimes being enough to provoke an orgasm. For Genet—in retrospect and probably in actuality—burglary was like rape. Entering the victim's room, he was entering a helpless man. 'He is a fluid element which I breathe, which enters into me, which swells my lungs.'

With Sade and Genet, as with other *poètes maudits*, the criss-crossing between life and art is complex and tangled. We owe our only knowledge of Genet the burglar to Genet the writer, but the same imagination was involved in house-breaking and in writing. Each experience has enriched the other with mental events and habits. With Sade, life and work could be said to have been conditioned by the same fantasies were it not for the fact that they were constantly developing, as he was, and it is important to see (as clearly as we can) how he represented himself to himself in each successive phase of his development. Even the books can be regarded, like Genet's, as efforts to regain mastery over his life. In neither case does this protect the reader from contagion. 'By injecting us with his evil,' wrote Sartre, 'Genet is getting rid of it. Each of his books is a cathartic crisis of possession . . . With each book, this possessed man goes further towards mastering the demon that possessed him.'

Sade's whole *oeuvre* could be viewed similarly as a massive attempt to get rid of his evil, to take vengeance against the mother who rejected him when he was four and the mother-in-law who caused him to spend more than half his adult life in prison; his formative novel, *Les 120 journées*, could not have been written

[1] *Faut-il brûler Sade?*, Cambridge, 1974.

by a free man. 'I would bet you imagined you were working wonders,' he wrote to Renée-Pélagie, 'in reducing me to an atrocious abstinence from the sins of the flesh. Well, you were quite mistaken. You were heating up my brain. You made me create phantoms which I must bring to life.' Genet's dependence on masturbation fantasies is remarkably similar: 'I exist only through those who do not exist except for the being they receive from me.'

There is no reason to doubt that Sade genuinely expected 'to disappear from human memory', or that he wanted to. If he still exists, it is not because his characters are so vivid. It is because he had the courage to go as far as it was possible to go in a direction he would never have taken if he had been given freedom of choice.

Bibliography

Sade's work:

Oeuvres complètes, 16 vols, Paris: Cercle du livre précieux, 1966–7

Correspondance inédite du Marquis de Sade de ses proches et ses familiers
(ed. Paul Bourdin), Paris: Libraire de France, 1929; Geneva:
Slatkine reprints, 1970

*Journal inédit. Deux cahiers retrouvés du journal inédit du Marquis de
Sade,* 1807–1808, 1814 (ed. Georges Daumas), Paris: Gallimard,
1970

Translations:

120 Days of Sodom (tr. Pieralessandro Cascavini), Paris: Olympia
Press, 1954

The Bedroom Philosophers (tr. Pieralessandro Cascavini), Paris:
Olympia Press, 1957

The Complete Justine, Philosophy in the Bedroom and other writings (tr.
Richard Seaver and Austryn Wainhouse), New York: Grove
Press, 1965

Juliette (tr. Austryn Wainhouse), New York: Grove Press, 1968

The Crimes of Love: Three Novellas (tr. Lowell Blair), New York:
Bantam Books, 1964

The Misfortunes of Virtue (tr. Harriet Sohmers), Paris: Obelisk
Press, 1953

Selected Writings of de Sade (Selected and translated by Leonard de
Saint-Yves), London: Peter Owen, 1953; New York: British
Book Centre, 1954

De Sade Quartet from *Contes et Fabliaux* (tr. Margaret Crosland),
London: Peter Owen, 1954

Selected Letters (tr. W. J. Strachan), London: Peter Owen, 1965

Bibliography:

CHANOVER, E. PIERRE, *The Marquis de Sade: a Bibliography,* New
Jersey: Scarecrow Press, 1973

Biography and Criticism of Sade:

1a) Books in French

BARTHES, ROLAND, *Sade, Fourier, Loyola*, Paris: Seuil, 1971

DE BEAUVOIR, SIMONE, *Faut-il brûler Sade?* Paris: Gallimard, 1955; (tr. Annette Michelson as *The Marquis de Sade*, London: Calder, 1962)

BLANCHOT, MAURICE, *Sade et Lautréamont*, Paris: Editions de Minuit, 1949

Centre Aixois d'Etudes et de recherches sur le 18ème siècle, *Le Marquis de Sade*, Paris, Armand Colin, 1968

CHÉRASSE, JEAN A. et GUICHENEY, G., *Sade, j'écris ton nom Liberté*, Paris: Pygmalion, 1976

DESBORDES, JEAN, *Le vrai visage du Marquis de Sade*, Paris: Editions de la nouvelle revue critique, 1939

DIDIER, BEATRICE, *Sade: une écriture du desir*, Paris: Denoël/Gonthier, 1976

HEINE, MAURICE, *Le Marquis de Sade*, Paris: Gallimard, 1950

KLOSSOWSKI, PIERRE, *Sade mon prochain*, Paris: Seuil, 1947

LELY, GILBERT, *Vie du marquis de Sade*, 2 vols, Paris: Gallimard, 1952–7; Revised I vol, Pauvert, 1965; (tr. Alec Brown, *The Marquis de Sade: A Biography*, London: Elek, 1961)

PAULHAN, JEAN, *Le Marquis de Sade et sa complice: ou les revanches de la pudeur*, Paris: Editions Lilac, 1951

ROGER, PHILIPPE, *Sade: la philosophie dans le pressoir*, Paris: Grasset, 1976

SWINBURNE, A. C., *Apologie de Sade*, London: printed for private circulation, 1906

1b) Books in English

GORER, GEOFFREY, *The Life and Ideas of the Marquis de Sade*, London: Peter Owen, 1953 (based on his book *The Revolutionary Ideas of the Marquis de Sade*, Wishart, 1934)

SOMMERS, MONTAGUE, *The Marquis de Sade, a Study in Algolagnia*, London: British Society for the Study of Sex Psychology, 1920

THOMAS, DONALD, *The Marquis de Sade*, London, Weidenfeld and Nicolson, 1977

2a) Essays and articles in French

BATAILLE, GEORGES, 'Sade' in *La Littérature et le mal*, Paris: Gallimard, 1957

CAMUS, 'La négation absolue' in *L'homme révolté*, Paris: Gallimard, 1951

LACAN, JACQUES, 'Kant avec Sade' in *Ecrits*, Paris: Seuil, 1966

SAINTE-BEUVE, 'Jugement sur Sade' in 'Quelques visites sur la situation en littérature', Paris: la Revue des deux mondes, Vol. 3, 1843

SOLLERS, PHILIPPE, 'Sade dans le texte' in *Logiques*, Paris: Seuil, 1968

Obliques, No. 12–13, Paris, 1977. Issue devoted to Sade

2b) Essays and articles in English

HASSAN, IHAB, 'Sade: The Prison of Consciousness' in *The Dismemberment of Orpheus: Towards a Postmodern Literature*, New York: Oxford University Press, 1971

RICKWORD, EDGELL, 'Notes for a Study of Sade' in *Essays and Opinions 1921–31*, Cheadle: Carcanet Press, 1974

WILSON, EDMUND, 'The Vogue of the Marquis de Sade' in *Eight Essays*, New York: Doubleday, 1954

—— 'The Documents on the Marquis de Sade' in *The Bit Between My Teeth*, New York: Farrar Straus and Giroux, 1965

2c) Study in German

ADORNO, THEODOR, *Dialektik der Aufklärung*, Amsterdam, 1947

Historical

ARIES, PHILIPPE, *Centuries of Childhood* (tr. R. Baldick), London: Cape, 1973

BARBER, ELINOR G., *The Bourgeoisie in 18th Century France*, New Jersey: Princeton University Press, 1955

COBB, RICHARD, *Paris and Its Provinces 1792–1802*, London: Oxford University Press, 1972

COBBAN, ALFRED, *A History of Modern France*, London: Penguin, 1957

DAKIN, DOUGLAS, *Turgot and the Ancien Régime in France*, London: Methuen, 1939

FORD, FRANKLIN L., *Robe and Sword*, Harvard University Press, 1953

DE GONCOURT, E. and J., *The Woman of the 18th Century* (tr. Jacques le Clerq and Ralph Roder), London: Allen and Unwin, 1928

GOODWIN, A., *The French Revolution*, London: Hutchinson, 1953

GOODWIN, A. (ed.), *The European Nobility in the 18th Century*, London: A. & C. Black, 1953

GROSSMAN, LIONEL, *French Society and Culture*, New Jersey: Prentice-Hall, 1972

HERBERT, SYDNEY, *The Fall of Feudalism in France*, London: Methuen, 1921

JOHNSON, DOUGLAS (ed.), *French Society and the Revolution*, Cambridge: Cambridge University Press, 1976

LEFEBVRE, G., *The Coming of the French Revolution* (tr. R. R. Palmer), Princeton University Press, 1949

LOUGH, JOHN, *Introduction to 18th Century France*, London: Longman, 1960

MACKRELL, J. Q. C., *The Attack on 'Feudalism' in 18th Century France*, London: Routledge, 1973

MCCLOY, SHELBY T., *The Humanist Movement in 18th Century France*, University of Kentucky Press, 1957

MICHELET, JULES, *History of the French Revolution* (tr. C. Cocks, ed. G. Wright), Chicago: 1967

MITFORD, NANCY, *Madame de Pompadour*, London: Hamish Hamilton, 1954

RUDE, GEORGE, *The Crowd in the French Revolution*, London: Oxford University Press, 1959

SOBOUL, ALBERT, *The French Revolution 1787–1799* (tr. Alan Forrest), London: NLB, 1974

DE TOQUEVILLE, ALEXIS, *The Ancien Régime and the French Revolution* (tr. Stuart Gilbert), New York: Doubleday, 1955; London: Fontana, 1966

VALLENTIN, ANTONINA, *Mirabeau: Voice of the Revolution*, London: Hamish Hamilton, 1948

Literary and Philosophical History

ADAM, ANTOINE, *Grandeur and Illusion: French Literature and Society 1600–1715* (tr. Herbert Tint), Weidenfeld and Nicolson, 1972

BRISSENDEN, R. F., *Virtue in Danger. Studies in the Novel of Sentiment from Sade to Richardson*, London: 1974

CROCKER, LESTER G., *Nature and Culture*, Baltimore: Johns Hopkins Press, 1963

—— *An Age of Crisis: Man and World in 18th Century French Thought*, Baltimore: Johns Hopkins Press, 1970

CRUICKSHANK, JOHN (ed.), *French Literature and Its Background,*
Vol. 3: The 18th Century, London: Oxford University Press,
1968

FOUCAULT, MICHEL, *Madness and Civilization: History of Insanity in*
the Age of Reason (tr. Richard Howard), London: Tavistock,
1967

FRANCE, PETER, *Rhetoric and Truth in France,* Oxford: 1972

HELLER, ERICH, *The Artist's Journey into the Interior and Other Essays,*
London: Secker and Warburg, 1966

NAGY, PIERRE, *Libertinage et revolution* (tr. (from Hungarian)
Christiane Gremillon), Paris: Gallimard, 1975

PRAZ, MARIO, *The Romantic Agony* (tr. Angus Davidson), London:
Oxford University Press, 1933, 1951

Psychological

BROWN, NORMAN O., *Life Against Death: The Psychoanalytical Mean-*
ing of History, London: Routledge, 1959

DELEUZE, GILLES, *Presentation de Sacher-Masoch,* Paris: Editions de
Minuit, 1967

ELLIS, HAVELOCK, *Psychology of Sex,* London: Heinemann, 1933

FREUD, SIGMUND, 'The Unconscious' in *The Standard Edition of*
Complete Psychological Works, Vol. IV (tr. ed. James Strachey),
London: Hogarth Press

—— *The Ego and the Id,* 'The Economic Problem of Masochism'
and 'Negation' in Vol. XIV

—— *Civilization and Its Discontents* and 'Dostoevsky and Parricide'
in Vol. XXI

KRAFFT-EBING, R., *Aberrations of Sexual Life* (tr. Arthur Burbury,
ed. Alexander Hartwick), London: Staples Press, 1951

LAING, R. D., *The Divided Self,* London: Tavistock, 1960

RICOEUR, PAUL, *Freud and Philosophy* (tr. Denis Savage), New
Haven: Yale University Press, 1970

Index